T0236450

Communications
in Computer and Information Science 433

Editorial Board

Frédéric Boniol   Virginie Wiels
Yamine Ait Ameur   Klaus-Dieter Schewe (Eds.)

ABZ 2014:
The Landing Gear
Case Study

Case Study Track,
Held at the 4th International Conference
on Abstract State Machines,
Alloy, B, TLA, VDM, and Z,
Toulouse, France, June 2-6, 2014
Proceedings

 Springer

Volume Editors

Frédéric Boniol
ONERA/DTIM, Toulouse, France
E-mail: frederic.boniol@onera.fr

Virginie Wiels
ONERA/DTIM, Toulouse, France
E-mail: virginie.wiels@onera.fr

Yamine Ait Ameur
INP-ENSEEIHT/IRIT, Toulouse, France
E-mail: yamine@enseeiht.fr

Klaus-Dieter Schewe
Software Competence Center Hagenberg, Austria
E-mail: kd.schewe@scch.at

ISSN 1865-0929   e-ISSN 1865-0937
ISBN 978-3-319-07511-2   e-ISBN 978-3-319-07512-9
DOI 10.1007/978-3-319-07512-9
Springer Cham Heidelberg New York Dordrecht London

Library of Congress Control Number: 2014939449

Typesetting: Camera-ready by author, data conversion by Scientific Publishing Services, Chennai, India

Printed on acid-free paper

Springer is part of Springer Science+Business Media (www.springer.com)

Preface

Case studies have played an essential role in the history of formal methods. They have allowed us to illustrate the application of formal techniques for modelling and verification so as to compare different methods in terms of expressivity, performance, and ease of use. They have also permitted us to enact the progress made by these methods. As formal methods have made much progress over the years, our aim at ABZ 2014 was to propose a complex case study, representative of industrial needs.

The proposed case study, a landing gear system for an aircraft, is very rich. It is composed of three parts: the pilot interface, the mechanical and hydraulic parts, and the digital part. The case study is thus not restricted to software, but involves complex system modelling (behavior of gears, doors, cylinders, electro-valves). The software part is in charge of controlling gears and doors, but also of monitoring the system and informing the pilot in case of an anomaly. Requirements to be verified on the system include normal mode and failure mode requirements. In both categories, requirements finely combine functional properties and timing constraints. This case study is indeed complex, both to model and to verify. Furthermore, it was not a priori a state-based oriented case study and a question was to see how the ABZ formal methods could accommodate this kind of system.

We were very happy that the case study attracted a lot of interest. The 11 selected papers use different formal techniques: B, ASM, Fiacre. They also propose different kinds of verification: proof, model checking, test generation, run-time monitoring, and simulation. The papers did not necessarily model all aspects of the case study, but the proposed modelling and analyses were very interesting.

In addition to the submissions, a lot of interest was expressed in this case study. We had a lively and stimulating track during the 4th edition of the ABZ 2014 conference in Toulouse, with fruitful discussions around the results obtained and the difficulties encountered, which fostered further modelling and verification.

This ABZ 2014 case study would not have succeeded without the deep investment and involvement of the Program Committee members who contributed by reviewing and selecting the best contributions. This event would not exist if the authors and contributors did not submit their proposals. We extend our thanks to all of them: reviewers, authors, Program Committee members, and Organizing Committee members.

A special thanks to Jean-Raymond Abrial and Egon Börger for their interest in the case study and the stimulating exchanges we had about it.

The EasyChair system was set up for the management of ABZ 2014 supporting the submission, review, and volume preparation processes. It proved to be a powerful framework.

Finally, ABZ 2014 received the support of several sponsors, among them Airbus, CNES, CNRS, CS, CRITT Informatique, ENSEEIHT Toulouse, FME, IRIT, INP Toulouse, Midi Pyrénées Region, ONERA, SCCH, and Université Paul Sabatier Toulouse. Many thanks for their support.

June 2014

Frédéric Boniol
Virginie Wiels
Yamine Ait Ameur
Klaus-Dieter Schewe

Organization

Program Committee

Jean-Raymond Abrial	Consultant, France
Yamine Ait Ameur	IRIT/INPT-ENSEEIHT, France
Richard Banach	University of Manchester, UK
Eerke Boiten	University of Kent, UK
Frédéric Boniol	ONERA, France
Michael Butler	University of Southampton, UK
Egon Börger	Università di Pisa, Italy
Ana Cavalcanti	University of York, UK
David Deharbe	Universidade Federal do Rio Grande do Norte, Brazil
John Derrick	University of Sheffield, UK
Juergen Dingel	Queen's University, UK
Kerstin Eder	University of Bristol, UK
Roozbeh Farahbod	SAP Research, Germany
Mamoun Filali-Amine	IRIT-Toulouse, France
John Fitzgerald	Newcastle University, UK
Marc Frappier	University of Sherbrooke, Canada
Vincenzo Gervasi	University of Pisa, Italy
Dimitra Giannakopoulou	NASA Ames, USA
Uwe Glässer	Simon Fraser University, Canada
Stefania Gnesi	ISTI-CNR, Italy
Lindsay Groves	Victoria University of Wellington, New Zealand
Stefan Hallerstede	University of Düsseldorf, Germany
Klaus Havelund	California Institute of Technology, USA
Ian J. Hayes	University of Queensland, Australia
Rob Hierons	Brunel University, UK
Thai Son Hoang	Swiss Federal Institute of Technology Zurich, Switzerland
Sarfraz Khurshid	The University of Texas at Austin, USA
Regine Laleau	Paris Est Creteil University, France
Leslie Lamport	Microsoft Research, USA
Peter Gorm Larsen	Aarhus School of Engineering, Denmark
Thierry Lecomte	ClearSy, France
Michael Leuschel	University of Düsseldorf, Germany
Yuan-Fang Li	Monash University, Australia

Additional Reviewers

Arcaini, Paolo
Attiogbe, Christian
Barbosa, Haniel
Coleman, Joey
Colvin, Robert
Couto, Luís Diogo
Cunha, Alcino
Ernst, Gidon
Esparza Isasa, José Antonio
Fantechi, Alessandro
Gervais, Frederic
Herbreteau, Frédéric
Iliasov, Alexei
Kossak, Felix

Ladenberger, Lukas
Leupolz, Johannes
Macedo, Nuno
Mammar, Amel
Nalbandyan, Narek
Neron, Pierre
Pfähler, Jörg
Sandvik, Petter
Senni, Valerio
Singh, Neeraj
Tarasyuk, Anton
Tounsi, Mohamed
Treharne, Helen
Yaghoubi Shahir, Hamed

Table of Contents

The Landing Gear System Case Study

Frédéric Boniol and Virginie Wiels

ONERA, 2 av. E. Belin, BP 74025, F-31055 Toulouse France
{firstname.name}@onera.fr

1 Introduction

This document presents a landing gear system. It describes the system and provides some of its requirements. We propose this case study as a benchmark for techniques and tools dedicated to the verification of behavioral properties of systems.

The landing system is in charge of maneuvering landing gears and associated doors. The landing system is composed of 3 landing sets: front, left and right. Each landing set contains a door, a landing-gear and associated hydraulic cylinders. A simplified schema of a landing set is presented in Figure 1.

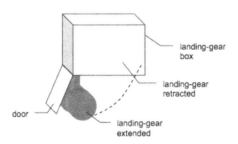

Fig. 1. Landing set

The system is controlled digitally in nominal mode and analogically in emergency mode. In this case study, we do not consider the emergency mode. However, in order to allow the pilot to activate the emergency command, the system has to elaborate health parameters for all the equipments involved in the landing gear function. This health monitoring part is in the scope of the case study.

In nominal mode, the landing sequence is: open the doors of the landing gear boxes, extend the landing gears and close the doors. This sequence is illustrated in Figure 2. After taking off, the retraction sequence to be performed is: open the doors, retract the landing gears and close the doors.

This system is representative of critical embedded systems. The action to be done at each time depends on the state of all the physical devices and on their temporal behavior. When considering such systems, the challenge is firstly to

F. Boniol et al. (Eds.): ABZ 2014 Case Study Track, CCIS 433, pp. 1–18, 2014.

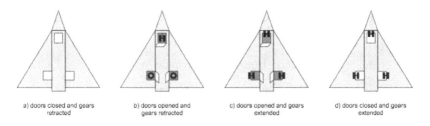

a) doors closed and gears retracted

b) doors opened and gears retracted

c) doors opened and gears extended

d) doors closed and gears extended

Fig. 2. The landing sequence

model and to program the software part controlling the landing and the retraction sequence, and secondly to prove safety requirements taking into account the physical behavior of hydraulic devices.

The document is organized as follows:

- Section 2 describes the architecture of the system;
- Section 3 describes the behavior of the hydraulic equipment;
- Section 4 specifies the expected behavior of the system, i.e. the behavior to be implemented by the control software;
- Section 5 presents the requirements of the system, that is the set of properties to be satisfied by the computing units of the system.

2   Architecture of the System

As shown in Figure 3, the landing gear system is composed of three parts:

- a mechanical part which contains all the mechanical devices and the three landing sets,
- a digital part including the control software,
- and a pilot interface.

2.1   The Pilot Interface

To command the retraction and outgoing of gears, an Up/Down handle is provided to the pilot. When the handle is switched to "Up" the retracting landing gear sequence is executed, when the handle is switched to "Down" the extending landing gear sequence is executed.

The pilot has a set of lights giving the current position of gears and doors, and the current health state of the system and its equipments. These lights are:

- one green light: "gears are locked down",
- one orange light: "gears maneuvering" ,
- one red light: "landing gear system failure",

No light is on when the gears are locked up. In case of failure, the pilot can manually activate the emergency hydraulic circuit. The expected consequence of this action is to lock the gears in the down position. In case of success and if the corresponding sensors are still working, the green light "gears are locked down" must be on.

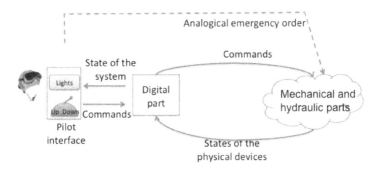

Fig. 3. Global architecture

2.2 The Mechanical and Hydraulic Parts

The architecture of the hydraulic part is described in Figure 4. As stated previously, the system is composed of three landing sets: front, left and right sets. Each set has got:

- a landing gear uplock box,
- and a door with two latching boxes in the closed position.

The landing gears and doors motion is performed by a set of actuating cylinders. The cylinder position corresponds to the door or landing gear position (when a door is open, the corresponding cylinder is extended). The landing system has the following actuating cylinders:

- For each door, a cylinder opens and closes the door.
- For each landing gear, a cylinder retracts and extends the landing gear.

Hydraulic power is provided to the cylinders by a set of electro-valves:

- One general electro-valve which supplies the specific electro-valves with hydraulic power from the aircraft hydraulic circuit.
- One electro-valve that sets pressure on the portion of the hydraulic circuit related to door opening.
- One electro-valve that sets pressure on the portion of the hydraulic circuit related to door closing.
- One electro-valve that sets pressure on the portion of the hydraulic circuit related to landing gear extending.
- One electro-valve that sets pressure on the portion of the hydraulic circuit related to the landing gear retracting.

Each electro-valve is activated by an electrical order coming from the digital part. In the specific case of the general electro-valve, this electrical order goes through an analogical switch in order to prevent abnormal behavior of the digital part (e.g. abnormal activation of the general electro-valve).

Note that the three doors (resp. gears) are controlled simultaneously by the same electro-valve. Put differently, it is not possible to control the doors (resp. gears) separately.

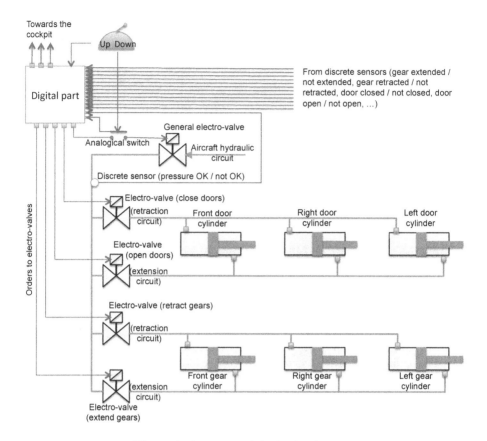

Fig. 4. Architecture of the hydraulic part

A set of discrete sensors inform the digital part about the state of the equipments:

– Front / right / left gear is locked / not locked in the extended position.
– Front / right / left gear is locked / not locked in the retracted position.
– Front / right / left gear shock absorber is on ground / in flight.
– Front / right / left door is in open / not open position.
– Front / right / left door is locked / not locked in the closed position.
– The hydraulic circuit (after the general electro-valve) is pressurized / not pressurized.
– The analogical switch between the digital part and the general electro-valve is closed / open.

In order to prevent sensor failures, each sensor is triplicated (i.e. each sensor is divided into three independent micro-sensors). It delivers simultaneously three discrete values describing the same situation (for instance "the left gear is locked in retracted position").

The behavior of the physical equipment involved in the hydraulic architecture is described in Section 3.

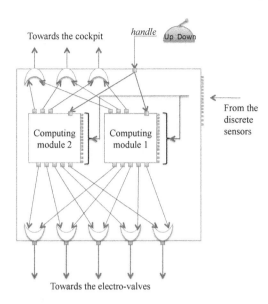

Fig. 5. Digital architecture

2.3 The Digital Part

The digital part is composed of two identical computing modules (see Figure 5). Each one executes in parallel the same control software. This software is in charge of controlling gears and doors, of detecting anomalies, and of informing the pilot about the global state of the system and anomalies (if any). It is part of a retroaction loop with the physical system, and produces commands for the distribution elements of the hydraulic system with respect to the sensors values and the pilot orders. The two computing modules receive the same inputs. These inputs are (remember that all the inputs are triplicated):

- $handle_i \in \{up, down\}$ $i = 1, 2, 3$
  $handle_i$ characterizes the position of the handle. If the handle is UP (resp. DOWN), then $handle_i = up$ (resp. $handle_i = down$).

- $analogical\_switch_i \in \{open, closed\}$ $i = 1, 2, 3$
  $analogical\_switch_i$ characterizes the position of the analogical switch: open or closed. See section 3.1.

- $gear\_extended_i[x] \in \{true, false\}$ $i = 1, 2, 3$, x in $\{front, right, left\}$
- $gear\_retracted_i[x] \in \{true, false\}$ $i = 1, 2, 3$, x in $\{front, right, left\}$
  $gear\_extended_i[x]$ is true if the corresponding gear is locked in the extended position and false in the other case.
  $gear\_retracted_i[x]$ is true if the corresponding gear is locked in the retracted position and false in the other case.
  See section 3.3 and Figure 11.

- $gear\_shock\_absorber_i[x] \in \{ground, flight\}$ $i = 1, 2, 3$, x in $\{front, right, left\}$
  $gear\_shock\_absorber_i[x]$ is returned by a sensor implemented directly on the corresponding gear (see Figure 11). It is true if and only if the aircraft is on ground.

- $door\_closed_i[x] \in \{true, false\}$ $i = 1, 2, 3$, x in $\{front, right, left\}$
- $door\_open_i[x] \in \{true, false\}$ $i = 1, 2, 3$, x in $\{front, right, left\}$
  $door\_closed_i[x]$ is true if and only if the corresponding door is locked closed.
  $door\_open_i[x]$ is true if and only if the corresponding door is locked open.
  See section 3.3 and Figure 12.

- $circuit\_pressurized_i \in \{true, false\}$ $i = 1, 2, 3$
  $circuit\_pressurized_i$ is returned by a pressure sensor on the hydraulic circuit between the general electro-valve and the maneuvering electro-valve (see Figure 4). $circuit\_pressurized_i$ is true if and only if the pressure is high in this part of the hydraulic circuit.

The total amount of input discrete values received by each computing module is 54 (3 *handle*, 3 *analogical_switch*, 9 *gear_extended*, 9 *gear_retracted*, 9 *gear_shock_absorber*, 9 *door_closed*, 9 *door_open* and 3 *circuit_pressurized*).

From these inputs, each module computes 5 electrical orders for the electro-valves:

- $general\_EV_k \in \{true, false\}$ $k = 1, 2$
- $close\_EV_k \in \{true, false\}$ $k = 1, 2$
- $open\_EV_k \in \{true, false\}$ $k = 1, 2$
- $retract\_EV_k \in \{true, false\}$ $k = 1, 2$
- $extend\_EV_k \in \{true, false\}$ $k = 1, 2$

where "EV" stands for "Electro-Valve" and k stands for the number of the considered computing module. These corresponding electrical orders outgoing from the two modules are physically produced on the same electrical line. The implicit composition of two outputs is an electrical "OR" as shown in Figure 5. For instance, let us consider the *general_EV* parameter. If the two modules produce the same value on $general\_EV_1$ and $general\_EV_2$, then this value is produced to the general electro-valve. Otherwise, if only one of them is *true* (because of a failure somewhere in the digital part), then the value *true* is produced to the electro-valve, even if it is not the correct value. The problem will anyway be detected at the next cycle when the module that produced the *false* value will detect an unexpected behavior with respect to its own orders. Then it will inform the pilot of a potential anomaly in the system.

Similarly the two modules produce global boolean state variables to the cockpit:

- $gears\_locked\_down_k \in \{true, false\}$ $k = 1, 2$
- $gears\_maneuvering_k \in \{true, false\}$ $k = 1, 2$
- $anomaly_k \in \{true, false\}$ $k = 1, 2$

These outputs are synthesized by each module from sensors data and from the situation awareness. Similarly to electrical orders provided to the electro-valves, the boolean state variables from the two modules are composed following a logical "OR" operation. If $gears\_locked\_down_k$ (for some k) is sent to the pilot interface with the value $true$, then the green light "gears are locked down" is on. If $gears\_maneuvering_k$ (for some k) is sent to the pilot interface with the value $true$, then the orange light "gears maneuvering" is on. If $anomaly_k$ (for some k) is sent to the pilot interface with the value $true$, then the red light "landing gear system failure" is on. The specification of the digital part is described in Section 4.

The output interface of each module is synthesized on Figure 6.

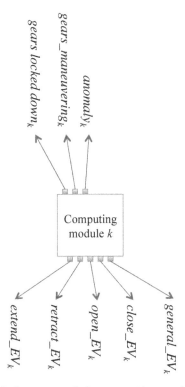

Fig. 6. Electrical outputs of the computing module k ($k = 1, 2$)

3   Behavior of the Hydraulic Equipment

3.1   The Analogical Switch (between the Digital Part and the General Electro-Valve)

The aim of this switch is to protect the system against abnormal behavior of the digital part. In order to prevent inadvertent order to the electro-valves, the general electro-valve can be stimulated only if this switch is closed. The switch is closed each time the "Up/Down" handle is moved by the pilot, and it remains

Analogical switch

Fig. 7. Interface of the analogical switch

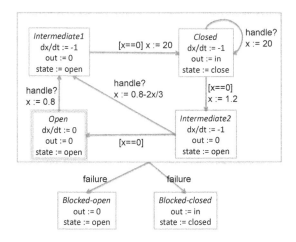

Fig. 8. Physical behavior of the analogical switch

closed 20 seconds. After this duration, the switch automatically becomes open. In the closed position, the switch transmits the electrical order from the digital part to the general electro-valve. In the open position, no electrical order is sent to the electro-valve. In that case, the oil pressure in the hydraulic circuit becomes down.

Because of inertial reasons, the transition from the two states closed and open takes a given amount of time:

– from open to closed: 0.8 second,
– from closed to open 1.2 seconds,

In addition to this normal behavior, the analogical switch can fail. We consider only permanent failures: the switch remains blocked in the closed or in the open position. A failure can occur at any time.

The global behavior of the switch, including failures, is specified by the model of Figure 7 and the hierarchical hybrid automaton of Figure 8. In this specification, *in* stands for the input value of the switch. In the global architecture of Figure 4, the *in* port of the analogical switch is connected to the *general_EV* output of the digital part (i.e., *in* = *general_EV*). The variable *out* stands for the electrical output of the switch. It is connected to the electrical port of the general electro-valve. The variable *state* is the logical output of the switch. It belongs to the set {*open, closed*}. It is connected to the input port *analogical_switch* of the digital part. Note that this output value is triplicated as explained in section 2.3. The event *handle?* stands for the detection of a movement of the pilot handle. This event is received each time the pilot moves the handle. And finally x is an internal continuous variable that evolves according to the differential equation in each state. The aim of this variable is to count the time in each state. For instance, in the state Open, x does not evolve, *state* is set to *open*, and *out* is set to 0 whatever the value of *in*. When *handle* is received, x is set to 0.8, the state Intermediate1 is reached and x begins to decrease. The values of *state* and *out* remain unchanged. 0.8 seconds later, x reached the null value. The transition from Intermediate1 to Close is fired and x is set to 20. *state* is now set to *closed* and *out* is set to *in*. And so on. The initial state of the automaton is Open.

Note that the switch is independent from the digital part.

3.2   Electro-Valves

All the electro-valves are supposed to have the same behavior. As shown in Figure 9, an electro-valve is an hydraulic equipment which has got two hydraulic ports *Hin* (hydraulic input port) and *Hout* (hydraulic output port), and an electrical port ($E \in \{true, textitfalse)$. Its behavior depends on the value of the electrical order connected to E.

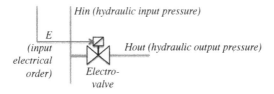

Fig. 9. An electro-valve equipment

- if $E = false$ (the voltage of the electrical order is down), then $Hout = 0$ (no pressure on the hydraulic output side, the hydraulic circuit is open);
- if $E = true$ (the voltage of the electrical order is high), then $Hout = Hin$ (the hydraulic circuit is closed);

Note that the electrical order must be sustained to *true* (i..e, at the high voltage) to maintain the electro-valve in the closed position. Put differently, the electrical order is not a discrete event, but can be seen as an analogical signal.

Because of inertial reasons, we suppose that from the open position to the closed position, the pressure grows up continuously from 0 to *Hin*. In this case study we suppose that the pressure grows up linearly, and that the total duration of the transition phase is 1 second. In the same way, the pressure goes down continuously from *Hin* to 0. We suppose that the pressure goes down linearly, and that the total duration of the transition phase is 3,6 seconds.

In addition to this normal behavior, any electro-valve can fail. We consider only permanent failures: the electro-valve remains blocked in the closed or the open state. A failure can occur at any time.

3.3   Cylinders

Cylinders are pure hydraulic equipments. As shown on Figure 10, they begin to move when they receive hydraulic pressure, and they stop to move when the pressure goes down or when they reach the end of their race.

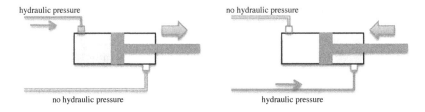

Fig. 10. Extension and retraction of a cylinder

Gear Cylinders. Gear cylinders are locked in high or down position by means of a latching box mechanism (the latching boxes are physically on the gears, one for each position). When a gear cylinder is locked in high (resp. down) position and when it receives pressure from the high (resp. down) hydraulic circuit,

- first it is unlocked from the high (resp. down) position
- then it moves to the down (resp. high) position
- and finally it is locked in the down (resp. high) position.

The behavior of the gear (including the values returned by the gear position sensors) is described on Figure 11.

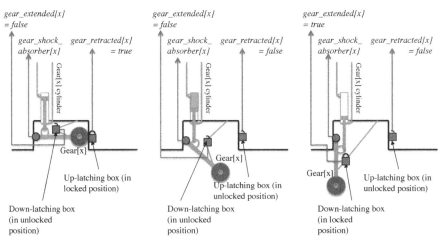

(a) gear in the retracted position (b) gear in the intermediate position (c) gear in the extended position

Fig. 11. Integration Gear - cylinder for the block $x \in \{front, right, left\}$ (the door is not represented)

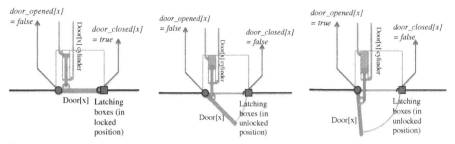

(a) door in the closed position

(b) door in the intermediate position

(c) door in the open position

Fig. 12. Integration Door - cylinder for the block $x \in \{front, right, left\}$ (the gear is not represented)

Door Cylinders. Door cylinders are locked (by means of two latching boxes on each door) only in closed position. Doors are maintained open by maintaining pressure in extension circuit. When a door cylinder is locked in closed position and when it receives pressure from the extension hydraulic circuit,

- first it is unlocked from the closed position
- then it moves to the open position
- and finally it is maintained in the open position as long as the pressure is maintained in the hydraulic extension circuit.

The behavior of the door (including the values returned by the door position sensors) is described on Figure 12.

Temporal Behavior for the Cylinders. All these operations are done automatically with the hydraulic pressure only. No electrical part is involved in cylinders. These operations take a certain amount of time, depending on the position of the cylinder in the aircraft and in the hydraulic circuit. The durations are given in the array below. The values are only mean values. The true durations can vary around these values up to 20%.

duration (in seconds) of ...	front gear	front door	right gear	right door	left gear	left door
unlock in down position	0.8	-	0.8	-	0.8	-
from down to high position	1.6	1.2	2	1.6	2	1.6
lock in high position	0.4	0.3	0.4	0.3	0.4	0.3
unlock in high position	0.8	0.4	0.8	0.4	0.8	0.4
from high to down position	1.2	1.2	1.6	1.5	1.6	1.5
lock in down position	0.4	-	0.4	-	0.4	-

Note that it is possible to stop and to inverse the motion of any cylinder at any time.

An example of the front-gear movement is given on Figure 13. This scenario is based on the mean values given in the previous table. Let us suppose that the front gear is locked in the extended position when the pressure arrives in the retraction circuit (first red arrow on the left). Then the gear is unlocked 0.4s later. It goes up during 1.6s. And finally it is locked in the retracted position 2.4s after the arrival of the pressure in the hydraulic circuit. Let us consider now that the pressure arrives in the extension circuit. The gear is unlocked 0.8s later. It begins moving down. Let us suppose now that the pressure is stopped. Then the cylinder stops as well in the current position. If the pressure arrives again in the retraction circuit, the gear goes up immediately from this current position at normal speed. In the same way, the last part of the scenario describes the extension phase without any interruption.

In addition to this normal behavior, any cylinder can fail. We consider only permanent failures: the cylinder remains blocked in the last position (down, high, or between these two positions). Any failure can occur at any time.

4   Software Specification

The aim of the software part of the system is twofold:

1. to control the hydraulic devices according to the pilot orders and to the mechanical devices positions;
2. to monitor the system and to inform the pilot in case of anomaly.

The first objective is described in section 4.1. The second one is described in section 4.3.

4.1   Expected Scenarios in Normal Mode

When the command line is working (in normal mode), the landing system reacts to the pilot orders by actioning or inhibiting the electro-valves of the appropriate cylinders. Two basic scenarios are considered: the outgoing sequence, and the retraction sequence.

Outgoing Sequence. The outgoing of gears is decomposed in a sequence of elementary actions. When the gears are locked in retracted position, and the doors are locked in closed position, if the pilot sets the handle to "Down", then the software should have the following sequence of actions:

1. stimulate the general electro-valve isolating the command unit in order to send hydraulic pressure to the maneuvering electro-valves,
2. stimulate the door opening electro-valve,
3. once the three doors are in the open position, stimulate the gear outgoing electro-valve,
4. once the three gears are locked down, stop the stimulation of the gear outgoing electro-valve,
5. stop the stimulation of the door opening electro-valve,

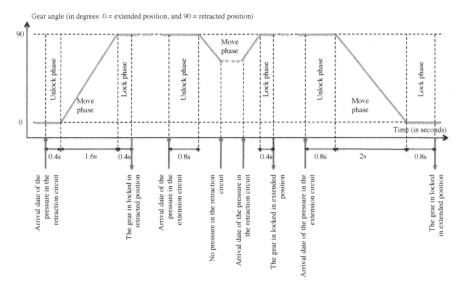

Fig. 13. Example of the front gear angle evolution (angle of the gear w.r.t the vertical: 0 (resp. 90) corresponds to the down (resp. up) position)

6. stimulate the door closure electro-valve,
7. once the three doors are locked in the closed position, stop the stimulation of the door closure electro-valve,
8. and finally stop stimulating the general electro-valve.

Retraction Sequence. In the same way, the retraction of gears is decomposed in a sequence of elementary actions. When the gears are locked in down position, and the doors are locked in closed position, if the pilot sets the handle to "Up", then the software should have the following sequence of actions:

1. stimulate the general electro-valve isolating the command unit, in order to send hydraulic pressure to the maneuvering electro-valves,
2. stimulate the door opening electro-valve,
3. once the three doors are in the open position, if the three shock absorbers are relaxed, then stimulate the gear retraction electro-valve and go to step 4, else (if one of the three shock absorbers is not relaxed) go to step 5,
4. once the three gears are locked up, stop the stimulation of the gear retraction electro-valve,
5. stop the stimulation of the door opening electro-valve,
6. stimulate the door closure electro-valve,
7. once the three doors are locked in the closed position, stop the stimulation of the door closure electro-valve,
8. and finally stop stimulating the general electro-valve.

The previous sequences should be interruptible by counter orders (a retraction order occurs during the let down sequence and conversely) at any time. In that case, the scenario continues from the point where it was interrupted. For instance, if an outgoing sequence is interrupted in the door closure phase (step 6 of the outgoing sequence) by an "Up" order, then the stimulation of the door closure electro-valve is stopped, and the retraction sequence is executed from step 2: the door opening electro-valve is stimulated and the doors begin opening again. Afterwards, the scenario continues up to the final step or up to a new interruption.

Interaction with the Cockpit. Each control software $k \in \{1, 2\}$[1] computes the three state booleans $gears\_locked\_down_k$, $gears\_maneuvering_k$ and $anomaly_k$.

- $gears\_locked\_down_k = true$ if and only if the three gears are seen as locked in extended position (sensor $gear\_extended[x] = true \; \forall x \in \{front, right, left\}$).
- $gears\_maneuvering_k = true$ if and only if at least one door or one gear is maneuvering, i.e., at least one door is not locked in closed position or one gear is not locked in extension or retraction position.
- $anomaly_k$ is specified in section 4.3.

4.2   Timing Constraints

Because of hydraulic constraints, timing constraints must be satisfied by the control software.

Electro-Valve Stimulation. Because of inertia of the oil pressure,

- stimulations of the general electro-valve and of the maneuvering electro-valve must be separated by at least 200ms,
- orders to stop the stimulation of the general electro-valve and of the maneuvering electro-valve must be separated by at least 1s.

Contrary Orders. Because of inertia of the oil pressure,

- two contrary orders (closure / opening doors, extension / retraction gears) must be separated by at least 100ms.

4.3   Health Monitoring and Expected Scenarios in Case of Inconsistency

The second objective of the control software is to detect anomalies and to inform the pilot. Anomalies are caused by failures on hydraulic equipment, electrical components, or computing modules.

---

[1] Remember that the digital part of the system is composed of two computing modules, each of them implements an instance of the control software.

Generic Monitoring. Each sensor is triplicated. The first activity of the control software is to select one of these three values. Let us call X a sensor and $X_i(t)$ $i = 1, 2, 3$ the three values of X received at time t:

- If at t the three channels are considered as valid and are equal, then the value considered by the control software is this common value.
- If at t one channel is different from the two others for the first time (i.e., the three channels were considered as valid up to t), then this channel is considered as invalid and is definitely eliminated. Only the two remaining channels are considered in the future. At time t, the value considered by the control software is the common value of the two remaining channels.
- If a channel has been eliminated previously, and if at t the two remaining channels are not equal, then the sensor is definitely considered as invalid.

An anomaly is detected each time a sensor is definitely considered as invalid.

Analogical Switch Monitoring

- If the analogical switch is seen open 1 second after the handle position has changed, then the switch is considered as invalid.
- If the analogical switch is seen closed 1.5 second after a time interval of 20 seconds during which the handle position has not changed, then the switch is considered as invalid.

In these two cases, an anomaly is detected.

Pressure Sensor Monitoring

- If the hydraulic circuit is still unpressurized 2 seconds after the general electro-valve has been stimulated, then an anomaly is detected in the hydraulic circuit.
- If the hydraulic circuit is still pressurized 10 seconds after the general electro-valve has been stopped, then an anomaly is detected in the hydraulic circuit.

Doors Motion Monitoring

- if the control software does not see the value *door_closed*[x] = *false* for all $x \in \{front, left, right\}$ 7 seconds after stimulation of the opening electro-valve, then the doors are considered as blocked and an anomaly is detected.
- if the control software does not see the value *door_open*[x] = *true* for all $x \in \{front, left, right\}$ 7 seconds after stimulation of the opening electro-valve, then the doors are considered as blocked and an anomaly is detected.
- if the control software does not see the value *door_open*[x] = *false* for all $x \in \{front, left, right\}$ 7 seconds after stimulation of the closure electro-valve, then the doors are considered as blocked and an anomaly is detected.
- if the control software does not see the value *door_closed*[x] = *true* for all $x \in \{front, left, right\}$ 7 seconds after stimulation of the closure electro-valve, then the doors are considered as blocked and an anomaly is detected.

Gears Motion Monitoring

- if the control software does not see the value *gear_extended*[*x*] = *false* for all
  x ∈ {*front, left, right*} 7 seconds after stimulation of the retraction electro-
  valve, then the gears are considered as blocked and an anomaly is detected.
- if the control software does not see the value *gear_retracted*[*x*] = *true* for all
  x ∈ {*front, left, right*} 10 seconds after stimulation of the retraction electro-
  valve, then the gears are considered as blocked and an anomaly is detected.
- if the control software does not see the value *gear_retracted*[*x*] = *false* for all
  x ∈ {*front, left, right*} 7 seconds after stimulation of the extension electro-
  valve, then the gears are considered as blocked and an anomaly is detected.
- if the control software does not see the value *gear_extended*[*x*] = *true* for all
  x ∈ {*front, left, right*} 10 seconds after stimulation of the extension electro-
  valve, then the gears are considered as blocked and an anomaly is detected.

Expected Behavior in Case of Anomaly. Whenever an anomaly is detected, the
system is globally considered as invalid. The data *anomaly$_k$* = *true* is sent to
the pilot interface (where *k* is the part number of the module that has detected
the anomaly). This message is then maintained forever. The effect of this action
is to put on the red light "landing gear system failure".

Otherwise (no anomaly ever happened), the data *anomaly$_k$* = *false* is sent
and maintained to the pilot interface. The effect of this action is to keep off the
red light "landing gear system failure".

5   Requirements / Properties

The requirements to be proved on the system are divided into two parts: normal
mode requirements, and failure mode requirements

5.1   Normal Mode Requirements

Requirement R_1

- (R_{11}) When the command line is working (normal mode), if the landing gear
  command handle has been pushed DOWN and stays DOWN, then the gears
  will be locked down and the doors will be seen closed less than 15 seconds
  after the handle has been pushed;
- (R_{12}) When the command line is working (normal mode), if the landing gear
  command handle has been pushed UP and stays UP, then the gears will be
  locked retracted and the doors will be seen closed less than 15 seconds after
  the handle has been pushed.

Note that a weaker version of these two requirements could be considered as
well. This weaker version does not take into account quantitative time.

- (R_{11}bis) When the command line is working (normal mode), if the landing
  gear command handle has been pushed DOWN and stays DOWN, then
  eventually the gears will be locked down and the doors will be seen closed;

- (R_{12}bis) When the command line is working (normal mode), if the landing gear command handle has been pushed UP and stays UP, then eventually the gears will be locked retracted and the doors will be seen closed.

Requirement R_2

- (R_{21}) When the command line is working (normal mode), if the landing gear command handle remains in the DOWN position, then retraction sequence is not observed.
- (R_{22}) When the command line is working (normal mode), if the landing gear command handle remains in the UP position, then outgoing sequence is not observed.

Requirement R_3

- (R_{31}) When the command line is working (normal mode), the stimulation of the gears outgoing or the retraction electro-valves can only happen when the three doors are locked open.
- (R_{32}) When the command line is working (normal mode), the stimulation of the doors opening or closure electro-valves can only happen when the three gears are locked down or up.

Requirement R_4

- (R_{41}) When the command line is working (normal mode), opening and closure doors electro-valves are not stimulated simultaneously.
- (R_{42}) When the command line is working (normal mode), outgoing and retraction gears electro-valves are not stimulated simultaneously.

Requirement R_5

- (R_{51}) When the command line is working (normal mode), it is not possible to stimulate the maneuvering electro-valve (opening, closure, outgoing or retraction) without stimulating the general electro-valve.

5.2   Failure Mode Requirements

Requirement R_6

- (R_{61}) If one of the three doors is still seen locked in the closed position more than 7 seconds after stimulating the opening electro-valve, then the boolean output *normal_mode* is set to *false*.
- (R_{62}) If one of the three doors is still seen locked in the open position more than 7 seconds after stimulating the closure electro-valve, then the boolean output *normal_mode* is set to *false*.
- (R_{63}) If one of the three gears is still seen locked in the down position more than 7 seconds after stimulating the retraction electro-valve, then the boolean output *normal_mode* is set to *false*.
- (R_{64}) If one of the three gears is still seen locked in the up position more than 7 seconds after stimulating the outgoing electro-valve, then the boolean output *normal_mode* is set to *false*.

Requirement R_7

- (R_{71}) If one of the three doors is not seen locked in the open position more than 7 seconds after stimulating the opening electro-valve, then the boolean output *normal_mode* is set to *false*.
- (R_{72}) If one of the three doors is not seen locked in the closed position more than 7 seconds after stimulating the closure electro-valve, then the boolean output *normal_mode* is set to *false*.
- (R_{73}) If one of the three gears is not seen locked in the up position more than 10 seconds after stimulating the retraction electro-valve, then the boolean output *normal_mode* is set to *false*.
- (R_{74}) If one of the three gears is not seen locked in the down position more than 10 seconds after stimulating the outgoing electro-valve, then the boolean output *normal_mode* is set to *false*.

Requirement R_8

- (R_{81}) When at least one computing module is working, if the landing gear command handle has been DOWN for 15 seconds, and if the gears are not locked down after 15 seconds, then the red light "landing gear system failure" is on.
- (R_{82}) When at least one computing module is working, if the landing gear command handle has been UP for 15 seconds, and if the gears are not locked retracted after 15 seconds, then the red light "landing gear system failure" is on.

Aircraft Landing Gear System: Approaches with Event-B to the Modeling of an Industrial System

Wen Su[1] and Jean-Raymond Abrial[2]

[1] School of Computer Engineering and Science, Shanghai University
wsu@shu.edu.cn
[2] Marseille, France
jrabrial@neuf.fr

Abstract. This paper describes the modeling, done using the Event-B notation, of the aircraft landing gear case study that is proposed in a special track of the ABZ'2014 Conference. In the course of our development, we discovered some problems in our initial modeling approach. This has led us to propose a second approach and then a third one. Each approach is more efficient than the previous one in terms of proof obligations (roughly speaking: 2000, 1000, 500). All this will be described in this paper. We also try to go beyond this specific case study and give some thoughts about large industrial modeling.

1 Introduction

This case study was proposed by Frédéric Boniol and Virginie Wiels (both from ONERA-DTIM) [4]. We found their description to be extremely well written. It is worth noticing it, as it is usually not the case in similar industrial systems. Their description of the aircraft landing gear is a prerequisite for the reading of this paper: we are not going to repeat it here. However, we decided to remove some parts of their case study, not because we found them to be not important, nor because we do no know how to model them, rather because we found that the modeling of them will not bring anything new with regards to some other parts we cover. In section 4 we make precise which parts have been omitted in our models.

Another prerequisite for reading this paper is a small knowledge of Event-B. As for the case study, we do not present any introduction to Event-B in this paper. There exist many introductions to Event-B in various papers [2,6].

We also recommend reading this paper together with the formal developments we have done with the Rodin Platform. These developments can be accessed in the following website [1]. The Rodin Platform can be freely downloaded together with the ProB and AnimB plug-ins (model-checker and animators) [9,8].

The paper is organized as follows. Section 2 is a general introduction to modeling. In Section 3, we introduce our methodology under the form of systematic

F. Boniol et al. (Eds.): ABZ 2014 Case Study Track, CCIS 433, pp. 19–35, 2014.
© Springer International Publishing Switzerland 2014

steps. Section 4 contains the precise requirements of what we take into account in our models. Sections 5, 6 and 7 contain the formal models of our three different approaches. Due to the lack of space, each of these three sections only contains a general introduction describing the modeling technique we use. This is followed by a conclusion and criticisms concerning the approach. As already mentioned, interested readers can access the precise formal developments where we have many explanations on the technical aspects of our approaches. Section 8 is a short conclusion together with the presentation of some future work in this area.

2   Purpose of Modeling

Before engaging in the modeling of a large embedding system like the one proposed in this case study, it is useful to make the purpose of modeling very precise. This view of modeling corresponds to our strong belief in this activity: it can be different to what can be encountered in the literature [7]. Here are a few elementary ideas about the purpose of modeling:

- Modeling is quite different from programming. It does not replace programming. It is performed before programming as a "blueprint" like the ones that can be found in other engineering disciplines.

- Within a model, we can formalize directly some of the properties of our future system. These properties are not an afterthought as is the case with programming. The proof of such properties are far easier to perform in this early stage than in the final program.

- Before the formal modeling, we must define precisely the requirements of the system under development. One purpose of modeling is thus to ensure that every requirement has been taken into account. But modeling also helps to identify the missing requirements, expected behavior, desired safety properties, and crystal clear specification of the system. In short, we can use modeling for making the requirements more precise.

- In modeling, we have a view of the system under study that is larger than that of the software alone. In fact, the software is only one (sometimes small) part of the complete system. Thus, we shall cover the software but also the environment within which this software is going to evolve.

- We shall not show the model directly to the "client" : he might have some difficulties understanding the mathematics used in the model. But, thanks to the animation of the model (using ProB or AnimB), we obtain a cheap executable prototype of the system. This is what we may show to the client. In view of this prototype execution, he can then decide to remove, modify, or add some requirements.

- Finally, the model helps us to prepare for a real implementation of the future software of the system and also make clear what we have to assume from the environment.

3   Methodology

Our approach is based on Event-B [2]. It is to be used together with the Rodin Platform [9]. We emphasize the usage of refinements and that of formal proofs in order to guarantee that some important properties of the system hold in all circumstances. But this is not sufficient to ensure that we can successfully solve the problem at hand. Facing a system like the one described in this case study raises many questions which cannot automatically find a solution with Event-B or, we think, with any other formal modeling approach: modeling is not an easy engineering task that can be solved by applying blindly some recipe. Here are a few questions:

- Where do we have to start from?
- Shall we work from inside-out or from outside-in? (that is, starting by mod- eling the software first and then the environment, or the other way around)
- How much of the environment do we have to incorporate in our model?
- When do we have to introduce the software module?
- How to handle timing constraints (leading to the discovery of anomalies)?
- Shall we use some traces to ensure a correct behavior?
- How to be sure that we do not forget any requirement?

It is not easy to answer these questions because there are certainly no definitive answers: they can be different from one project to the next. Even sometimes several distinct answers are possible (as is the case with the second question). All this can be seen in this paper where three distinct approaches are proposed: each of them present different answers to these questions. So, rather than trying to give definitive answers which is not possible, we propose a light *methodology* (already mentioned in [10]) made of several steps within which these answers can be given and discussed:

1. **Informal Requirements.** Give informal requirements to the system (this is done in section 4). During the requirement definitions, we use the require- ment tool ProR [8,5].

2. **Refinement Strategy.** Give a refinement strategy explaining what is done in each refinement and check that all requirements are taken into account (this is done in sections 5.2, 6.2, and 7.2).

3. **Formal Model.** Develop the formal model by means of several refinements without forgetting to perform all proofs, in particular the partial deadlock freeness proofs (this can be seen on the website [1]). During the formal developments, we use the model-checker of ProB [8] and also the animators of ProB and AnimB.

4 Requirements

4.1 Introduction

As was announced in the introduction, we simplified some properties proposed in the case study or we omitted some of them. Here are these properties.

We simplified the timing constraints by just taking them in the anomalies occuring if the reaction of the system is too slow after some electro-valves stimulations (this is summarized in section 4.8 where various inconsistencies are described).

We omitted completely the redundancies of the inputs (three wires that are chosen by a majority voting) because it was not clear for us how the software can make the difference between a wire sending "false" and a broken wire. Likewise, we did not introduce two identical pieces of software running in different computers. Again, it was not clear to us how these distinct software could detect that they are delivering different outputs. In all these cases of redundancies, the timing constraints we take into account will anyway detect some inconsistencies if the response of the environment is too slow or simply missing.

The architecture of the system we are going to model is the one presented in the figure below. It is a simplification of a similar figure that can be seen in the case study document. Here we have omitted the hydraulic parts: we connect directly each electro-valve to the corresponding part of equipment.

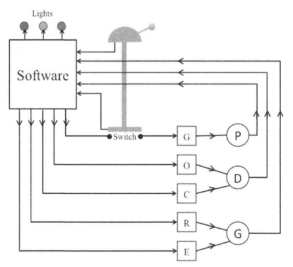

G: General Electro-valve
O: Opening electro-valve   P: Hydraulic pressure
C: Closing electro-valve   D: Doors
R: Retracting electro-valve   G: Gears
E: Extending Electro-valve

4.2 Labeling

The various requirements that can be seen in the next section are numbered and labeled. Here are the labels we use:

- For functional requirements: FUN
- For environment assumptions: ENV
- For anomaly requirements: ANM

4.3 Basic Elements

In this first section of the requirements, we describe the main elements of the system: gears, doors, and software. We also mention the two modes of the system and the limit of its behavior (when it stops because of some inconsistencies).

| The system has three landing sets situated in the front, the left, and the right part of the aircraft | ENV-1 |

| Each landing set contains a gear that can be retracted, extended, or maneuvered | ENV-2 |

| Each landing set also contains a door that can be open, closed, or maneuvered | ENV-3 |

| The system is controlled by a piece of software | ENV-4 |

| The system can be in two modes: nominal or emergency | FUN-1 |

| The emergency mode can be detected by the software (see ANM-1 to ANM-7) | FUN-2 |

| In emergency mode, the system stops | FUN-3 |

4.4 The Pilot Interface and Main Functions of the System

In this section of the requirements, we describe how the extension and retraction of the gears are performed after some action of the pilot on the handle at his disposal. We also indicate how the pilot is informed about the state of the system.

| The pilot has a handle with two positions: UP and DOWN | ENV-5 |

| When gears are retracted and the handle is going from UP to DOWN, the extending sequence is performed | FUN-4 |

The extending sequence is the following: open doors, extend gears, close doors	FUN-5

When gears are extended and the handle is going from DOWN to UP, the retracting sequence is performed	FUN-6

The retracting sequence is the following: open doors, retract gears, close doors	FUN-7

At any time during a door/gear maneuver, this maneuver can be stopped and reversed by the pilot moving the handle in the other direction	FUN-8

We have three lights in the cockpit: green, orange, and red	ENV-6

Gears extended, the green light is lit	FUN-9

Gears maneuvering, the orange light is lit	FUN-10

In emergency mode the red light is lit	FUN-11

4.5   The Mechanical and Hydraulic Parts

Here we give some information about the electro-valves situated in between the software and the basic equipment described in section 4.3.

There are 5 electro-valves (one general and four specific): - one general electro-valve providing or removing pressure in the hydraulic circuit - two electro-valves opening or closing doors - two electro-valves retracting or extending gears	ENV-7

Each electro-valve can be ON or OFF	ENV-8

When the general electro-valve is ON stimulated, the pressure will be eventually provided in the hydraulic circuit	ENV-9

When the general electro-valve is OFF stimulated, the pressure will be removed from the hydraulic circuit	ENV-10

When the status of the handle is changed, the general electro-valve is set to ON if it is OFF	FUN-12

When a gear operation is complete the general electro-valve is set to OFF	FUN-13

A specific electro-valve can be set to ON only when the pressure in the hydraulic circuit is provided	ENV-11

When the door closing or opening electro-valves are ON stimulated then the doors will be eventually closed or open	ENV-12

When the gear retracting or extending electro-valves are ON stimulated then the gears will be eventually retracted or extended	ENV-13

4.6 The Analogical Switch

An important characteristic of the equipment is the switch situated between the general electro-valve and the software.

Within the connection between the software and the general electro-valve, there is an analogical switch	ENV-14

The analogical switch can be closed or open	ENV-15

If not already closed, the analogical switch is mechanically closed each time there is a change in the handle by the pilot	ENV-16

40 seconds after the last handle change, the switch is mechanically turned open	ENV-17

Only when the switch is closed can the software send information successfully to the general electro-valve	ENV-18

4.7   The Software Input and Outputs

Here we summarize the inputs and outputs of the software.

The software receives the following inputs:
  - one from handle
  - one from analogical switch
  - one from circuit pressurized
  - three from gear extension
  - three from gear retraction
  - three from door closed
  - three from door opened
	ENV-19

The software sends the following outputs:
  - one to the general electro-valve
  - one to the close door electro-valve
  - one to the open door electro-valve
  - one to the retraction electro-valve
  - one to the extension electro-valve
	ENV-20

The software sends the following outputs to the cockpit:
  - gears maneuvering (then: orange light on)
  - gears locked down (then: green light on)
  - anomaly (then: red light on)
	ENV-21

4.8   Cases of Inconsistencies

In this section of the requirements, we show the various timings implying some anomaly in the behavior of the system.

Analogical switch still opened 160ms after stimulation	ANM-1

Circuit still unpressurized 2 seconds after stimulation	ANM-2

Circuit still pressurized after 10 seconds after stimulation	ANM-3

Doors still closed 7 seconds after stimulation	ANM-4

Doors still opened 7 seconds after stimulation	ANM-5

Gears not retracted 10 seconds after stimulation	ANM-6

Gears not extended 10 seconds after stimulation	ANM-7

4.9   Summary of Requirements

Here is a summary of the requirements and assumptions we are going to consider in our approaches:

- 21 Environnement assumptions (ENV)
- 13 Functional requirements (FUN)
- 7 Anomaly requirements (ANM)
- 41 Total

5   First Approach

Reading this section (and the following two as well) will be made easier by consulting the formal developments made with the Rodin Platform. This developments are available from the following website [1].

5.1   Introduction

In this approach (the first one we developed), we initially apprehend the system from outside in, starting by modeling the environment first and then the software. In other words, we introduce the software after some refinements only. We apply here a systematic approach that is usually *very successful* in the modeling of embedded systems.

This approach consists in first determining what are the basic equipment of our system. In our case, we have three main devices: the handle, the doors, and the gears. In this system, we have three doors and three gears, but at the initial level of abstraction we consider them *globally* as if there were a unique gear and a unique door. Such abstract door and gear are data-refined in the last two refinements to be three gears and three doors.

In a first abstraction, we express the *degree of freedom* of each device *independently* of others. For instance, the doors can be closed, or in the process of opening, or open, or finally in the process of closing.

Then we explain in a refinement what are the relationship between these devices. In fact, each device is not free as mentioned in the abstraction: it is constrained by others. For instance, the gears can be extending or retracting only when the doors are open. Likewise, starting the opening of the doors is constrained by a change in the handle position. At this level of abstraction, each device is *directly* influenced by others: we have no intermediate agent doing that job. It is as if each device were *mechanically connected* to others in order to influence them or be influenced by them.

In a subsequent refinement, we introduce the software. Devices are again independent, but the introduced piece of software contains the intelligence that influence their behavior. At this level of abstraction the software is directly connected to the devices. Of course, the software has to be aware of the state of each device and it has to send some commands to each of them: this is done by means of messages received from and sent to the devices. For example, in the following figure we can see how the boolean messages *door_opn* and *door_cls* are elaborated by the environment (plain lines) and received by the software (dashed lines).

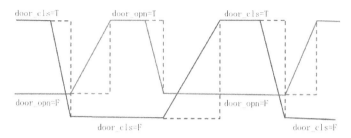

The non-vertical plain lines are due to the fact that the equipment (here the doors) take a certain time to move.

So far, our approach is quite general and can be applied to many similar embedded systems. In the next refinement, we become more specific: we introduce some intermediate pieces of equipment (in our case, the electro-valves) that are situated in between the software and the devices. The electro-valves transmit to the devices some hydraulic power able to move them. Some other peculiarity due to the hydraulic technology are introduced in a subsequent refinement (the general electro-valve).

It is fundamental to ensure that our embedded system behave in a correct fashion. The problem is to detect that some incorrect behavior has occurred. The most common way to do this is to check that each device responds to the stimulation of the software within a certain pre-defined time: the hydraulic technology implies that each device take a certain maximum predefined time to move. This is the purpose of the next refinement. Here we apply a technique that we already developed for modeling hybrid systems in [11] and [3].

5.2   Refinement Strategy

The general explanations given in the previous section are made more precise in the following refinement list. We have an initial model followed by nine refinements:

0. Free movements of handle, doors and gears

1. Synchronizing handle with doors and gears

2. Controlling doors and gears by means of the software

3. Introducing boolean wires

4. Introducing door Electro-Valves and gear Electro-Valves

5. Introducing general Electro-Valve

6. Introducing timing constraints

7. Introducing lights in the cockpit

8. Introducing three doors

9. Introducing three gears

The following table summarize the connections between the refinement strategy and the requirements defined in section 4: this ensures, a priori, that all requirements are indeed covered by our approach.

Refinement	Environment	Function	Anomaly
0	ENV-1(p),2,3,	-	-
1	ENV-5	FUN-4(p),5(p),6(p),7(p),8(p)	-
2	ENV-4,19(p)	FUN-4,5,6,7,8	-
3	ENV-19(p)	-	-
4	ENV-7(p),8(p),12,13,20(p)	-	-
5	ENV-7-11,14-16,17(p),18,20	FUN-12,13	-
6	-	FUN-1,2,3	ANM-1-7
7	ENV-6,21	FUN-9,10,11	
8	ENV-1(p),19(p)	-	-
9	ENV-1,19	-	-

(p) means the related requirement is PARTIALLY taken into account.

5.3   Problems Encountered with This Approach

The main problem we had in this development was the mastering of *partial deadlock freeness*. This property is the following: when no elementary operation can be performed any more (pressurizing, depressurizing, moving doors, moving gears, etc) then the system must have reached a *stable state* (gear and handle being coherent) where the only possible operation is that of the pilot changing the handle position. Notice that this partial deadlock freeness property is stronger than pure deadlock freeness where it is shown that some events can always be enabled (that is, the system is not blocked).

Another interesting property of such a system is *reachability*. In this case, it consists in proving that the pilot can always extend or retract the gears provided no handler modification is performed for a sufficiently large time. We develop a specific modeling to prove this property: it can be seen on the website [1].

At each refinement step, we tried to prove this property but it happened to be rather difficult: not difficult to prove when true but difficult to make it true.The difficulty is essentially due to the fact that the direction of the handle can be modified in the middle of doors or gears movements (even in the middle of a hydraulic circuit pressurizing or depressurizing, or in the middle of the opening of the analogical switch).

In order to solve this partial deadlock freeness problem, many intermediate events were added in the software and to the environment. This was done in a rather *unsystematic way* (a kind of hacking) and generated many additional proof obligations. This resulted eventually in 2258 proof obligations that were, fortunately, all proved automatically. But all this was clearly *very unsatisfactory*, so we decided to start a new development with a slightly different approach.

6   Second Approach

6.1   Introduction

In this second approach, we consider three physical "devices": the hydraulic circuit (whose state is pressurized or depressurized), the gears (whose state is retracted or extended), and the doors (whose state is open or closed). Any modification in the state of these devices takes a certain time. As a consequence, we always consider two environment events for such modifications: that is a "begin modification" and "end modification". More precisely, we have events "beg_prs", "end_prs" (for hydraulic circuit pressurization), "beg_opn", "end_opn" (for door opening), etc.

Events "begin modification" are initiated by the software stimulating some electro-valves: general_EV, open_EV, retract_EV, extend_EV, or closed_EV. When an environment event "end modification" occurs (always after the occurrence of a corresponding "begin modification" event), the environment sends an information to the software, which can then stimulate the next electro-valve, and so on.

At this level of abstraction, besides the electro-valves needed to open or close the doors, and the ones needed to retract or extend the gears, we suppose to have two "electro-valves" for pressurizing (pressurize_EV) or depressurizing (depressurize_EV) the hydraulic circuit. This is introduced in order to unify the electro-valves treatments. But, of course, this is only an abstraction. In reality, the pressurization and depressurization is not done by two electro-valves but by one only: the general electro-valve (general_EV). These two abstract "electro-valves", pressurize_EV and depressurize_EV, are data-refined to general_EV in the last refinement.

More precisely, the software contains the following events: act1, act2, ..., act6. Such software events stimulate the environment by means of some electro-valves. In response to this, the environment send messages to the software telling it that the corresponding device has change state. Then the software stimulates the next electro-valve, and so on. Here are the details of the electro-valve stimulations by the software:

      no EV

act1 : sending pressurized_EV
     receiving response

act2 : sending open_EV
     receiving response

act3 : sending retract_EV or extend_EV
     receiving response

act4 : sending closed_EV
     receiving response

act5 : sending depressurize_EV
     receiving response

act6 : no EV

At any moment, the software can also send to the environment the stimulation of an electro-valve which happen to be the "reverse" electro-valve of the one it last sent. These events are the following: chg2, chg3, ..., chg6. For example the event ch3 is possibly sent by the software after the event act2 that sent "open_EV" to the environment: in this case, the event chg3 send the "reverse" electro-valve, that is "close_EV". We have similar behavior with other chg events. This "reverse" electro-valve can be received by the environment just before the occurrence of an event "begin modification", or after it but before the occurrence of the corresponding "end modification", or finally, just after it. Depending on these cases, the reaction of the software and that of the environment will be different. The following tables show how the software and the environment events interact:

```
        ext = TRUE                                ext = FALSE

  ENVT        SOFT                        ENVT        SOFT
              act1                                    act1
      ↙    chg2  →    act6                    ↙    chg2  →    act6
beg_prs                              beg_prs
    ↓      chg2  →  end_dpr                 ↓      chg2  →  end_dpr
end_prs → act2  chg2  →  beg_dpr     end_prs → act2  chg2  →  beg_dpr
      ↙    chg3  →    act5                    ↙    chg3  →    act5
beg_opn                              beg_opn
    ↓      chg3  →  end_cls                 ↓      chg3  →  end_cls
end_opn → act3  chg3  →  beg_cls     end_opn → act3  chg3  →  beg_cls
      ↙    chg4  →    act4                    ↙    chg4  →    act4
beg_rtr                              beg_ext
    ↓      chg4  →  end_ext                 ↓      chg4  →  end_rtr
end_rtr → act4  chg4  →  beg_ext     end_ext → act4  chg4  →  beg_rtr
      ↙    chg5  →    act3                    ↙    chg5  →    act3
beg_cls                              beg_cls
    ↓      chg5  →  end_opn                 ↓      chg5  →  end_opn
end_cls → act5  chg5  →  beg_opn     end_cls → act5  chg5  →  beg_opn
      ↙    chg6  →    act2                    ↙    chg6  →    act2
beg_dpr                              beg_dpr
    ↓      chg6  →  end_prs                 ↓      chg6  →  end_prs
end_dpr → act6  chg6  →  beg_prs     end_dpr → act6  chg6  →  beg_prs
```

Here is an illustrating examples with the event chg3 (sending "close_EV"): the effect of this event can be received BEFORE beg_opn (opening has not started yet), AFTER beg_opn and BEFORE end_opn (opening has started but is not finished yet) or AFTER end_opn (opening is finished). If the new electro-valve stimulation (close_EV) is received before the doors start to open, then the next step for the software consists in depressurizing (since the software still believe that the doors are closed). This corresponds to the following trace:

$$act1 \rightarrow beg\_prs \rightarrow end\_prs \rightarrow act2 \rightarrow \underline{\underline{chg3}} \rightarrow act5 \rightarrow beg\_dpr \rightarrow end\_dpr$$

If the change occurs while the doors are opening (but the doors are not completely open yet), then the next step in the environment consists in closing the door and then depressurizing. Here is the corresponding trace:

act1 → beg_prs → end_prs → act2 → beg_opn → chg3 → end_cls → act5 →
beg_dpr → end_dpr

If the change occurs once the doors are open, then the next steps consist for the environment to start closing the doors, then closing them, and then depressurizing. Here is a final trace:

act1 → beg_prs → end_prs → act2 → beg_opn → end_opn → chg3 → beg_cls →
end_cls → act5 → beg_dpr → end_dpr

An important idea in this new approach is to consider the problem of partial deadlock freeness right from the beginning. With the systematic treatment we have briefly explained, this is done now in a very systematic fashion.

6.2   Refinement Strategy

From the third refinement step on, the strategy is the same as in the previous approach:

0. Introducing the connection between the software and the environment

1. Introducing the handle

2. Introducing analogical switch

3. Introducing timing constraints

4. Introducing lights in the cockpit

5. Introducing three doors

6. Introducing three gears

7. Refining Electro-valves

Again, the following table summarize the connections between the refinement strategy and the requirements defined in section 4: this ensures, a priori, that all requirements are indeed covered by our approach.

Refinement	Environment	Function	Anomaly
0	ENV-1(p),2-4,7(p),9(p)-13(p),19(p),20(p)	FUN-4-8,12(p),13(p)	-
1	ENV-5	-	-
2	ENV-14,15,16,17(p),18,19(p)	-	-
3	EVN-17	FUN-1,2,3	ANM-1-7
4	ENV-6,21	FUN-9,10,11	-
5	ENV-1(p),19(p)	-	-
6	ENV-1,19	-	-
7	ENV-7-13,20	FUN-12,13	-

(p) means the related requirement is PARTIALLY taken into account.

6.3 About This Approach

This approach has far less proof obligations than the previous one: 1099 only. Moreover, we now completely master the partial deadlock freeness. However we found that many invariants and events are very similar. So, we think that it could be further simplified. This is the purpose of the next approach.

7 Third Approach

7.1 Introduction

In this approach, the idea is to *tabulate* the behavior of the system. For this, we introduce three constants "tables": the relation N (for next), the function R (for reverse) and the function T (for timing). The relation N defines the order in which the various electro-valves have to be stimulated by the software:

$$N = \{\; no\_ev \mapsto prs\_ev, \quad prs\_ev \mapsto opn\_ev, \quad opn\_ev \mapsto rtr\_ev, \\ rtr\_ev \mapsto cls\_ev, \quad opn\_ev \mapsto ext\_ev, \quad ext\_ev \mapsto cls\_ev, \\ cls\_ev \mapsto dpr\_ev, \quad dpr\_ev \mapsto no\_ev \;\}$$

The function R determines which electro-valves the software has to stimulate in case of a modification of the handle position during a move:

$$R = \{\; prs\_ev \mapsto dpr\_ev, \quad dpr\_ev \mapsto prs\_ev, \quad opn\_ev \mapsto cls\_ev, \\ cls\_ev \mapsto opn\_ev, \quad rtr\_ev \mapsto ext\_ev, \quad ext\_ev \mapsto rtr\_ev \;\}$$

The function T determine the various timings to be checked depending on the stimulated electro-valve:

$$T = \{\; prs\_ev \mapsto 2000, \quad opn\_ev \mapsto 7000, \quad rtr\_ev \mapsto 10000, \\ ext\_ev \mapsto 10000, \quad cls\_ev \mapsto 7000, \quad dpr\_ev \mapsto 10000 \;\}$$

7.2 Refinement Strategy

The refinement strategy is similar to that used in the previous approach.

7.3 About This Approach

The tabulation done in this approach is very efficient with regards to the number of proof obligations: we have 341 of them only. The events (in the software or in the environment) appear to be *generic events* interpreting tables N, R, and T. This technique is very interesting as it is now very easy to extend the system by just modifying the tables, and this *without modifying the events*.

8   Conclusion

In this paper, we presented three modeling approaches to the "Aircraft Landing Gear" case study. We could have presented the last one only (the more efficient) but it seemed to us that, from a methodological point of view, it was quite interesting to show how we progressed in this project. It is also interesting to motivate the fact that there is not a unique way to develop the model of a relatively large industrial system.

In a system like this one, there are many actions that are performed in parallel with others: the software works in parallel with the environment, the pilot can modify the handle position in parallel with the hydraulic equipment, the three doors as well as the three gears are all moved simultaneously. Have we taken this into account in our modeling? The answer is positive. By introducing some "begin modification"-"end modification" events, we state implicitly that between them, other events can occur. For instance, when the three doors are opening (between event "beg_opn" and "end_opn"), the pilot can change the position of the handle resulting in the occurrence of events "chg_..." (this is explained in Section 6).

The main original impulse to our development of several models was the problem of partial deadlock freeness. In fact, this problem is very important for complex embedded systems like the one we study here. Clearly, the presence of deadlocks in certain circumstances can have terrible consequences (think of the pilot being suddenly unable to extend the landing gears). All this motivates us to pursue further some practical investigations in this domain, in particular the question of the relationship between deadlock freeness and refinement. Next is a quick description of this question.

Unlike invariants which are maintained from an abstraction to its refinement, deadlock freeness is not maintained: it is quite possible to have an abstraction that is deadlock free whereas its refinement is not, this is due essentially to guard strengthening occurring in refinements. Moreover, deadlock freeness proofs are usually a bit complicated because they involve the disjunction of all the event guards. So, such complicated proofs have to be redone within each refinement. An interesting problem is that of doing such new deadlock freeness proofs by taking account of the fact that deadlock freeness has already been proved in the abstraction. In other words, can we only do a simple additional proof in a refinement instead a completely new proof? We shall study this in some further work.

Acknowledgements. We would like to thank the anonymous reviewers for their helpful feedback. Wen Su was supported in part by the Open Project of Shanghai Key Laboratory of Trustworthy Computing (No. 07dz22304201303). Jean-Raymond Abrial was partly funded by FP7 ADVANCE Project (No. 287563).

References

1. http://www.lab205.org/case-landing
2. Abrial, J.-R.: Modeling in Event-B: System and Software Engineering. Cambridge University Press (2010)

3. Abrial, J.-R., Su, W., Zhu, H.: Formalizing hybrid systems with Event-B. In: Derrick, J., Fitzgerald, J., Gnesi, S., Khurshid, S., Leuschel, M., Reeves, S., Riccobene, E. (eds.) ABZ 2012. LNCS, vol. 7316, pp. 178–193. Springer, Heidelberg (2012)
4. Boniol, F., Wiels, V.: The Landing Gear System Case Study. In: Boniol, F. (ed.) ABZ 2014 Case Study Track. CCIS, vol. 433, pp. 1–18. Springer, Heidelberg (2014)
5. Hallerstede, S., Jastram, M., Ladenberger, L.: A method and tool for tracing requirements into specifications. Science of Computer Programming, 36 (2013)
6. Hoang, T.S., Fürst, A., Abrial, J.-R.: Event-B patterns and their tool support. Software and System Modeling 12(2), 229–244 (2013)
7. Larman, C.: Applying UML and Patterns: An Introduction to Object-Oriented Analysis and Design and Iterative Development. Prentice Hall (2004)
8. Leuschel, M., Butler, M.J.: ProB: an automated analysis toolset for the B method. STTT 10(2), 185–203 (2008)
9. Rodin, http://www.event-b.org/
10. Su, W., Abrial, J.-R., Huang, R., Zhu, H.: From requirements to development: Methodology and example. In: Qin, S., Qiu, Z. (eds.) ICFEM 2011. LNCS, vol. 6991, pp. 437–455. Springer, Heidelberg (2011)
11. Su, W., Abrial, J.-R., Zhu, H.: Complementary methodologies for developing hybrid systems with Event-B. In: Aoki, T., Taguchi, K. (eds.) ICFEM 2012. LNCS, vol. 7635, pp. 230–248. Springer, Heidelberg (2012)

Modeling and Analyzing Using ASMs: The Landing Gear System Case Study

Paolo Arcaini[1], Angelo Gargantini[1], and Elvinia Riccobene[2]

[1] Dipartimento di Ingegneria, Università degli Studi di Bergamo, Italy
{paolo.arcaini,angelo.gargantini}@unibg.it
[2] Dipartimento di Informatica, Università degli Studi di Milano, Italy
elvinia.riccobene@unimi.it

Abstract. The paper presents an Abstract State Machine (ASM) specification of the Landing Gear System case study, and shows how the ASMETA framework can be used to support the modeling and analysis (validation and verification) activities for developing a rigorous and correct model in terms of ASMs. We exploit the two fundamental concepts of the ASM method, i.e., the notion of ground model and the refinement principle, and we achieve model development and model analysis by the combined use of formal methods for specification and for verification.

1 Introduction

The *Abstract State Machine* (ASM) method is a system engineering method that guides the development of software and embedded hardware-software systems seamlessly from requirements capture to their implementation. Within a precise but simple conceptual framework, the ASM method allows a *modeling technique* which integrates dynamic (*operational*) and static (*declarative*) descriptions, and an *analysis technique* that combines *validation* (by simulation and testing) and *verification* methods at any desired level of detail. The method has been successfully applied in different fields as: definition of industrial standards for programming and modeling languages, design and re-engineering of industrial control systems, modeling e-commerce and web services, design and analysis of protocols, architectural design, language design, verification of compilation schemes and compiler back-ends, etc.

ASMs are an extension of Finite State Machines, obtained by replacing unstructured control states by states comprising arbitrarily complex data [7]. The method has, therefore, a rigorous mathematical foundation [9], but a practitioner needs no special training to use the method since ASMs can be correctly understood as pseudo-code or virtual machines working over abstract data structures.

We here propose an ASM specification of the Landing Gear System (LGS), proposed in the ABZ conference as a real-life case study [5] with the aim of showing how different formal methods can be used for the specification, design and development of a complex system.

The ASM modeling process is based on the concept of a *ground model* representing a precise but concise high-level formalization of the system, and on the

F. Boniol et al. (Eds.): ABZ 2014 Case Study Track, CCIS 433, pp. 36–51, 2014.

refinement principle that allows to capture all details of the system design by a sequence of refined models till the desired level of detail.

After a brief introduction to ASMs in Section 2, Section 3 presents the modeling approach, and it also overviews a variety of model analysis activities that can be performed by using the ASMETA framework [4,12], a set of tools for the ASMs.

Section 4 reports the results of the modeling activity, and of the model validation and verification performed at each level of refinement. We start from a ground model that is the description of the *core* system, namely one landing set whose behavior is captured in terms of user input and doors' and gears' alleged state. Then we refine the model by adding the actuators' behavior in terms of electro-valves' and cylinders' operations; subsequently the sensors are added. The system with one landing component is then generalized to a system with three landing sets, and in the last refinement the health monitoring is included.

Section 5 discusses the strengths and the weaknesses of the approach, and outlines some future research directions. Since no other solutions of modeling and analysis of the LGS case study are available at the moment of writing this paper, we are not able to report any related work. Of course, many successful applications exist in literature regarding the use of the ASMs for complex system modeling and analysis. Due to their multiplicity, we prefer to refer to [9] for a complete introduction on the ASM method and the presentation of the great variety of its successful applications.

2 Abstract State Machines

Abstract State Machines (ASMs), whose complete presentation can be found in [9], are an extension of FSMs, where unstructured control states are replaced by states with arbitrary complex data. The *states* of an ASM are multi-sorted first-order structures, i.e., domains of objects with functions and predicates defined on them. ASM states are modified by *transition relations* specified by "rules" describing the modification of the function interpretations from one state to the next one. There is a limited but powerful set of *rule constructors* that allow to express guarded actions (`if-then`), simultaneous parallel actions (`par`) or sequential actions (`seq`). Appropriate rule constructors also allow nondeterminism (existential quantification `choose`) and unrestricted synchronous parallelism (universal quantification `forall`).

An ASM state *s* is represented by a set of couples (*location, value*). ASM *locations*, namely pairs (*function-name, list-of-parameter-values*), represent the abstract ASM concept of basic object containers (memory units). Location *updates* represent the basic units of state change and they are given as assignments, each of the form *loc* := *v*, where *loc* is a location and *v* its new value.

Functions are classified as *derived*, i.e., those coming with a specification or computation mechanism given in terms of other functions, and *basic* which can be *static* (never change during any run of the machine) or *dynamic* (may change as a consequence of agent actions or *updates*). Dynamic functions are distinguished between *monitored* (only read by the machine and modified by the environment), and *controlled* (read and written by the machine).

A *computation* of an ASM is a finite or infinite sequence $s_0, s_1, \ldots, s_n, \ldots$ of states of the machine, where s_0 is an initial state and each s_{n+1} is obtained from s_n by simultaneously firing all the transition rules which are enabled in s_n. The (unique) *main rule* is a transition rule and represents the starting point of the computation. An ASM can have more than one *initial state*. It is possible to specify state *invariants*.

3   Modeling Process and Supporting Tools

The process of *requirements capture* results in constructing rigorous *ground models* which are precise but concise high-level system blueprints ("system contracts"), formulated in domain-specific terms, using an application-oriented language which can be understood by all stakeholders. The developer starts from the textual description of the informal requirements, and an ASM model is developed simply translating the text in terms of transition rules capturing the behavior of the system at a very high level of abstraction. This sketchy first model is usually neither "correct" nor "complete". Rather, it tries on purpose to expose errors, ambiguities, or incompletenesses in the original text. Correctness can be achieved through an iterative process reasoning on requirements till producing a ground model.

From the ground model, by step-wise refined models, further details are added to capture the major design decisions and provide descriptions of the complete software architecture and component design of the system. In this way the complexity of the system can be always taken under control, and it is possible to bridge, in a seamless manner, the gap between specification and code.

Still from its ground level, a model can be *validated* and *verified*. Model validation should be applied at the early stages of the system development, in order to ensure that the specification really reflects the user needs and statements about the system, and to detect faults in the specification as early as possible with limited effort. Validation should precede the application of more expensive and accurate methods, like formal requirements analysis and verification of properties, that should be applied only when a designer has enough confidence that the specification captures all informal requirements.

Tools allowing different forms of model analysis can surely help the developer in reaching model correctness. For the ASM method, the ASMETA (ASM mETAmodeling) framework[1] [4,12] provides basic functionalities for ASM models creation and manipulation (as editing, storage, interchange, access, etc.), as well as advanced model analysis techniques (as validation, verification, testing, model review, requirements analysis, runtime monitoring, etc.). The tools are strongly integrated in order to permit reusing information about models during several development phases.

---

[1] http://asmeta.sourceforge.net/

The concrete syntax AsmetaL is available for model *editing*. Model *simulation* is possible using AsmetaS [11]. The tool allows *invariant checking* to guarantee that the executed model always satisfies given properties, *consistent updates checking* for revealing inconsistent updates, *random simulation* where random values for monitored functions are provided by the environment, and *interactive simulation* when required inputs are provided interactively during simulation.

A more powerful validation approach is based on *scenario construction* by the ASM validator AsmetaV [10]. The validator is based on the AsmetaS simulator and on the Avalla modeling language. This last provides constructs to express execution scenarios in an algorithmic way as interaction sequences consisting of (a) *actions* committed by the user to set the environment, to check the machine state, and to ask for the execution of certain transition rules, and (b) the *reaction* of the machine to make one (or a sequence of) step(s) in response of the user actions.

A further validation technique is *model review* which aims at determining if a model not only fulfills the intended requirements, but it is of sufficient *quality* to be easy to develop, maintain, and enhance. Model review allows to identify defects early in the system development, reducing the cost of fixing them, so it is useful to apply this technique on models just sketched. The AsmetaMA tool [2] permits *automatic* review of ASMs. Typical vulnerabilities and defects a developer can introduce during the modeling activity using the ASMs are checked as violations of suitable meta-properties. The violation of a meta-property means that some attributes (minimality, completeness, redundancy, etc.) are not guaranteed and indicates the presence of actual faults, or only of potential faults.

Formal verification of ASMs is possible by means of AsmetaSMV [1]. This tool takes in input models written in AsmetaL and maps them into specifications for the model checker NuSMV. AsmetaSMV supports both the verification of *Computation Tree Logic* (CTL) and *Linear Temporal Logic* (LTL) formulas.

Tools for model-based testing and runtime verification are available in the ASMETA framework; we do not use them in this work, since we do not have any implementation to test. However, such techniques are explained and used in a separate paper regarding the sub-case study of the voting system of sensors [3], for which a Java implementation was developed.

3.1 Model Refinement

For complex systems, the complete specification can be reached by step-wise refinement, namely by a chain of models each of which is proved to be a correct refinement of the previous one. According to the notion of ASM refinement method presented in [6,8], to refine an ASM M to an ASM M^*, the following items must be defined:

- a notion of *refined state*;
- a notion of *states of interest* and of *correspondence* between M-states S and M^*-states S^* of interest, i.e., the pairs of states in the runs one wants to relate through the refinement, including usually the correspondence of initial and (if there are any) of final states;

Ground model: - doors & gears	1st refinement: - electro-valves - cylinders	2nd refinement: - sensors	3rd refinement: - three landing sets	4th refinement: - health monitoring

Fig. 1. Models chain

- a notion of abstract *computation segments* $\tau_1, \ldots, \tau_m$, where each τ_i represents a single M-step, and of corresponding refined computation segments $\sigma_1, \ldots, \sigma_n$, of single M^*-steps σ_j, which in given runs lead from corresponding states of interest to (usually the next) corresponding states of interest;
- a notion of *locations of interest* and of *corresponding* locations, i.e., pairs of (possibly sets of) locations one wants to relate in corresponding states;
- a notion of equivalence $\equiv$ of the data in the locations of interest; these local data equivalences usually accumulate to a notion of equivalence of corresponding states of interest.

According to this scheme, an ASM refinement allows one to combine a change of the signature (data refinement) with a change of the control (operation refinement), while many notions of refinement in the literature keep these two features separated.

Once the notions of corresponding states and of their equivalence have been determined, one can define that M^* is a correct refinement of M as follows:

Definition 1. *Fix a notion $\equiv$ of equivalence of states and of initial and final states. An ASM M^* is a correct refinement of an ASM M if and only if for each M^*-run $s_1^*, s_2^*, \ldots$, there is an M-run $s_1, s_2, \ldots$ and sequences $i_0 < i_1 < \ldots, j_0 < j_1 < \ldots$ such that $i_0 = j_0 = 0$ and $S_{i_k} \equiv S_{j_k}^*$ for each k and either*
- *both runs terminate and their final states are the last pair of equivalent states;*
   or
- *both runs and both sequences $i_0 < i_1 < \ldots, j_0 < j_1 < \ldots$ are infinite.*

The states S_{i_k} and $S_{j_k}^*$ are the corresponding states of interest. They represent the end points of the corresponding computation segments (those of interest) for which the equivalence is defined in terms of a relation between their corresponding locations (those of interest).

4   Models Chain of the LGS

In the following sections we present the five steps of the refinement process for modeling the case study[2]. Fig. 1 depicts the relationship existing between the models and, for each model, the system elements introduced with respect to the previous model. We start from the high level description (ground model) of

---

[2] All the models are available online at
http://fmse.di.unimi.it/sw/landingGearSystem.zip

```
asm LandingGearSystemGround

signature:
    enum domain HandleStatus = {UP | DOWN}
    enum domain DoorStatus = {CLOSED | OPENING | OPEN | CLOSING}
    enum domain GearStatus = {RETRACTED | EXTENDING | EXTENDED |
                                                          RETRACTING}
    dynamic monitored handle: HandleStatus
    dynamic controlled doors: DoorStatus
    dynamic controlled gears: GearStatus

definitions:
    rule r_closeDoor =
        switch doors
            case OPEN: doors := CLOSING
            case CLOSING: doors := CLOSED
            case OPENING: doors := CLOSING
        endswitch

    rule r_retractionSequence =
        if gears != RETRACTED then
            switch doors
                case CLOSED: doors := OPENING
                case CLOSING: doors := OPENING
                case OPENING: doors := OPEN
                case OPEN:
                    switch gears
                        case EXTENDED: gears := RETRACTING
                        case RETRACTING: gears := RETRACTED
                        case EXTENDING: gears := RETRACTING
                    endswitch
            endswitch
        else
            r_closeDoor[]
        endif


rule r_outgoingSequence =
    if gears != EXTENDED then
        switch doors
            case CLOSED: doors := OPENING
            case OPENING: doors := OPEN
            case OPEN:
                switch gears
                    case RETRACTED: gears := EXTENDING
                    case EXTENDING: gears := EXTENDED
                    case RETRACTING: gears := EXTENDING
                endswitch
        endswitch
    else
        r_closeDoor[]
    endif

invariant over gears, doors:
(gears = EXTENDING or gears = RETRACTING) implies
doors = OPEN

invariant over gears, doors:
doors = CLOSED implies
(gears = EXTENDED or gears = RETRACTED)

main rule r_Main =
    if handle = UP then
        r_retractionSequence[]
    else
        r_outgoingSequence[]
    endif

default init s0:
    function doors = CLOSED
    function gears = EXTENDED
```

Code 1. Ground model

the system *core*, i.e., one landing set whose behavior is captured in terms of user input and doors' and gears' alleged state. Then we refine the model by adding the behavior of the actuators: electro-valves and cylinders. In the third step the sensors are added. The fourth refinement generalizes the system, moving from one landing component to a system with three equal landing sets. In the last refinement, the health monitoring is included.

For the first two refinement steps we prove that a model is a correct refinement of the more abstract one. For the further levels, the proof technique is similar and it has been skipped. On the ground model we apply different validation techniques (simulation, scenario construction, model review) that, due to lack of space, are not repeated in the other levels. If a refinement step is proved correct, all the properties already verified in the high-level model do not need to be verified again in the refined model. However, since the refinement process was guided by the requirements, and each refinement introduces new elements in the model, new properties regarding the newly added requirements have been added and verified at each suitable level.

4.1 Ground Model

In the first model we have only modeled the doors and the gears and how their status changes. The model does not contain valves, cylinders, sensors, and the health monitoring. The complete ground model in shown in Code 1. Function **doors** represents the status of the doors that can be OPEN, CLOSED, OPENING

```
rule r_retractionSequence =
    if gears != RETRACTED then
        switch doors
            ...
            case OPEN:
                switch gears
                    case RETRACTING: gears := EXTENDED //error. It should be RETRACTED
                    ...
```

Code 2. Wrong ground model – Error in `r_retractionSequence`

or CLOSING. Function `gears` represents the status of the gears that can be EXTENDED, RETRACTED, RETRACTING or EXTENDING.

The state transitions are driven by the value of the monitored function `handle`. As long as the `handle` is UP, the *retraction sequence* [5] is executed, and, instead, as long as the `handle` is DOWN, the *outgoing sequence* [5] is executed. Let's see, as an example, how the retraction sequence works: so we assume that, in each state, the `handle` is UP. In the initial state, the `doors` are CLOSED and the `gears` are EXTENDED; then the `doors` start OPENING. When the `doors` become OPEN, the `gears` start RETRACTING. When the `gears` become RETRACTED, the `doors` start CLOSING. The retraction sequence terminates with the `doors` CLOSED and the `gears` RETRACTED. The outgoing sequence behaves similarly. Note that, a retraction (resp. an outgoing) sequence can be always interrupted by switching the value of the `handle`; in this case, an outgoing (resp. a retraction) sequence begins, starting from the status of the `doors` and the `gears` reached in the previous sequence.

An invariant checks that, if the `gears` are moving (i.e., they are EXTENDING or RETRACTING), the `doors` must be OPEN; another invariant checks that, if the `doors` are CLOSED, then the `gears` must be stopped (i.e., they are EXTENDED or RETRACTED).

Model Review. As first validation activity, we have checked the model with the model advisor. The first model we wrote actually contained an error, as shown in Code 2. Indeed, during a retraction sequence, the `gears` became EXTENDED instead of RETRACTED. The model advisor has discovered two meta-property violations (among the seven proposed in [2]):

- MP_5 requires that, for every domain element e, there exists a location which has value e. In the faulty model, MP_5 is violated since element RETRACTED of domain `GearStatus` is never used.
- MP_6 requires that every controlled location can take any value in its codomain. In the faulty model, MP_6 is violated since function `gears` does not take the value RETRACTED of its codomain.

Obviously, both meta-property violations are caused by the same error in the model. Note that behavioral faults often reveal themselves as stylistic defects and therefore they can be captured by the model advisor.

Simulation. By simulation we were able to identify the state in which the erroneous rule was executed. Fig. 2 shows the simulation trace of the wrong ground

```
Insert a symbol of HandleStatus   Insert a symbol of HandleStatus   Insert a symbol of HandleStatus   Insert a symbol ofHandleStatus
in [UP, DOWN] for handle:         in [UP, DOWN] for handle:         in [UP, DOWN] for handle:         in [UP, DOWN] for handle:
UP                                UP                                UP                                UP
<State 0 (monitored)>             <State 1 (monitored)>             <State 2 (monitored)>             <State 3 (monitored)>
handle=UP                         handle=UP                         handle=UP                         handle=UP
</State 0 (monitored)>            </State 1 (monitored)>            </State 2 (monitored)>            </State 3 (monitored)>
<State 1 (controlled)>            <State 2 (controlled)>            <State 3 (controlled)>            <State 4 (controlled)>
doors=OPENING                     doors=OPEN                        doors=OPEN                        doors=OPEN
gears=EXTENDED                    gears=EXTENDED                    gears=RETRACTING                  gears=EXTENDED
</State 1 (controlled)>           </State 2 (controlled)>           </State 3 (controlled)>           </State 4 (controlled)>
```

Fig. 2. Simulation of the wrong ground model

```
Insert a symbol of HandleStatus          Insert a symbol of HandleStatus          Insert a symbol of HandleStatus
in [UP, DOWN] for handle:                in [UP, DOWN] for handle:                in [UP, DOWN] for handle:
UP                                       UP                                       UP
<State 0 (monitored)>                    <State 2 (monitored)>                    <State 4 (monitored)>
handle=UP                                handle=UP                                handle=UP
</State 0 (monitored)>                   </State 2 (monitored)>                   </State 4 (monitored)>
<State 1 (controlled)>                   <State 3 (controlled)>                   <State 5 (controlled)>
doors=OPENING                            doors=OPEN                               doors=CLOSING
gears=EXTENDED                           gears=RETRACTING                         gears=RETRACTED
</State 1 (controlled)>                  </State 3 (controlled)>                  </State 5 (controlled)>
Insert a symbol of HandleStatus          Insert a symbol of HandleStatus          Insert a symbol of HandleStatus
in [UP, DOWN] for handle:                in [UP, DOWN] for handle:                in [UP, DOWN] for handle:
UP                                       UP                                       UP
<State 1 (monitored)>                    <State 3 (monitored)>                    <State 5 (monitored)>
handle=UP                                handle=UP                                handle=UP
</State 1 (monitored)>                   </State 3 (monitored)>                   </State 5 (monitored)>
<State 2 (controlled)>                   <State 4 (controlled)>                   <State 6 (controlled)>
doors=OPEN                               doors=OPEN                               doors=CLOSED
gears=EXTENDED                           gears=RETRACTED                          gears=RETRACTED
</State 2 (controlled)>                  </State 4 (controlled)>                  </State 6 (controlled)>
```

Fig. 3. Simulation of the correct ground model – Complete retraction sequence

scenario lgsGround1
load LandingGearSystemGround.asm
 	
set handle := UP;
step
check doors = OPENING and gears =EXTENDED;
	set handle := UP;
	step
	check doors = OPEN and gears =EXTENDED;
	
	set handle := UP;
	step
	check doors = OPEN and gears =RETRACTING;
		set handle := UP;
		step
		check doors = OPEN and gears =RETRACTED;

Code 3. Scenario reproducing the simulation that leads to the error

model. During an interactive simulation, at each step the user is asked for the values of the monitored functions (in this case the function `handle`).

Fig. 3 shows the simulation, over the correct ground model, of the complete retraction sequence described previously.

Scenario-Based Validation. We have then built a scenario describing the simulation that brings to the execution of the erroneous rule shown in Code 2; a scenario permits to automatize the execution of a run that must be executed more than once. Code 3 shows the scenario in which, before each step, the value of the monitored function `handle` is set to UP, and, after the simulation step, the values of functions `doors` and `gears` are checked. The scenario execution consists in a simulation, similar to that seen in Fig. 2. However, the simulation is not interactive, since the values of the monitored functions are set according to the values specified in the scenario. Moreover, the scenario execution also checks for the specified properties. Fig. 4 shows the output of the scenario execution over

```
<State 1 (controlled)>                                  <State 3 (controlled)>
doors=OPENING                                           doors=OPEN
gears=EXTENDED                                          gears=RETRACTING
handle=UP                                               handle=UP
</State 1 (controlled)>                                 </State 3 (controlled)>
"check succeeded: doors = OPENING and gears = EXTENDED" "check succeeded: doors = OPEN and gears = RETRACTING"
<State 2 (controlled)>                                  <State 4 (controlled)>
doors=OPEN                                              doors=OPEN
gears=EXTENDED                                          gears=EXTENDED
handle=UP                                               handle=UP
</State 2 (controlled)>                                 </State 4 (controlled)>
"check succeeded: doors = OPEN and gears = EXTENDED"    "CHECK FAILED: doors = OPEN and gears = RETRACTED at step 4"
```

Fig. 4. Execution of the scenario shown in Code 3 over the wrong ground model

the faulty ground model; we can notice that, in the fourth step, the specified property has been violated. We have later executed the scenario over the correct model and all the checks have been successful. Scenarios may be thought as use cases that drive the development of the model in a sort of Behaviour-Driven Development: a model is enhanced and/or fixed until all the scenarios execute without failures.

Model Checking. In the ground model we have been able to verify four normal mode requirements among those reported in the case study: $R_{11}bis$, $R_{12}bis$, R_{21}, and R_{22}. For example, requirement $R_{11}bis$ requires that, *when the command line is working (normal mode), if the landing gear command handle has been pushed DOWN and stays DOWN, then eventually the gears will be locked down and the doors will be seen closed.*

We have verified the following four CTL properties:

```
ag(ag(handle = DOWN) implies af(gears = EXTENDED and doors = CLOSED)) //R₁₁ bis
ag(ag(handle = UP) implies af(gears = RETRACTED and doors = CLOSED)) //R₁₂ bis
ag(ag(handle = DOWN) implies ax(ag(gears != RETRACTING))) //R₂₁
ag(ag(handle = UP) implies ax(ag(gears != EXTENDING))) //R₂₂
```

4.2   First Refinement: Adding the Electro-Valves and the Cylinders

In this model we have refined the ground model by adding the representation of the electro-valves and of the cylinders. Code 4 shows the new elements introduced in the model. We have added the functions for the general electro-valve (`generalEV`) and the electro-valves related to the opening/closing of the doors (`openDoorsEV` and `closeDoorsEV`) and the retracting/extending of the gears (`retractGearsEV` and `extendGearsEV`), that represent the actuators of the system. These functions have been declared controlled.

Functions `cylindersDoors` and `cylindersGears` represent the status of cylinders that move the doors and the gears. The functions have been declared as *derived*, since they can be defined in terms of the values of functions `doors` and `gears`. For example, the cylinders of the doors are extended/retracted when the doors are open/closed, and extending/retracting when the doors are opening/-closing. A similar relation exists between the gears and their cylinders.

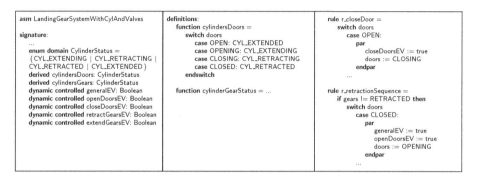

Code 4. Model with cylinders and electro-valves

Model Review. The model advisor signals that functions `cylindersDoors` and `cylindersGears` are useless, since they are never used (never read). Indeed, we have added the cylinders only for documentation purposes, but they could be omitted from the model, since their status is given by a straightforward relation with the status of the doors/gears.

Correctness of the Model Refinement. Let us call M the ground model `Landing-GearSystemGround` and M^* the refined model `LandingGearSystemWithCylAnd-Valves`. At M-level, the locations of interest are those for functions `doors` and `gears`, which have corresponding locations for the same function names at level M^* (since the refinement simply extends the signature of machine M). Two states $s \in S$ and $s^* \in S^*$ are equivalent, i.e., $s \equiv s^*$, iff $[\![doors]\!]_s = [\![doors]\!]_{s^*} \wedge [\![gears]\!]_s = [\![gears]\!]_{s^*}$. In order to prove the correctness of the refinement, we apply Def. 1.

Let $s_0^*, s_1^*, \ldots, s_n^*$ be an M^* run. Let us consider the sequence $t = ([\![handle]\!]_{s_0^*}, [\![handle]\!]_{s_1^*}, \ldots, [\![handle]\!]_{s_{n-1}^*})$. If we apply sequence t to M, we obtain a run $s_0, s_1, \ldots, s_n$ such that $s_i \equiv s_i^*, \forall i = 0, \ldots, n$.

Model Checking. In this model, we have been able to verify the normal mode requirements $R_{31}, R_{32}, R_{41}, R_{42}$, and R_{51}. For example, requirement R_{31} requires that, *when the command line is working (normal mode), the stimulation of the gears outgoing or the retraction electro-valves can only happen when the three doors are locked open.*

We have verified the following four CTL properties:

```
ag((extendGearsEV or retractGearsEV) implies doors = OPEN) //R31
ag((openDoorsEV or closeDoorsEV) implies
                    (gears = RETRACTED or gears = EXTENDED)) //R32
ag(not(openDoorsEV and closeDoorsEV)) //R41
ag(not(extendGearsEV and retractGearsEV)) //R42
ag((openDoorsEV or closeDoorsEV or extendGearsEV or retractGearsEV)
                    implies generalEV) //R51
```

```
asm LandingGearSystemWithCylValvesAndSensors       rule r_retractionSequence =
                                                       if gears != RETRACTED then
signature:                                                 switch doors
   ...                                                         case CLOSED:
   dynamic monitored gearsExtended: Boolean                       par
   dynamic monitored gearsRetracted: Boolean                         generalEV := true
   dynamic monitored doorsClosed: Boolean                            openDoorsEV := true
   dynamic monitored doorsOpen: Boolean                              doors := OPENING
                                                                  endpar
definitions:                                                   case OPENING:
                                                                  if doorsOpen then
   rule r_closeDoor =                                                 par
      switch doors                                                       openDoorsEV := false
         case CLOSING:                                                   doors := OPEN
            if doorsClosed then                                       endpar
               par                                                 endif
                  generalEV := false                         ...
                  closeDoorsEV := false
                  doors := CLOSED       invariant over doorsClosed, doorsOpen: not(doorsClosed and doorsOpen)
               endpar                   invariant over gearsExtended, gearsRetracted: not(gearsExtended and gearsRetracted)
            endif
      ...
```

Code 5. Model with cylinders, electro-valves, and sensors

4.3   Second Refinement: Adding the Sensors

The model presented in this section extends the model described in Section 4.2 by adding the modeling of the sensors. Code 5 shows the new elements introduced in the model. Four boolean monitored functions are used to indicate whether the gears are extended (gearsExtended) or retracted (gearsRetracted), and whether the doors are closed (doorsClosed) or open (doorsOpen). In ASMs, monitored functions represent quantities that are not determined by the system, but that come from the *environment*; usually, they are used in transitions rules (e.g., in the guard of a conditional rule or in the right part of an update rule) to modify the state of the system. For this reason, we chose to model the sensors as monitored functions, because, in the landing gear system, the sensors can be seen as inputs that determine the status of the system: for example, whenever the sensor gearsExtended is seen turned on, the gears are considered extended by the system.

In this model, we have refined some rules by adding the reading of sensors. Some update rules have been guarded by conditional rules checking the value of the monitored functions; for example, we can see in Code 5 that, if the doors are CLOSING, they become CLOSED only if the sensor doorsClosed is turned on (i.e., the guard of conditional rule is true).

In this paper, we do not model the sensor voting module, that is modeled and analysed in [3]. Moreover, we assume that impossible combinations of sensor values (e.g., both sensors doorsClosed and doorsOpen turned on) cannot appear. In order to check that only admissible combinations of sensor values are provided by the environment, we add to the model two invariants specifying that doorsClosed and doorsOpen cannot be turned on together, and that gearsExtended and gearsRetracted cannot be turned on together (see Code 5). An alternative solution could be to make the model more robust, by accepting any combination of sensor values, but modifying the ASM state only upon the observation of correct combinations: this would require to make the guards of the transition rules more complex.

asm LandingGearSystemWithCylValvesAndSensors3LS	definitions:
	function gearsExtended =
signature:	(forall $s in LS with gearsExtended($s))
...	
enum domain LS = {FRONT | LEFT | RIGHT}	function gearsRetracted =
dynamic monitored gearsExtended: LS —> Boolean	(forall $s in LS with gearsRetracted($s))
dynamic monitored gearsRetracted: LS —> Boolean	
dynamic monitored doorsClosed: LS —> Boolean	function doorsClosed =
dynamic monitored doorsOpen: LS —> Boolean	(forall $s in LS with doorsClosed($s))
derived gearsExtended: Boolean	
derived gearsRetracted: Boolean	function doorsOpen =
derived doorsClosed: Boolean	(forall $s in LS with doorsOpen($s))
derived doorsOpen: Boolean	...

Code 6. Model with cylinders, electro-valves, and sensors – Three landing sets

Correctness of the Model Refinement. Let us call M the model LandingGear-SystemWithCylAndValves and M^* the refined model LandingGearSystemWith-CylValvesAndSensors. At M-level, the locations of interest are those as in the previous refinement. Two states s and s^* are equivalent, i.e., $s \equiv s^*$, iff $[\![doors]\!]_s = [\![doors]\!]_{s^*} \wedge [\![gears]\!]_s = [\![gears]\!]_{s^*}$. Let $updLocs(s_i^*)$ be the set of locations that are non-trivially updated in state s_i^* (so having a different value in state s_{i+1}^*). In order to prove the correctness of the refinement, we apply Def. 1.

Let $s_0^*, s_1^*, \ldots, s_n^*$ be an M^* run; we say that a state s_i^* is of interest if $i = 0 \vee \mathsf{doors} \in updLocs(s_{i-1}^*) \vee \mathsf{gears} \in updLocs(s_{i-1}^*)$. Given the sequence of states of interest $s_{j_0}^*, s_{j_1}^*, \ldots, s_{j_m}^*$, such that $j_0 = 0$ and $j_0 < j_1 < \ldots < j_m \leq n$, we build the sequence $t = ([\![handle]\!]_{s_{j_1-1}^*}, [\![handle]\!]_{s_{j_2-1}^*}, \ldots, [\![handle]\!]_{s_{j_m-1}^*})$. If we apply sequence t to M, we obtain a run $s_0, s_1, \ldots, s_m$ such that $s_i \equiv s_{j_i}^*, \forall i = 0, \ldots, m$.

Model Checking. The introduction of the sensors do not require to verify any further requirement.

4.4 Third Refinement: Adding the Three Landing Sets

The model presented in this section extends the model described in Section 4.3 by adding the modeling of the three landing sets. Code 6 shows the new elements introduced in the model and how some functions have been modified. The enumerative domain LS represents the three landing sets (FRONT, LEFT, and RIGHT). The sensors have been refined by explicitly modeling, for each sensor type, the sensor on each landing set; four new unary monitored functions with domain LS have been added to the model. For example, the unary monitored function **gearsExtended** represents the three sensors associated with the three landing sets, that detect the extension of the gears: specifically, each location of the function (gearsExtended(FRONT), gearsExtended(LEFT), and gearsExtended(RIGHT)) is a sensor of a landing set.

The 0-ary functions that in the previous model (Section 4.3) are declared as monitored, in this model are declared as derived, because now their value depends on the value of the corresponding unary functions having the same name. Indeed, each derived function describes if all the corresponding sensors on the three landing sets are turned on, or if at least one is turned off.

```
asm LandingGearSystemWithHealthMon3LS

signature:
    ...
    derived aGearExtended: Boolean
    derived aGearRetracted: Boolean
    derived aDoorClosed: Boolean
    derived aDoorOpen: Boolean
    derived greenLight: Boolean
    derived orangeLight: Boolean
    derived redLight: Boolean
    dynamic monitored timeout: Boolean
    dynamic controlled anomaly: Boolean

definitions:
    function aGearExtended = (exist $s in LS with gearsExtended($s))
    function aGearRetracted = (exist $s in LS with gearsRetracted($s))
    function aDoorClosed = (exist $s in LS with doorsClosed($s))
    function aDoorOpen = (exist $s in LS with doorsOpen($s))

    function greenLight = (gears = EXTENDED)
    function orangeLight = (gears = EXTENDING or gears = RETRACTING)
    function redLight = anomaly
    ...
```

```
rule r_healthMonitoring =
    if timeout then
        if (openDoorsEV and not(doorsOpen)) or
           (closeDoorsEV and aDoorOpen) or
           (retractGearsEV and aGearExtended) or ...
            anomaly := true
        endif
    endif

main rule r_Main =
    if not(anomaly) then
        par
            if handle = UP then
                r_retractionSequence[]
            else
                r_outgoingSequence[]
            endif
            r_healthMonitoring[]
        endpar
    endif

default init s0:
    function anomaly = false
    ...
```

Code 7. Model with cylinders, electro-valves, and sensors – With failure mode

Note that AsmetaL permits function overloading, i.e., having different functions with the same name, but a different arity and/or a different domain.

Correctness of the Model Refinement. The proof of the correctness of the model refinement is straightforward, and it should be done as seen for the two previous models.

Model Checking. The introduction of the three landing sets do not require to verify any further requirement.

4.5 Fourth Refinement: Adding the Health Monitoring System

The model presented in this section extends the model described in Section 4.4, by adding the modeling of the health monitoring system (Section 4.3 of the case study in [5]). We only consider the doors motion monitoring and the gears motion monitoring. A possible way to model the monitoring of the sensors is described in [3]. Since the analogical switch and the pressure sensor are not considered in this work, we do not model their monitoring.

Code 7 shows the new elements introduced in the model. The health monitoring is executed by rule r_healthMonitoring that, whenever a *timeout* has occurred, checks that the values of the sensors are as expected. The detection of an anomaly in the system is modeled by the update to *true* of the boolean function anomaly; in the main rule, the system is executed only if there is no anomaly (i.e., anomaly is false). The timeout is modeled through the boolean monitored function timeout. Note that, at this level of abstraction, we do not need to explicitly handle the time, neither to distinguish between different time intervals: it is sufficient to know if, in a given system configuration, the maximum allowed time interval, after which the system configuration should be observed changed, has elapsed. For example, if the electro-valve responsible for the opening of the doors is turned on and the doors are not open (openDoorsEV and not(doorsOpen)), if the timeout has elapsed, then an anomaly has been detected[3].

In the monitoring rules, sometimes we need to know if, given a sensor type, at least one single sensor is turned on. For example, one monitoring rule states that *if the control software does not see the value door_open[x] = false for all x = {front, left, right} ...*; in order to implement this rule, we must check if at least one door is open, but this can not be inferred through function doorsOpen. In order to model this kind of rules, we have introduced in this model the functions aDoorOpen, aDoorClosed, aGearExtended, and aGearRetracted that signal if there is at least one of the corresponding sensors turned on.

Correctness of the Model Refinement. The proof of the correctness of the model refinement is straightforward.

Model Checking. In this model, we have been able to verify the failure mode requirements R_{61}, R_{62}, R_{63}, R_{64}, R_{71}, R_{72}, R_{73}, and R_{74}. For example, requirement R_{61} requires that, *if one of the three doors is still seen locked in the closed position more than 7 seconds after stimulating the opening electro-valve, then the boolean output normal mode is set to false.*

We have verified the following eight CTL properties:

```
ag((openDoorsEV and aDoorClosed and timeout) implies ax(ag(anomaly))) //R₆₁
ag((closeDoorsEV and aDoorOpen and timeout) implies ax(ag(anomaly))) //R₆₂
ag((retractGearsEV and aGearExtended and timeout) implies ax(ag(anomaly))) //R₆₃
ag((extendGearsEV and aGearRetracted and timeout) implies ax(ag(anomaly))) //R₆₄
ag((openDoorsEV and not(doorsOpen) and timeout) implies ax(ag(anomaly))) //R₇₁
ag((closeDoorsEV and not(doorsClosed) and timeout) implies ax(ag(anomaly))) //R₇₂
ag((retractGearsEV and not(gearsRetracted) and timeout) implies ax(ag(anomaly))) //R₇₃
ag((extendGearsEV and not(gearsExtended) and timeout) implies ax(ag(anomaly))) //R₇₄
```

5   Discussion and Conclusion

The paper presents an ASM specification of the Landing Gear System case study [5]. The modeling process exploits the two fundamental concepts of the ASM method, i.e., the concept of ground model and the refinement principle.

The use of the refinement approach helped us to manage the complexity of the case study and to achieve the verification of the given requirements. Actually the refinement was guided by the requirements to be verified, since they gave the hint on how to proceed in adding details at each refinement step. Indeed, every refinement step came with a set of suitable novel properties to be verified. Even though, thanks to the proof of refinement correctness, properties already verified at a given step were guaranteed in the refined steps, we have kept the whole set of properties and verified them by model checking at each step.

Among the possible views proposed in the informal requirements – functional, architectural, real time, reliability, etc. – we do not cover real time aspects.

---

[3] In the case study, this behavior is described as follows: *if the control software does not see the value door_closed[x] = false for all x ∈ {front, left, right} 7 seconds after stimulation of the opening electro-valve, then the doors are considered as blocked and an anomaly is detected.*

Although reactive timed ASMs [13] have been proposed for dealing with time in ASMs, they are not supported by our tools for model analysis. This is the reason why, for properties R_1 (see Section 5.1 in [5]), we verified the weaker version. We modeled the time passing by means of a suitable monitored function *timeout* which was enough for achieving the automatic verification of all the properties regarding *failure mode requirements* (see Section 5.2 of [5]).

From the functional view, we abstracted from the analogical switch and the pressure sensor, while, from the architecture view, we simplified the digital architecture by only considering *one* computing module. Both abstractions are not due to limitations of the method, but simply to the lack of space. Both these functional and architectural abstractions are, however, straightforward to detail. Abstracting from the analogical switch and the pressure sensor also influenced the modeling of the health monitoring. Therefore, regarding the system reliability, we did not deal with scenarios involving these two devices.

In the specification presented here, also the model of the sensor voting is missing. Indeed it has been considered as case study in a separate paper [3] to present two approaches for checking the implementation conformance: an offline model-based testing approach and an online runtime monitoring approach.

By using the simulator and the validator for scenarios construction, we were able to reproduce the expected scenarios of the LGS operating in normal mode (see Section 4.1 in [5]), even if this simulation is not reported here.

The model development and the model analysis have been made possible by the combined use of formal methods for modeling and for verification. In fact, the behavioral specification is expressed in terms of ASMs, while the verification of the properties, as well as other forms of model analysis (e.g., model review), is conducted by the use of the NuSMV model checker. The advantage, in our case, is that all methods are integrated in the same framework, ASMETA, so the user does not need to worry about translating the ASM specification into the language of the model checker. The mapping from an ASM model into a NuSMV model is automatic and the CTL properties can be directly expressed as part of the ASM model itself.

What is missing in the method, apart from the real time aspects, is a mechanical support by theorem provers for verifying the refinement correctness, and the definition of refinement patterns that could be useful to guide the refinement process. For this case study, the refinement steps were suggested by the properties to verify and the refinement correctness was proved by hand. These topics will be arguments for future research, as well as the possibility to integrate the ASM method with other approaches, as the Event-B, that are better structured in this respect.

References

1. Arcaini, P., Gargantini, A., Riccobene, E.: AsmetaSMV: A way to link high-level ASM models to low-level NuSMV specifications. In: Frappier, M., Glässer, U., Khurshid, S., Laleau, R., Reeves, S. (eds.) ABZ 2010. LNCS, vol. 5977, pp. 61–74. Springer, Heidelberg (2010)

2. Arcaini, P., Gargantini, A., Riccobene, E.: Automatic Review of Abstract State Machines by Meta Property Verification. In: Muñoz, C. (ed.) Proceedings of the Second NASA Formal Methods Symposium (NFM 2010), pp. 4–13. NASA (2010)
3. Arcaini, P., Gargantini, A., Riccobene, E.: Offline model-based testing and runtime monitoring of the sensor voting module. In: Boniol, F. (ed.) ABZ 2014 Case Study Track. CCIS, vol. 433, pp. 95–109. Springer, Heidelberg (2014)
4. Arcaini, P., Gargantini, A., Riccobene, E., Scandurra, P.: A model-driven process for engineering a toolset for a formal method. Software: Practice and Experience 41, 155–166 (2011)
5. Boniol, F., Wiels, V.: The Landing Gear System Case Study. In: Boniol, F. (ed.) ABZ 2014 Case Study Track. CCIS, vol. 433, pp. 1–18. Springer, Heidelberg (2014)
6. Börger, E.: The ASM refinement method. Formal Aspects of Computing 15, 237–257 (2003)
7. Börger, E.: The ASM method for system design and analysis. A tutorial introduction. In: Gramlich, B. (ed.) FroCos 2005. LNCS (LNAI), vol. 3717, pp. 264–283. Springer, Heidelberg (2005)
8. Börger, E.: Construction and analysis of ground models and their refinements as a foundation for validating computer based systems. Formal Aspects of Computing 19, 225–241 (2007)
9. Börger, E., Stärk, R.: Abstract State Machines: A Method for High-Level System Design and Analysis. Springer (2003)
10. Carioni, A., Gargantini, A., Riccobene, E., Scandurra, P.: A Scenario-Based Validation Language for ASMs. In: Börger, E., Butler, M., Bowen, J.P., Boca, P. (eds.) ABZ 2008. LNCS, vol. 5238, pp. 71–84. Springer, Heidelberg (2008)
11. Gargantini, A., Riccobene, E., Scandurra, P.: A Metamodel-based Language and a Simulation Engine for Abstract State Machines. J. Universal Computer Science 14(12), 1949–1983 (2008)
12. Gargantini, A., Riccobene, E., Scandurra, P.: Model-Driven Language Engineering: The ASMETA Case Study. In: Int. Conf. on Software Engineering Advances, ICSEA, pp. 373–378 (2008)
13. Slissenko, A., Vasilyev, P.: Simulation of Timed Abstract State Machines with predicate logic model-checking. J.UCS 14(12), 1984–2006 (2008)

Context-Aware Verification
of a Landing Gear System

Philippe Dhaussy and Ciprian Teodorov

UEB, Lab-STICC Laboratory UMR CNRS 6285
ENSTA Bretagne, France
`{firstname.name}@ensta-bretagne.fr`

Abstract. Despite the high level of automation, the practicability of formal verification through model-checking of large models is hindered by the combinatorial explosion problem. In this paper we apply a novel context-aware verification technique to the Landing Gear System Case Study (LGS) [2]. The idea is to express and verify requirements relative to certain environmental situations. The system environment is decomposed into several independent scenarios (contexts), which are successively composed with the system during reachability analysis. These contexts are specified using a language called CDL (*Context Description Language*), based on activity and message sequence diagrams. The properties to be verified are specified with observer automata and attached to specific regions in the context. This approach enables an automated context-guided decomposition of the verification into smaller problems, hence effectively reducing the state-space explosion problem. In the case of the LGS this technique enabled the fully-automated decomposition of the verification into 885 smaller model-checking problems.

Keywords: formal verification, context-aware model-checking, OBP, observer-automata.

1 Introduction

Software verification is an integral part of the software development lifecycle, the goal of which is to ensure that software fully satisfies all the expected requirements. Reactive systems are becoming extremely complex with the huge increase in high technologies. Among reactive systems, the asynchronous systems communicating by exchanging messages via buffer queues are often characterized by a vast number of possible behaviors. To cope with this complexity, manufacturers of industrial systems make significant efforts in testing and simulation to successfully pass the certification process. Nevertheless revealing errors and bugs in this huge number of behaviors remains a very difficult activity. An alternative method is to adopt formal methods, and to use exhaustive and automatic verification tools such as model-checkers.

Model-checking algorithms can be used to verify requirements of a model formally and automatically. However, because of the internal complexity of the

F. Boniol et al. (Eds.): ABZ 2014 Case Study Track, CCIS 433, pp. 52–65, 2014.

developed systems, model-checking can lead to an unmanageable large state-space, a problem known as the state-space explosion problem [6,16]. Numerous techniques, such as symbolic model-checking [4], and partial-order reduction [20], have been proposed to reduce the impact of this problem effectively pushing the limits of model-checking further and further.

In this paper, we use a novel technique, dubbed context-aware verification [10], to model and analyze the Landing Gear System Case Study LGS [2]. This technique proposes to reduce the set of possible behaviors (and thus the state-space) by closing the system-under-study (SUS) with a well defined environment (context). In the context of embedded reactive systems, the environment of each system is finite and well known. Hence, we claim that the explicit and formal specification of this context enables at least three different state-space reduction axes: *a*) the environment can be decomposed in contexts, thus isolating different operating modes; *b*) each individual context can automatically be subdivided in independent verification problems; *c*) the requirements, specified as observer automata, are focused on specific environmental conditions.

For the LGS , we have modeled one top-level context which was automatically decomposed into 885 isolated smaller scenarios, enabling us to iteratively perform reachability analysis on each of them. Even though, some of these scenarios fail due to the state-space explosion problem we show that our context-aware verification approach pushes the limits of reachability analysis, enabling an automatic divide-and-conquer approach to model-checking. Because the limited size of this paper, we briefly present the SUS modeling and requirement specification, we deliberately focus the presentation on our context-guided state-space reduction technique.

Paper Organization. Section 2 presents the related techniques addressing the state-space explosion problem. Section 3 overviews the principles of our approach for context-aware formal verification. The LGS model is presented, in Section 4, along with the results obtained with OBP *Observation Engine.* Section 5 concludes this study giving some future research directions.

2   Related Work

Model checking is a technique that relies on building a finite model of a system of interest, and checking that a desired property, typically specified as a temporal logic formula, holds for that model. Since the introduction of this technology in the early 1980s [18], several model-checker tools have been developed to help the verification of concurrent systems [15,1].

However, while model-checking provides an automated rigorous framework for formal system validation and verification, and has successfully been applied on industrial systems it suffers from the state-space explosion problem. This is due to the exponential growth of the number of states the system can reach with respect to the number of interacting components. Since its introduction, model checking has progressed significantly, with numerous research efforts focused on reducing the impact of this problem, thus enabling the verification of ever larger systems. Some of these approaches focus on the use of efficient data-structures such as BDD [4] for achieving compact state-space representation, others rely on algorithmic advancements and the maximal use of the available resources such as external memories [11]. To prune the state-space, techniques such as partial-order reduction [14,17,20,14] and symmetry reduction [7] exploit fine-grain transition interleaving symmetries and global system symmetries respectively. Yet other approaches, like bounded model-checking [5] exploit the observation that in many practical settings the property verification can be done with only a partial (bounded) reachability analysis.

The successful application of these methods to several case studies (see for instance [3] for aerospace examples) demonstrates their maturity in the case of synchronous embedded systems. However, even though these techniques push the limits of model-checking ever further, the state-space explosion problem remains especially in the case of large and complex asynchronous systems.

Besides the previously cited techniques that approach the property verification problem monolithically, compositional verification [13] focus on the analysis of individual components of the system using assume/guarantee reasoning (or design-by-contract) to extract (sometimes automatically) the interactions that a component has with its environment and to reduce the model-checking problem to these interactions. Once each individual component is proved correct the composition is performed using operators that preserve the correctness.

Our approach can be seen as a coarse-grain compositional verification, where instead of analyzing the interactions of individual components with their neighboring environment we focus on the interactions of the whole system with its surrounding environment (context). Conversely to "traditional" techniques in which the surrounding environment is often implicitly modeled in the system (to obtain a closed system), we explicitly describe it separately from the model. By explicitly modeling the environment as one (or more) formally defined context(s) and composing it with the system-under-study we can conduct the full system verification. Using the "context" knowledge the verification problem is decomposed, following a fully automatic divide-and-conquer algorithm, in smaller problems (with smaller state-space) which are analyzed independently.

3   Context-Aware Model-Checking

In this section, we present a formal verification approach that aims primarily at reducing the state-space explosion problem in the context of exhaustive verification through model-checking. This approach, dubbed *context-aware model-checking*, focuses on the explicit modeling of the environment as one or more contexts, which then are iteratively composed with the system-under-study (SUS). The requirements are associated and verified in the contexts that correspond to the environmental conditions in which they should be satisfied, and automated context-guided state-space reduction techniques can be used to further push the limits of reachability analysis. All these developments are implemented in the OBP *Observation Engine*[9] and are publicly available[1].

When verifying properties, through explicit-state model checking, the system explores all the behaviors possible in the SUS and checks whether the verified properties are true or not. Due to the exponential growth of system states relative to the number of interacting components, most of the time the number of reachable configurations is too large to be contained in memory. Besides using techniques like the ones described in Sec. 2, to alleviate this problem the system designers manually tune the SUS to restrict its behaviors to the ones pertinent relative to the specified requirements. This process is tedious, error prone and poses a number of methodological challenges since different versions of the SUS should be kept sound, in sync and maintained. To address these issues, we propose to restrict model behavior by composing it with an explicitly defined environment that interacts with the SUS. The environment enables a subset of the behavior of the model. This technique reduces the complexity of the exploration by limiting its scope to a reduced set of behaviors related to specific environmental conditions. Moreover, this approach solves the methodological issues, since it decouples the SUS from its environment, thus allowing their refinement in isolation.

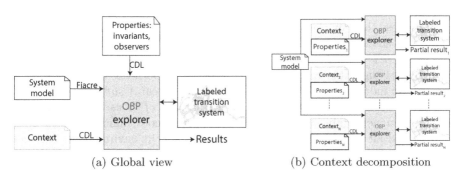

(a) Global view   (b) Context decomposition

Fig. 1. Context-aware model-checking

Fig. 1a shows a global overview of the OBP *Observation Engine*. The *System model* representing the SUS is described using the formal language Fiacre [12], which enables the specification of interacting behaviors and timing constraints through a timed-automata based approach. The surrounding environment and the requirements are specified with the *Context Description Language* (CDL). The CDL formalizes the environment through a number of contexts that interact asynchronously with the SUS. Moreover, the CDL enables the specification of requirements through properties that are verified by OBP *Observation Engine*. These properties expressed through property-pattern definitions[10] are based on events (eg. variable x changed) and predicates which are composed to express either invariants or observers. It should be noted that most of the safety properties that we are studying can be expressed using observer automata, moreover in

---

[1] OBP Observation Engine website: http://www.obpcdl.org

[19] the authors present an automated approach for reducing liveness checking to safety verification by observer-based model instrumentation.

The OBP *Observation Engine* verifies the given set of properties with a reachability strategy using a breath-first-search algorithm on the implicit graph induced by the parallel composition of the SUS with the context. During the exploration the *Observation Engine* captures the occurrences of events and evaluates the predicates after the atomic execution of each transition. It then updates the invariants and the status of all observers involved in the run, thus effectively performing an exhaustive state-space analysis. A report is generated, at the end of the exploration, showing the truth values of all invariants and the status of the attached observers. Moreover, the resulting Labelled Transition System (LTS) can be queried to find either the system states invalidating a given invariant or to generate a counter-example based on the *success/reject* state of a given observer, hence effectively guiding the user through the process of the SUS evaluation against the given requirements.

Environment Modeling with CDL Formalism

In the context of reactive embedded systems, the environment of each component of the system is often well known. It is therefore more effective to identify and better express this environment than trying reduce the state-space of the SUS. However, it should be noted that the proof relevance is based on the following hypothesis: *It is possible to specify the sets of bounded behaviors in a complete way.* Even though this can be seen as a strong hypothesis we argue that it expresses no more than the following well accepted idea: *A software system can be correctly developed only if we know the constraints of its use.* So, we suppose that the designer is able to identify the perimeter (constraints, conditions) of the SUS and all possible interactions between it and its environment. Another important observation is that the properties are often related to specific use cases (such as initialization, reconfiguration, degraded modes). Therefore, it is not necessary for a given property to take into account all possible behaviors of the environment, but only the ones concerned by the verification.

To formalize the context specification in [8] we introduced the CDL formal language to capture the interactions with the environment. A CDL^2 model describes the surrounding environment of a SUS and the properties to be checked in this environment. The interleaving of context actors described by a CDL specification generates a graph representing all executions of the environment actors, which can be fed as input to traditional model-checkers, see [8] for more details.

Moreover, if all the identified contexts are finite and acyclic (there are no infinite loops in the interaction between the system and its environment) then the *interleaved context graph* is also finite and acyclic. This is the case with many command systems or communication protocols. Based on this observation we have developed a powerful context-guided state-space reduction technique which relies on the automated recursive partitioning (splitting) of a given context in indepen-

---

^{2} For the detailed syntax, see www.obpcdl.org

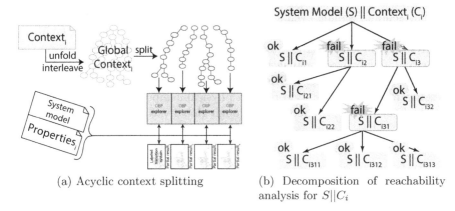

(a) Acyclic context splitting

(b) Decomposition of reachability analysis for $S||C_i$

Fig. 2. Context-guided state-space reduction and verification

dent sub-contexts. This technique, schematically presented in Fig. 2a, is systematically applied by OBP *Observation Engine* when a given reachability analysis ($S||C_i$ in Fig. 2b) fails due to lack of memory resources to store the state-space. After splitting $context_i$, the sub-contexts are iteratively composed with the model for exploration, and the properties associated with $context_i$ are checked for all sub-contexts. Therefore, the global verification problem for $context_i$ is effectively decomposed into K_i smaller verification problems. Hence, verifying the properties on all these K_i problems is equivalent to verifying them on the initial system.

Context-aware reduction of system behavior is particularly interesting in the case of complex embedded system, such as avionics, since they exhibit clearly identified operating modes with specific properties associated with these modes. Unfortunately, only few existing approaches propose practical ways to precisely capture these contexts in order to reduce formal verification complexity and thus improve the scalability of existing model checking approaches. Moreover, a clear methodology that formalizes the context coverage with respect to the full system behavior and assist the user on initial context specification is required for these techniques to be used on industrial-scale critical systems.

4   Case-Study: The Landing Gear System

In this section we apply our context-aware verification approach to the LGS case-study [2] of the ABZ 2014 conference. Before presenting our results, we overview the LGS modeling using the fiacre language, the environment specification using CDL, and we introduce two properties which should be verified on the system.

4.1   Modeling the SUS

The FIACRE LGS model, presented in Fig. 3a, is composed of two parts: a model of the software part, and a model of the physical part, communicating through urgent signals. The environment of the LGS is composed of two agents: the pilot sending *handle* events to change the handle position (from down to up or vice-versa), and a a virtual agent called *Perturbator* injecting failures in the physical components (Fig. 3b). The interactions from the environment (i.e., *handle* and *failures*) are managed by a specific component called *Dispatcher*. Inputs are received through a FIFO channel and are dispatched immediately to the software part (*handle*) and to each physical component (*failures*). Outputs (i.e., the lights status) are modeled through global variables set by the software part.

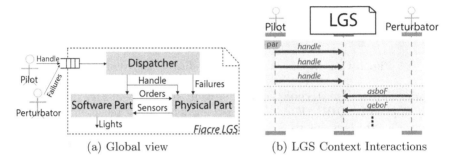

(a) Global view   (b) LGS Context Interactions

Fig. 3. Landing gear system model

The physical part is the parallel composition of 12 instances of the following FIACRE processes: *a) Analog Switch*, implementing the behavior of the analog switch; *b) General_EV*, implementing the behavior of the general electro-valve; *c)* a generic process *Generic_EV*, implementing the behavior of one electro-valve; *d)* a generic process *Gear*, implementing the behavior of one gear; *e)* a generic process *Door*, implementing the behavior of one door. Table 1 shows the number

Table 1. Fiacre processes for the Physical Part

	Analog Switch	General_EV	Generic_EV	Gear	Door
# of states	18	34	24	23	20
# of instances	1	1	4	3	3

of states of each of these processes along with the number of times each one is instantiated in the model.

Each process is a FIACRE automaton. As illustration, Fig. 4 shows the automaton of the process `AnalogSwitch` composed of 18 states. This process implements a loop from *open* to *closed* and from *closed* to *open* through numerous intermediate states including timers as required in the general description of the case study. The two final states at the right of the automaton implements the failure state *blockedOpen* to *blockedClosed*. These states are reached from anywhere in the automaton whenever a failure event is received from the *Perturbator* through the *Dispatcher*.

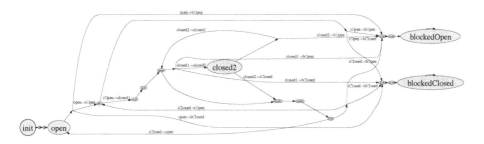

Fig. 4. Automaton of the *Analog Switch* process

Similarly, the software part is the parallel composition of 8 instances of the following FIACRE processes: *a*) a generic process *Door sensor synthesis*, which computes the door state (*closed, open,* or *intermediate*) from the values returned by the sensors; *b*) a generic process *Gear sensor synthesis*, which computes the gear state (*retracted, extended,* or *intermediate*) from the values returned by the sensors; *c*) *EV Manager*, which executes the extension and retraction sequences according to the handle position and the values returned by the sensors; *d*) *Status Manager*, which computes the status (on or off) of the three lights in the cockpit. Table 2 shows the number of states of each of these processes along with the number of times each one is instantiated in the model.

Table 2. Fiacre processes for the Software Part

	Door sensor synth.	Gear sensor synth.	EV Manager	Status Manager
# of states	8	8	52	10
# of instances	3	3	1	1

The FIACRE model of the LGS described in the previous paragraphs has more than 3,000 lines of code, and it is available at http://www.obpcdl.org along with the OBP *Observation Engine* toolset.

Assumptions and Restrictions. With respect to the general description of the case study, two more restrictions have been introduced:

1. Firstly, we consider only one software module (and not two as required in the general description), which is assumed failure-free.
2. Secondly, we consider only one failure-free wire for each sensor (and not three as required in the general description). Put differently, we suppose that sensors are safe, i.e., without any failure mode. Nevertheless, we assume that all the physical equipment can fail at anytime. However, failures are assumed to be permanent, such that if a equipment (a gear for instance) becomes blocked, then it remains blocked forever.

Except these restrictions, all the other specification have been taken into account. Particularly the timing constraints: the automata of the gears, doors, electro-valves, and analog-switch implement the timed behavior as required in the general description. Similarly, the *EV-manager* allows the pilot to change the sequence (from retraction to extension or vice-versa) at anytime during the sequence. Finally, *EV-manager* monitors the physical equipment through the electrical values returned by the sensors. Whenever one of these values is not equal to the one expected by the software part (for instance the right door is still seen closed 7 seconds after activation of the opening electro-valve), then an *anomaly* state is reached and the red light is turned on.

4.2 Modeling the Context

As mentioned in the previous section the environment of the LGS is composed of the interleaved actions of two context actors, namely the pilot sending up/-down commands through its handle, and a virtual actor (named Perturbator) introducing failures into the system. Using the CDL formalism the pilot behavior is represented through an activity composed of a sequence of *handle* events sent to the *Dispatcher* process (see first two lines of Listing. 1).

Table 3. Overview of the considered failures along with the affected components

analog switch		general EV		door electro-valves				gear electro-valves			
				extension		retraction		extension		retraction	
Opened	Closed	Opened	Closed	Opened	Closed	Opened	Closed	Opened	Closed	Opened	Closed
$asboF$	$asbcF$	$gboF$	$gbcF$	$deboF$	$debcF$	$drboF$	$drbcF$	$geboF$	$gebcF$	$grboF$	$grbcF$
exclusive		exclusive		exclusive		exclusive		exclusive		exclusive	

door			gear		
Front	Left	Right	Front	Left	Right
fdF	ldF	rdF	fgF	lgF	rgF

The *Perturbator* actor encodes all considered failure configurations composed of sequences of 1 up to 3 failures taken from the total 18 failures that have been identified, see Table 3 for the complete list of the failures classified according to the affected component. It should be noted that between the first 12 failures there are groups of 2 exclusive failures (ex. the analog-switch cannot be blocked in the opened and closed state at the same time). Taking these exclusion rules into account it follow that there are 885 possible failure configurations as follows: *a*) 18 possible configurations with 1 failures. *b*) 147 possible configurations with 2 failures (and 6 excluded failures). *c*) 720 possible configurations with 3 failures (and 96 excluded failures). Each of these failure scenarios as encoded as a CDL activity (Listing 1 lines 5–6), named $FailureContext_k^x$, where $x \in [1 \ldots 3]$ is the number of failures and k is the id of a given configuration from the set of the ones possible with x failures (ex. $k \in [1 \ldots 147], for\ x = 2$). The *Perturbator* actor is then represented as a CDL activity that non-deterministically chooses one of these failure configuration to play, see lines 8–11 in Listing 1.

The CDL specification of the global environment, Listing 1 lines 13–16, consists of the initialization of the SUS (line 15) followed by the asynchronous

interleaving of the *Pilot* events with the *Perturbator* failure sequences. Note
also the association of the properties to be verified (described in the following
paragraphs) with the context (lines 14).

Listing 1. Overview of the CDL environment description

```
1   event Handle is   {send HANDLE to {Dispatcher}1}
2   activity PILOT is { event Handle; event Handle; event Handle}
3
4   event asbof is {send ASBO_FAILURE to {Dispatcher}1}
5   activity FailureContext^1_k is { event k^{th} failure }
6   activity FailureContext^{2..3}_k is {
7   ··· // all permutations of the k^{th} 2(or 3) failures }
8   activity Perturbator is {
9       FailureContext^1_1 [] ··· [] FailureContext^1_{18}
10      [] FailureContext^2_1 [] ··· [] FailureContext^2_{147}
11      [] FailureContext^3_1 [] ··· [] FailureContext^3_{720} }
12
13  cdl scenario_885_failure_configurations is {
14      properties oR_1, oR_2 // reference to the observers for R_1, and R_2
15      init is { act_init } // initialization sequence
16      main is { PILOT || Perturbator } //scenario }
```

4.3   Specifying the Properties

To illustrate the property specification aspects of the CDL language, let us consider the following two requirements:

- **Requirement** R_1**:** The red light should always be off.
- **Requirement** R_2**:** At the end of each *Pilot* interaction the green light
  should be on.

Listing 2. CDL-based property specification

```
1   predicate pRed is { {SYS}1:red_light=true }
2   event evt_red is { pRed becomes true }
3   ···
4   property oR_1 is { start —— / / evt_red / -> reject }
5   property oR_2 is {
6       clock ck;
7       start —— / / evt_orange / ck := 0 -> maneuvering;
8       maneuvering —— / / evt_green / ck := -1 -> success;
9       start —— ck >= 15000 / / / ck := -1 -> reject;
10  }
```

In CDL, R_1 is an observer that reaches the *reject* state when the *red_light*
turns on, line 4 in Listing 2. The $\{SYS\}1$ prefix indicates the fiacre component where the *red_light* variable is defined. The second requirement, R_2, is
represented using an observer automaton that follows the system execution and
produces a *success* event whenever the green light is turned on before the *ck*
deadline. The observer declaration (line 5) is introduced with the *property* keyword and defines a transition from the **start** state to the **maneuvering** state

initializing the timer ck when the evt_orange is present, a transition from the **maneuvering** state to the **success** state (disabling the timer), and a transition from the **start** state to the **reject** state if the timer expired. These observers are references in the context in which they should be checked and composed with the system during reachability analysis.

4.4   Experimental Results

This section presents some experimental results obtained using our context-aware verification approach [9] on the LGS . All results where obtained using OBP v.1.4.5 on a 64-bit Linux machine that has 64GB of memory.

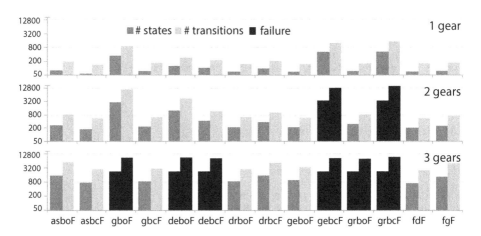

Fig. 5. Reachability analysis results for one/two/three-gear(s) LGS with 1 failure injected interleaved with 3-handle interactions (results in thousands). The black bars indicate the state-space explosion cases, showing the number of states/transitions explored before failure.

While the environment model presented in Sec. 4.2 considers only a single top-level context, our explicit-context modeling approach also enables the analysis of partial system behavior, for instance, by simply running the automatic context split on the *Perturbator* actor we obtain the set of simpler environments that does not take into account the possible model failures. Considering such a context in which the *Pilot* actor sends 3-handle interactions followed by the injection of 2 failures ($drboF$, fdF) by the *Perturbator* in a 3 gear system we get a state-space of 1,451,144 states and 4,969,518 transitions in 2,598 sec. However, just by adding one more failure ($geboF$), at the end of the preceding sequence of interactions, the exploration fails (due to lack of memory) after analyzing 1,908,556 states and 6,484,681 transitions.

Even though we could not analyze the whole LGS system using the current version of OBP *Observation Engine*, we have been able to analyze a large number of reachable states of the system. In Fig. 5 we show the results obtained on a

Table 4. Number of sub-context and state-space approximation with respect to the number of gears after two context splitting step

	1 gear	2 gears	3 gears
split 1	391	606	885
split 2	1936	3100	4632
state-space aprox.	1.13×10^8	5.55×10^8	6.72×10^9
Cumulated result for 1 failure with 3 pilot interactions (3-handle)			
# of sub-contexts	14	16	18
states	2 328 635	14 156 119	26 585 225
transitions	5 766 682	53 104 972	98 135 315
time (sec.)	2 387	16 942	46 216

simplification of the model using all 1 failure configurations introduced in Table 3 (the ldF, lgF, rdF, rgF are not included in the Fig. since the 1-gear case does not include them, however the results are comparable with fdF and fgF). Compared to the 1-gear case in the second case the size of the obtained LTS is in average 4.63X(6.44X) bigger in terms of states(transitions), with the $deboF$ giving a 10X(15.5X) bigger LTS. It is interesting to note that if in the case of the 2-gear case we reduce the number of $Pilot$ interactions to one (1-handle) the size of the resulting LTS drops in average (over the 16-failure cases) by 86.5X(98.4X) states(transitions), with a peak in the case of the $gboF$ failure which gives a 146X(174X) smaller system. In the second and third case it should be noted that the 64GB memory space on our machine did not suffice for exploring the context injecting some failures, like $gebcF$ and $grbcF$ failures. [3] Table 4 shows the number of elementary sub-contexts after one and respectively 2 automatic split levels. The state-space approximation line provides a rough optimistic prediction of the number of reachable states by multiplying the lowest number of states presented in Fig. 5 by the number of sub-context after the second split. The lowest half of Table 4 shows the cumulated results, in terms of LTS size and size, of the exploration of the 1-failure 3-handle contexts shown in Fig. 5.

In Fig. 6 we show a visual representation of the LTS obtained for 3-gear/2 $Pilot$ interactions without failures[4]. Two distinct operating modes of the LGS system are shown: at the left we can identify the initialization sequence of the LGS comprising of 7,348 states and 30,605 transitions, while at the right the behavior of the system during a down/up gear sequence is exposed.

Our splitting technique did not suffice for completing the reachability analysis of a 3-gear/3-$Pilot$ interactions with failures. However, we argue that despite this setback, the context-aware verification approach introduces a new state-space reduction axis complementary with more holistic approaches such as partial-order reduction [20], and symmetry-reduction [7]. Moreover, the possibility to partially

---

[3] It should be noted that the instantiation of the model with 1, 2 or 3 gears is can be seen also as a partitioning of the verification on the model-side as opposed to the context-side.

[4] The layout is obtained using Grapviz sfdp layout using a simple linear color scheme where the shorter transitions are red while the longer ones are blue.

Fig. 6. LGS behaviors during a gear down/up sequence (no failures)

analyze the system gives valuable insights on particular context-dependent behaviors enabling the designer to better focus its verification efforts.

5 Conclusion and Perspectives

In this paper, we apply a novel context-aware verification technique to the Landing Gear System. This approach based on Fiacre and CDL languages and in the
OBP *Observation Engine*to OBP proposes to reduce the set of possible behaviors (and thus the state-space) by closing the system-under-study with a well
defined environment (context). For LGS we have modeled one top-level context which was automatically decomposed into 885 isolated smaller scenarios,
enabling us to iteratively perform reachability analysis on each of them. Even
though, some of these scenarios fail due to the state-space explosion problem,
we show that our context-aware verification approach pushes the limits of reachability analysis, enabling an automatic divide-and-conquer approach to model-
checking. We are currently working on improving our context-aware verification
approach by providing a clear methodological framework that formalizes the
context coverage with respect to the full system.

Acknowledgments. We wish to thank Dr Frederic Boniol for his valuable and
constructive suggestions related to this paper.

References

1. Bengtsson, J., Larsen, K.G., Larsson, F., Pettersson, P., Yi, W.: UPPAAL — a
Tool Suite for Automatic Verification of Real–Time Systems. In: Alur, R., Sontag,
E.D., Henzinger, T.A. (eds.) HS 1995. LNCS, vol. 1066, pp. 232–243. Springer,
Heidelberg (1996)

2. Boniol, F., Wiels, V.: The Landing Gear System Case Study. In: Boniol, F. (ed.) ABZ 2014 Case Study Track. CCIS, vol. 433, pp. 1–18. Springer, Heidelberg (2014)
3. Boniol, F., Wiels, V., Ledinot, E.: Experiences using model checking to verify real time properties of a landing gear control system. In: Embedded Real-Time Systems (ERTS), Toulouse, France (2006)
4. Burch, J.R., Clarke, E.M., McMillan, K.L., Dill, D.L., Hwang, L.J.: Symbolic model checking: 10^{20} states and beyond. In: 5th IEEE Symposium on Logic in Computer Science, pp. 428–439 (1990)
5. Clarke, E., Biere, A., Raimi, R., Zhu, Y.: Bounded model checking using satisfiability solving. Formal Methods in System Design 19(1), 7–34 (2001)
6. Clarke, E., Emerson, E., Sistla, A.: Automatic verification of finite-state concurrent systems using temporal logic specifications. ACM Trans. Program. Lang. Syst. 8(2), 244–263 (1986)
7. Clarke, E., Enders, R., Filkorn, T., Jha, S.: Exploiting symmetry in temporal logic model checking. Formal Methods in System Design 9(1-2), 77–104 (1996)
8. Dhaussy, P., Boniol, F., Roger, J.-C.: Reducing state explosion with context modeling for model-checking. In: 13th IEEE International High Assurance Systems Engineering Symposium (Hase 2011), Boca Raton, USA (2011)
9. Dhaussy, P., Boniol, F., Roger, J.C., Leroux, L.: Improving model checking with context modelling. Advances in Software Engineering ID 547157, 13 pages (2012)
10. Dhaussy, P., Pillain, P.-Y., Creff, S., Raji, A., Le Traon, Y., Baudry, B.: Evaluating context descriptions and property definition patterns for software formal validation. In: Schürr, A., Selic, B. (eds.) MODELS 2009. LNCS, vol. 5795, pp. 438–452. Springer, Heidelberg (2009)
11. Edelkamp, S., Sanders, P., Šimeček, P.: Semi-external LTL model checking. In: Gupta, A., Malik, S. (eds.) CAV 2008. LNCS, vol. 5123, pp. 530–542. Springer, Heidelberg (2008)
12. Farail, P., Gaufillet, P., Peres, F., Bodeveix, J.P., Filali, M., Berthomieu, B., Rodrigo, S., Vernadat, F., Garavel, H., Lang, F.: FIACRE: an intermediate language for model verification in the TOPCASED environment. In: European Congress on Embedded Real-Time Software (ERTS), SEE, Toulouse (January 2008)
13. Flanagan, C., Qadeer, S.: Thread-modular model checking. In: Ball, T., Rajamani, S.K. (eds.) SPIN 2003. LNCS, vol. 2648, pp. 213–224. Springer, Heidelberg (2003)
14. Godefroid, P.: The Ulg partial-order package for SPIN. In: SPIN Workshop (1995)
15. Holzmann, G.J.: The model checker SPIN. Software Engineering 23(5), 279–295 (1997)
16. Park, S., Kwon, G.: Avoidance of state explosion using dependency analysis in model checking control flow model. In: Gavrilova, M.L., Gervasi, O., Kumar, V., Tan, C.J.K., Taniar, D., Laganá, A., Mun, Y., Choo, H. (eds.) ICCSA 2006. LNCS, vol. 3984, pp. 905–911. Springer, Heidelberg (2006)
17. Peled, D.: Combining Partial-Order Reductions with On-the-fly Model-Checking. In: Dill, D.L. (ed.) CAV 1994. LNCS, vol. 818, pp. 377–390. Springer, Heidelberg (1994)
18. Queille, J.P., Sifakis, J.: Specification and verification of concurrent systems in cesar. In: Dezani-Ciancaglini, M., Montanari, U. (eds.) Programming 1982. LNCS, vol. 137, pp. 337–351. Springer, Heidelberg (1982)
19. Schuppan, V., Biere, A.: Liveness checking as safety checking for infinite state spaces. Electronic Notes in Theoretical Computer Science 149(1), 79–96 (2006)
20. Valmari, A.: Stubborn sets for reduced state space generation. In: Rozenberg, G. (ed.) APN 1990. LNCS, vol. 483, pp. 491–515. Springer, Heidelberg (1991)

Validation of the ABZ Landing Gear System Using ProB⋆

Dominik Hansen, Lukas Ladenberger, Harald Wiegard,
Jens Bendisposto, and Michael Leuschel

Universität Düsseldorf Institut für Informatik,
Universitätsstr. 1, D-40225 Düsseldorf
{hansen,ladenberger,wiegard,bendisposto,leuschel}@cs.uni-duesseldorf.de

Abstract. In this paper we present our formalisation of the ABZ landing gear case study in Event-B. The development was carried out using
the Rodin platform and mainly used superposition refinement to structure the specification. To validate the model we complemented proof with
animation and model checking. For the latter, we used the PROB animator and model checker. Graphical representation of the model turned
out to be crucial in the development and validation of the model; this
was achieved using a new version of BMotion Studio integrated into
PROB 2.0.

1 Introduction

The "classical" B-method [1] and its successor the Event-B method [2] are refinement based formal methods. While the B-method is geared towards software
development, the Event-B method is more tailored towards systems modelling.
Refinement can be used to structure the development and proofs, and allows introducing complexity gradually. In Event-B the concept of refinement has been
considerably extended: events can be added, extended, split up or merged, parameters can be refined, removed or added, witnesses can be provided for automatic refinement proofs, event termination (convergence) can be proven or
delayed to other refinement layers, etc. Model structuring, on the other hand,
is much simpler in Event-B than in classical B: at one particular refinement
level an Event-B model consists of a main machine which contains variables and
events and a series of contexts which contain constants and sets. Composition
and decomposition notions have been developed [10] for Event-B, but are not
part of the core Event-B method and we have not used them in our case study.

In this paper, we present our results and experiences in formalising and validating the ABZ case study [6] in Event-B. To carry out the study, we have chosen
the Rodin [3], PROB [9] and BMotion Studio [8] tools. The tools are tightly integrated. Rodin enables the use of the Event-B method and supports rigorous

---

⋆ The work in this paper is partly funded by ADVANCE, an European Commission
Information and Communication Technologies FP7 project.

F. Boniol et al. (Eds.): ABZ 2014 Case Study Track, CCIS 433, pp. 66–79, 2014.

reasoning by formal proving. PROB can animate and modelcheck Event-B models, as well as provides a lot of features, for instance the inspection of the desired behaviour of a model. BMotion Studio is a framework for creating visualizations for formal models.

Structure of the Paper. Sect. 2 describes the Event-B model of the landing gear system and its refinement hierarchy. In Sect. 3 we demonstrate different approaches to validate our model. Sect. 4 describes the graphical representation of the model and outlines its use and benefits. Finally, Sect. 5 contains the conclusion and discusses future work.

Additional Material. For more information and resources, we refer the reader to our website:

http://stups.hhu.de/ProB/index.php5/ABZ14

The website contains the model, visualization, and video material.

2 The Event-B Model and Its Refinement Hierarchy

In this section, we describe our Event-B model of the landing gear system. This section may give the impression that the development was a linear process; in reality we started several times from scratch and adapted prior refinements. Initially, we also experimented with a classical B model, where structuring is easier but the stricter refinement concept makes environment modelling more difficult. We specify both the digital part and the environment in the same Event-B model. Hence, we obtain a integrated view of the system where we try to make a clear separation between both parts. Each event is associated either with the digital part or with the environment. The same applies to the variables, except for some shared variables (sensors and digital orders) which are used for the interaction of both parts. Fig. 1 shows the interaction of the digital part and its environment. The figure may look like a clone of a picture from the original case-study specification, but it is actually part of the interactive visualization of our model.

2.1 Door and Landing Gear

We start by specifying the mechanical part of the landing gear system. The top-level abstraction of our development only models one door and one landing gear. The door is represented as a variable with the following possible states:

- closed
- door_moving
- open

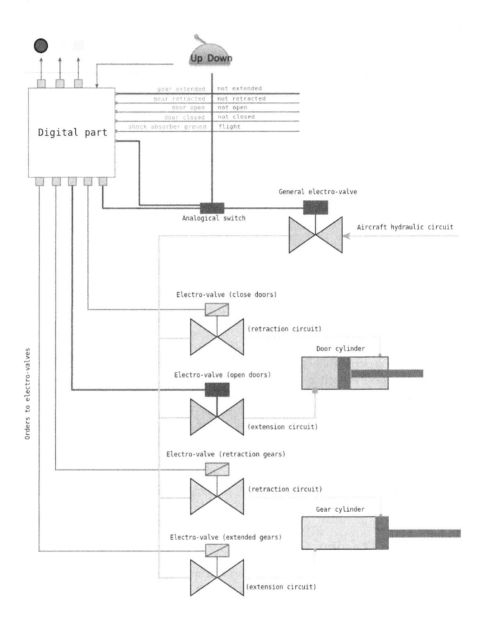

Fig. 1. Interaction of the digital part and the environment

The states of the landing gear variable are:

- retracted
- gear_moving
- extended

In addition, we define events to change the states of these variables as illustrated in Fig. 2. Thus, at this point we only forbid direct jumps from closed (or retracted) to open (or extended) or back. We do not define a fixed sequence of states, and the behaviours of the gear and the door are fully independent of each other.

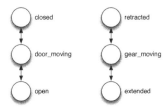

Fig. 2. Possible Door and Landing Gear States and Transitions

2.2 Electro-valves

In the first refinement step we add hydraulic elements to our specification. For each valve except for the general valve[1] we add a variable with the possible states *valve_open* and *valve_closed*. We define events to change the state of each valve. Moreover, we connect the behaviour of the door and the gear to the states of the corresponding valves. This is done by adding additional guards to the events that change state of the door and the gear. For example, the event that moves the door from the closed position to the moving positing can only be executed if the variable *open_door_valve* has the state *valve_open*. No movement of the door/gear is possible if two contrary valves (e.g. *open_door_valve* and *close_door_valve*) are simultaneously open. In this case the door/gear remains in its current position.

2.3 Outputs of the Digital Part

Next, we connect the electric orders of the digital part to the electro-valves of the hydraulic part. The electric orders are modelled as boolean variables. In this refinement we only regard the electric orders stimulating the electro-valves introduced in the last refinement step. We add events to change the states of electric orders. Now, we only allow a behaviour of the electric-valves if the corresponding orders come from the digital part. Moreover we forbid stimulating two contrary orders (open door/close door, extend/retract gear) simultaneously by adding additional guards to the events. We specify the requirement R_4 explicitly as these two invariants:

---

[1] The general valve is introduced in a later refinement step.

invariants
$R41$: ¬($open\_EV = TRUE \land close\_EV = TRUE$)
$R42$: ¬($retract\_EV = TRUE \land extend\_EV = TRUE$)

Note that the electric orders only enable events that change the states of the valves and do not execute them. This is important in order to later introduce failing electro-valves.

2.4 Controller Sensors

In this refinement step we introduce the input sensors of the digital part. We abstract the sensors by only considering the common value of the different channels. We add the following sensors:

- door_closed
- door_open
- gear_extended
- gear_retracted

The sensors are set by the events which change the state of the door and the gear. They directly reflect the state of the mechanical part but it would also be possible to introduce new events to update the sensor states according to their mechanical counterpart. After this refinement the controller only allows moving orders to the gear when the door is open, i.e. the *door_open* sensor is TRUE (R_{31}). Analogously, the controller only allows moving orders for the door when the gear is extended or retracted (R_{32}). These requirements are modelled as guards.

2.5 Controller Behaviour

In this refinement we define the sequence of output orders produced by the digital part. We abstract the digital part to consist of one controller producing the synthesized outputs of both computing modules. The sequence executed by the controller depends on the handle that can be moved by the pilot. We add a variable representing the handle and an event to change the state of the handle from *up* to *down* and vice versa. The handle event can be executed at any time. Moreover, the shock absorber sensor affects the behaviour of the controller. There must not be an order to retract the gear if the shock absorber is not relaxed, i.e., the aircraft is landed.

It is not difficult to define the uninterrupted outgoing and retraction sequence. However, allowing an interruption of the sequences by a counter order of the handle at any time makes this refinement step complex and tricky. We managed this by using some additional internal variables and adding guards to the events which change the states of the output orders. For example, the electric order towards the retraction valve can not occur if the handle is in the down position (R_{21}) and the order towards the extension valve can not occur if the handle is in the up position (R_{22}).

2.6 Analogical Switch and General Electro-valve

The analogical switch is intended to prevent the hydraulic part against abnormal behaviour. We add a variable for analogical switch and two events to change its state from *open* to *closed* and back. Moreover, we need an internal controller variable to record a handle movement and add this boolean variable as guard to the event which closes the switch. The general electro-valve is needed to supply the other electro-valves with hydraulic power from the aircraft hydraulic circuit. We add a variable for the electrical order (*general_EV*) coming from the digital part and events to change its state. The order for the general electro-valve must occur before the controller can produce an order to the other electro-valves. Hence, we add guards to all events which stimulate the other electro-valves. The following invariants ensure this behaviour:

> **invariants**
> $R511$: $open\_EV = TRUE \implies general\_EV = TRUE$
> $R512$: $close\_EV = TRUE \implies general\_EV = TRUE$
> $R513$: $extend\_EV = TRUE \implies general\_EV = TRUE$
> $R514$: $retract\_EV = TRUE \implies general\_EV = TRUE$

Furthermore we add a variable for the general electro-valve and events to change it state. A behaviour of the gear/door can only occur if the general electro-valve and the corresponding maneuvering valve is open.

2.7 Cockpit Lights

Besides the orders to the hydraulic part, the controller produces three further output signals to the cockpit:

- gears_locked_down
- gears_maneuvering
- anomaly

We add three boolean variables to represent these output signals and events to change it state. The two signals representing the state of gear can be easily computed by regarding the input sensors from the mechanical part. The *gears_locked_down* output directly correspond to the *gear_extended* input sensor. The *gears_maneuvering* output equals TRUE if the *gear_extended* and *gear_retracted* sensors are both FALSE.

In this refinement we abstract all possible inconsistent behaviours by one *anomaly* variable. We introduce a single event to set the variable to TRUE (without any guards). This event represents that the controller has detected an inconsistent behaviour.

In addition to the signals produced by the controller, we add three variables to represent the signal lights in the cockpit. The events to switch the lights on/off are connected to the output signals of the controller.

2.8   Further Refinement Steps

Several further refinement steps are needed to cover the complete specification of the landing gear system. For example, a further refinement step should introduce time and timing constraints. We experimented by introducing discrete time and an environment event (tick) incrementing the time. This approach works well from a theoretical point of view. Whenever an event with a time-based requirement is executed, the current time is saved in a designated variable. When the handle is pushed up, the current time will be saved to the variable $timerHandleUp$. This variable will be set to -1 if the handle is moved down. This allows us to formulate liveness conditions such as the requirement R_1 (stronger version) as an invariant:

---

invariants
   $R11s$: $anomaly = FALSE \land timerHandleUp > -1 \land$
         $time \geq timerHandleUp + 150 \implies$
         $gear\_retracted = TRUE \land door\_closed = TRUE$

However, in practice, it is very complex to introduce timers for each timing constraint of the specification. Hence, we did not finished this refinement step due to the lack of time. Another refinement step should break up the abstractions we did so far (e.g. triplicating the sensors). We stopped at this point by getting a sufficient model to control the graphical visualization we made. Moreover, our model allows us to validate some of the "normal mode" requirements of the specification.

3   Validating the Model

This section describes validations carried out using PROB. In that setting the graphical visualization of the landing gear system was important. The latter is described separately in Sect. 4.

3.1   Invariants

As already mentioned, the requirements R_4 and R_5 are specified as invariants on different refinements levels. Our approach to validate an invariant is as follows: Before proving the invariants, we always run the model checker PROB. Sometimes the model checker provides us with a counter-example violating an invariant. In such cases we revisited and fixed our model by adding or modifying some guards. Moreover, we used another feature of PROB which is called constrained based model checking. In this mode of operation, PROB does not explore all reachable states starting from the initial state(s), but checks whether applying a single operation can result in an invariant violation independently of the particular initialization of the Event-B machine. If the constraint based checker finds a counter-example, this indicates that the model may contain a problem. The sequence of operations discovered by the constraint based checker leads from a valid state (satisfying the invariant) to a invariant violation, meaning that the B machine may have to be corrected. The valid state is not necessarily reachable from a valid initial state. However, this situation indicates that it will be impossible to prove the machine using the Event-B proof rules.

If PROB does not provide a counter-example we start proving the invariants. For the invariants specified in our final model the Rodin's provers are able to automatically discharge all generated proof obligations.

3.2   Animation and Model Testing

The animation feature of PROB had a major impact on our modelling process. Each time we added some new events to our Event-B model we ran the animator to check the new behaviour. To validate the complex behaviour of the controller (Sec. 2.5) we automated this approach. We used the animator to create valid traces (sequence of executed events) of the controller interacting with the environment. For example, we animated the complete outgoing and retraction sequence by letting the environment react in regular way. Additionally, we create traces by interrupting both sequences at each position by a counter order of the handle. All traces were saved and used as regression tests to validate further modifications of the model.

3.3   Temporal Formulas

The requirements R_{11} and R_{12} (weaker version) describe a temporal behaviour of the system. The desired goal is to show that if the handle is pushed up/down the end of the retraction/extension sequence will be reached. Normally we would write such a liveness condition using the following simple LTL pattern:

$$\Box(t \Rightarrow \Diamond g)$$

where t is a trigger (handle movement) and g is the goal state which should be finally reached (gear are retracted/extened and the door is closed). However on the path from the handle movement to the end of the corresponding sequence several conditions must to be ensured. For example the handle must stay in its position and no anomaly should occur. To ensure these conditions we use a more complex LTL pattern:

$$\Box(t \Rightarrow ((g \ R \ s) \Rightarrow \Diamond g))$$

In this pattern, we only regard the paths (after the handle movement) that satisfy the condition s. The condition s must be satisfied only until the goal state is reached. Therefore the goal predicate releases (R) the condition s. Note that the release operator does not require that the goal state is finally reached. For example, the whole LTL formula for R_{12} is as follows:

$\Box(handle = up \Rightarrow$
$\quad(((gear\_retracted = TRUE \wedge door\_closed = TRUE)$
$\quad\quad R \quad (handle = up \wedge gear\_shock\_absorber = flight \wedge anomaly = FALSE))$
$\quad\quad \Rightarrow \Diamond(gear\_retracted = TRUE \wedge door\_closed = TRUE)))$

In contrast to invariants, LTL formulas are not automatically satisfied by further refinement steps and we have to re-check them at each level. Sometimes this requires some additional conditions such as fairness for certain events. We use the LTL model checker of PROB to validate the LTL formulas for the requirements R_{11} and R_{12}.

3.4   Relative Deadlock Freedom and Determinism Checking

The classical deadlock notion is not very useful for our model as the environment contains events that are always enabled. Instead we developed and used a new feature of PROB to check if a controller event is always possible. The feature is called relative deadlock checking and is able to only regard a certain selection of events. We checked the refinement described in Sect. 2.3 for relative deadlock freedom. In this refinement step, the controller does not have to wait for an environment behaviour, hence a controller event should always be possible.

Another important point is that the controller should behave in a deterministic way. In our model the controller behaviour is divided into several events. Therefore we have to ensure that for the same inputs the controller always produces the same outputs. To verify this, we developed and used another new feature of PROB checking that only one controller event is enabled at the same time (see Fig. 3). More formally, the user selects a set of events $e_1, \ldots, e_k$ and the PROB model checker verifies that for every reachable state exactly one event e_i is enabled. We believe that this feature will be of interest for other Event-B system developments. In particular, it would have been handy for the case study reported in [7].

4   Graphical Visualization

To visualize our model we used the new version of BMotion studio in PROB 2.0. We have not yet released PROB 2.0 officially, but the source code is available from [4]. Nightly builds are available from a Rodin updatesite [5]. One of the main differences between the current PROB Plug-in for Rodin and PROB 2.0 is that the latter is no longer based on Eclipse but rather uses standard Browser technology as its GUI. This allows to integrate PROB into a wide range of tools. Rodin is one of them but it is also possible to integrate PROB into a regular website or a presentation tool.

Another very important difference between PROB 2.0 and its predecessor is the tight integration with the Groovy scripting language. PROB 2.0 is implemented as if it was a library for Groovy. Basically everything from the constraint solver to the user interface is exposed to the scripting language. This makes it very easy to programatically control PROB 2.0.

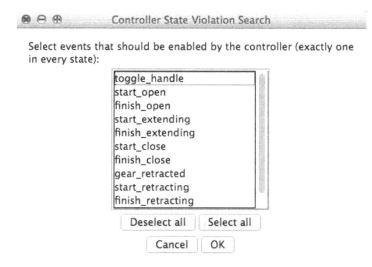

Fig. 3. Controller Violation Search Dialog

The graphical interface consists of HTML, CSS and optionally JavaScript. This makes the user interface very flexible and compositional. We can design and implement each bit of the application separately and compose them in ways that are almost arbitrary. For the Rodin integration we bundle information into components, that are then displayed inside an Eclipse view. For instance, one component consists of the list of events that can be executed in a given state and some control buttons to execute random animation steps and to go back and forth in time. This component is shown in the Events view within Rodin.

The new version of BMotion Studio [8] is just a view like every other view. It translates a state into a graphical representation. Once an animation is started, BMotion Studio is notified about every state change and then updates the graphical representation according to the state of the animation.

Originally BMotion Studio [8] was developed as a separate plug-in for Rodin. It used the Eclipse Graphical Editing Framework (GEF) to provide an editor to create visualizations of a model. While this was a very convenient approach to create simple visualizations, the visual editor makes it hard to create complex visualizations. For instance, creating a large table or a railroad track layout is very cumbersome.

BMotion Studio for PROB 2.0 follows the same principles as PROB 2.0. Most parts of BMotion Studio are accessible via the Groovy scripting language. Additionally the user interface can make use of JavaScript. This makes is much easier to create complex or dynamic visualizations. A track layout, for example, can be created by any graphic program that is able to produce a SVG vector graphic. One advantage of the SVG format is that it is very easy to manipulate graphical components.

4.1   Visualization of the Landing Gear System

Our landing gear visualization consists of two parts, a graphical part, and an observer part. Simple SVG widgets, like shapes represent the different aspects of the architecture of the hydraulic part of the landing gear system as shown in Fig. 1. The observer part acts as the link between the formal model and the graphical part. It defines expressions and predicates written in B that are evaluated by PROB in the current state of the simulation. The results of the expressions and predicates are used by the observers to update the visualization. For instance, the colour of the lines that represent the electric orders to the elector-valves is switched from red to green and from green to red whenever the corresponding variable is set to true or false respectively. This is shown in Fig. 1, where the electric order to the open door electro valve is coloured in green whereas the other electric orders are coloured in red. The blue coloured lines represent the current circulation of pressure.

Another example is the position of the door cylinder: It is shifted in respect of the state of the door (*closed, door_moving* and *open*). In Fig. 1 the door cylinder illustrates the *door_moving* state. We also created a separate view of the physical environment as shown in Fig. 4 that represents beside the state of the cylinders, the current state of the physical door and gear.

The strict separation into a graphical part and an observer part makes the visualization reusable for other Event-B or even Classical B models of the landing gear system. Indeed, to adapt the visualizations for a different formal model one simply has to change the the observer part of the visualization, but not the graphical part.

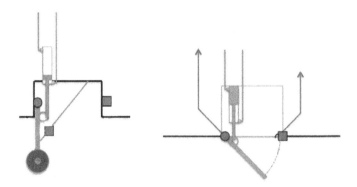

Fig. 4. Visualization of the physical environment

In addition, the visualization is subdivided into components, where each component reflects a specific refinement level of the model. A component is only displayed if the corresponding refinement level is part of the running simulation. The visualization shown in Fig. 1 illustrates the last refinement step that is described in Sect. 2.7. In that sense the visualization is created to be extensible, for instance with new refinement levels.

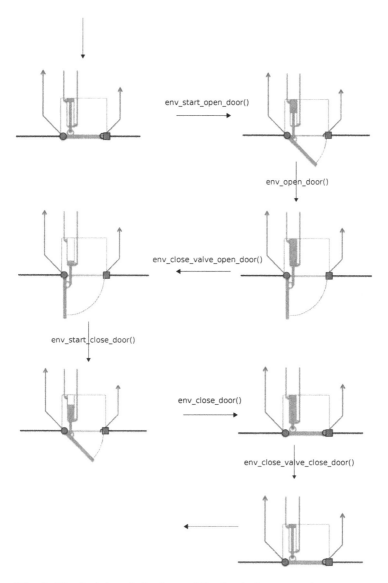

Fig. 5. Physical door behaviour while simulating retraction sequence

The visualization can be used for different purposes. For instance, BMotion Studio is able to replay user defined traces within the visualization. This feature helped us to check whether the two basic scenarios: the outgoing sequence and the retraction sequence are realized accurately in our model. Beside analysing the two basic scenarios, we also used this feature to replay traces that lead to invariant violations found by PROB. A stepwise visualization of door behaviour while simulating the retraction sequence is demonstrated in Fig. 5. It was also used to communicate the model between the people involved in this case study.

5 Conclusion

In this paper we presented our Event-B model of the ABZ landing gear case study. By using refinement we were able to add stepwise more details to our model and make a formal development of system manageable. Even if our model does not cover the complete specification of the system, we were able to validate some "normal mode" requirements of the system. For example, our model is capable to perform the full landing gear retraction and extension sequences, both of which can be reversed at any moment in time.

Our main goal was to verify that our toolchain is able to deal with the case study. We used the following techniques to validate our model:

- Model checking
- Constraint based model checking
- Proving
- LTL model checking
- Animation based simulation
- Trace checking
- Determinism checking
- Relative deadlock checking

Initiated by the requirements of the case study, we developed a determinism checker and relative deadlock checker. We believe these new PROB features are also useful for future projects.

We used BMotion Studio to create a visualization of the model that was crucial in the development and validation of the model. Conversely, we used the case study to experiment with the development version of BMotion Studio and PROB 2.0.

Although developing a visualization required extra effort, the benefits of the visualization were tremendous. The visualization helped to get a common understanding about the model. It revealed problems and errors in the model. The arrangement of the visualization into different refinement steps allowed us to hide some of the complexity of the system and to focus on a specific problem. We strongly believe that the ability to animate and visualize the system is crucial for correctness and for reducing modelling effort when developing non-trivial formal models.

6 Possible Future Work

As part of the research project Advance we have developed a co-simulation framework that allows to use PROB together with another simulator for continuous systems. The framework uses the Functional Mock-up Interface (FMI) standard to exchange information between the simulators. We could use the framework to simulate the controller of the landing gear system in PROB and the environment (or parts of it) in another simulator, e.g. Dymola.

Another interesting work would be to use our visualizations for formalisations of the other case study solutions, including those that are specified in CSP, TLA$^+$

or Z. The visualization could be also enhanced with interactive components (e.g. buttons) to drive the simulation.

Acknowledgements. We are grateful to Stefan Hallerstede for various discussions and support in developing the formal Event-B model. Finally, we are thankful to anonymous referees for their useful feedback.

References

1. Abrial, J.-R.: The B-Book. Cambridge University Press (1996)
2. Abrial, J.-R.: Modeling in Event-B: System and Software Engineering. Cambridge University Press (2010)
3. Abrial, J.-R., Butler, M., Hallerstede, S., Voisin, L.: An open extensible tool environment for Event-B. In: Liu, Z., Kleinberg, R.D. (eds.) ICFEM 2006. LNCS, vol. 4260, pp. 588–605. Springer, Heidelberg (2006)
4. Bendisposto, J., Birkhoff, M., Clark, J., Dobrikov, I., Fontaine, M., Fritz, F., Goebbels, R., Hansen, D., Kantner, P., Koerner, P., Krings, S., Ladenberger, L., Luo, L., Leuschel, M., Plagge, D., Spermann, C.: ProB 2.0 source code, http://github.com/bendisposto/prob2
5. Bendisposto, J., Birkhoff, M., Clark, J., Dobrikov, I., Fontaine, M., Fritz, F., Goebbels, R., Hansen, D., Kantner, P., Koerner, P., Krings, S., Ladenberger, L., Luo, L., Leuschel, M., Plagge, D., Spermann, C.: ProB 2.0 Update Site for Rodin, http://nightly.cobra.cs.uni-duesseldorf.de/experimental/updatesite/
6. Boniol, F., Wiels, V.: The Landing Gear System Case Study. In: Boniol, F. (ed.) ABZ 2014 Case Study Track. CCIS, vol. 433, pp. 1–18. Springer, Heidelberg (2014)
7. Gmehlich, R., Grau, K., Hallerstede, S., Leuschel, M., Lösch, F., Plagge, D.: On fitting a formal method into practice. In: Qin, S., Qiu, Z. (eds.) ICFEM 2011. LNCS, vol. 6991, pp. 195–210. Springer, Heidelberg (2011)
8. Ladenberger, L., Bendisposto, J., Leuschel, M.: Visualising Event-B Models with B-Motion Studio. In: Alpuente, M., Cook, B., Joubert, C. (eds.) FMICS 2009. LNCS, vol. 5825, pp. 202–204. Springer, Heidelberg (2009)
9. Leuschel, M., Butler, M.J.: ProB: An automated analysis toolset for the B method. STTT 10(2), 185–203 (2008)
10. Silva, R., Butler, M.: Shared event composition/decomposition in Event-B. In: Aichernig, B.K., de Boer, F.S., Bonsangue, M.M. (eds.) FMCO 2010. LNCS, vol. 6957, pp. 122–141. Springer, Heidelberg (2011)

Modeling a Landing Gear System in Event-B

Amel Mammar[1] and Régine Laleau[2]

[1] Institut Mines-Télécom/Télécom SudParis, CNRS UMR 5157 SAMOVAR, France
amel.mammar@telecom-sudparis.eu
[2] Université Paris-Est, LACL, IUT Sénart Fontainebleau, France
laleau@u-pec.fr

Abstract. This paper describes the Event-B modeling of the landing gear system of an aircraft whose the complete description can be found in [3]. This real-life case study has been proposed by the ABZ'2014 track that takes place in Toulouse, the European capital of the aeronautic industry. Our modeling is based on the Parnas and Madey's 4-Variable Model that permits to consider the different parts of a system. These parts are incrementally introduced using the Event-B refinement technique. The entire development has been carried out under the Rodin toolset. To validate and prove the different components, we use the Atelier B, SMT and ML provers which are plugged to Rodin.

1 General Overview of the System

The objective of the landing gear system is to permit a safe extension/retraction of the gears when the plane is going to land/fly. Each gear is placed in a landing-gear box equipped with a door that must be open when a gear is extending/retracting and closed when it becomes completely extended/retracted and locked. To this aim, the controller (See Figure 1) reads, periodically through a set of sensors, the states of the different elements (doors, gears, handler, etc.) and sends orders to a set of electro-valves that make, for instance, the gears extend/retract or the doors open/close. More details will be introduced throughout the modeling of this system.

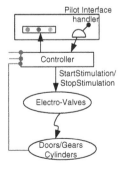

Fig. 1. The overall structure of the landing gear system

F. Boniol et al. (Eds.): ABZ 2014 Case Study Track, CCIS 433, pp. 80–94, 2014.

To model this system in Event-B [2], we suggest following the classification of modeling variables according to the four-variable model of Parnas and Madey [8]. We distinguish two groups of variables *environment* and *controller* variables:

1. *Environment variables*: represent the status of the elements outside the controller. Two kinds of variables are distinguished:
   - *Monitored variables*: the values of these variables are not calculated by the controller but can be monitored. For example, the actual states of the doors/gears.
   - *Controlled variables*: the values of these variables are determined by the controller. For example, the status of the valves and the lights.
2. *Controller variables*: denote values inside the controller system. Mainly, they represent the values of some elements as seen by the controller but also the different orders it sends.
   - *Inputs*: the values stored in the controller and provided by some sensors. For example, $door\_open_i[x]$, $handle_i$, $gear\_extended_i[x]$, etc.
   - *Outputs*: they are the orders sent by the controller toward the different environmental elements. For example, $general\_EV$, $retract\_EV$, $gears\_ma$ $neuvring$, $anomaly$, etc.

The system can be seen as continuously executing the following sequence of actions:

Do
    Read Inputs from some sensors
    Process Inputs
    Produce outputs
Until *a failure is detected*

In the following sections, we are going to develop the modeling of this system in six main steps:

1. *Modeling the monitored variables*: we describe the behavior of the physical components like the doors, the gears, cylinders, but also the handler, the switch and the shock absorbers. The variables modeling these components are suffixed with "_p" because they represent their actual (physical) status (See Section 3).
2. *Modeling the controlled variables*: we describe in this phase the behavior of the valves that permit to act directly on the doors, gears and cylinders (See Section 4). We also describe the behavior of the lights that inform the pilot about the status of the system in general. Again, the variables modeling these components are suffixed with "_p" because they represent their actual status (See Section 4).
3. *Modeling the controller/output variables*: we describe how the controller reads information from the sensors, sends orders to the valves and how it updates the values of the lights (See Section 5).
4. *Modeling timing aspects*: to facilitate the design, we have chosen to elaborate a first modeling of the system without considering any timed constraints. The timed aspects are taken into account later by refinement (See Section 6).

5. *Modeling the failure cases*: in this step, we take into account the system's anomalies caused by failures on the different elements of the system (See Section 7).
6. Finally, we describe how properties are verified (See Section 8).

In each of the previous steps, the different elements are gradually introduced thanks to the Event-B refinement mechanism. The next section gives a brief description of the Event-B method together with its refinement technique.

2   Event-B Method

Event-B [2] is the successor of the B method [1] permitting to model discrete systems using mathematical notations. The complexity of a system is mastered thanks to the refinement concept that allows to gradually introduce the different parts that constitute the system starting from an abstract model to a more concrete one. An Event-B specification is made of two elements: *context* and *machine*. A context describes the static part of an Event-B specification; it consists of constants and sets (user-defined types) together with axioms that specify their properties. The dynamic part of an Event-B specification is included in a machine that defines variables and events. The possible values that the variables hold are restricted using an invariant written using a first-order predicate on the state variables. An event can be executed if it is enabled, i.e. all the conditions, named guards, prior to its execution hold. Among all enabled events, only one is executed. In this case, substitutions, called actions, are applied over variables. The execution of each event should maintain the invariant. To this aim, proof obligations are generated for each event. To discharge these proof obligations, the Rodin[1] platform offers an automatic prover but also the possibility to plug additional external provers like the SMT and Atelier B provers.

3   Modeling the Monitored Variables

In the system, we have the following monitored variables: *gears, doors, doors/gears cylinders, handler, hydraulic circuit* and *switch*. These elements are introduced according to the following refinement strategy:

- Initial model (Component *Gears*): we start by describing the behavior of the gears, that can be made extended or not, since this is the main objective of the system.
- 1st refinement (Component *GearsIntermediateStates*): we refine the state where a gear is not extended by distinguishing two different sub-states: retracted or partly-extended.
- 2nd and 3rd refinements (Components *Doors* and *DoorsIntermediateStates*): like for the gears, we describe the state of a door as open or not, then we add an intermediate state to model a partly-open door.

---

[1] http://www.event-b.org/install.html

- 4th refinement (Component *Cylinders*): in this step, we introduce the cylinders that allow the motion of the doors and gears.
- 5th refinement (Component *HandlerSwitchShockAbsorber*): we model in this phase the handler, the analogical switch, the hydraulic circuit and the shock absorbers.

In the following sub-sections, we detail each step.

3.1 Gears Modeling: The Initial Model and the First Refinement

We first introduce a context with set **PositionsDG** representing the three possible cases for gears/doors/etc.: *front, left* or *right*. Then, we define a Boolean variable *gear_extended_p* to formalize whether a gear is extended or not:

> **inv1:** $gear\_extended\_p \in PositionsDG \rightarrow BOOL$

To make the gears extended or not, we define the following two events:

Make_GearExtended	Start_GearRetracting
ANY *po* **WHERE**	**ANY** *po* **WHERE**
$po \in PositionsDG \wedge$	$po \in PositionsDG \wedge$
$gear\_extended\_p(po)$=FALSE	$gear\_extended\_p(po)$=TRUE
THEN	**THEN**
$gear\_extended\_p(po)$:=TRUE	$gear\_extended\_p(po)$:=FALSE
END	**END**

When a gear is not extended, it can be retracted or partly-extended. So, we refine the previous specification by introducing a new Boolean variable *gear_retracted_p* that is true if the gear is entirely retracted. This variable is defined by two invariants (**inv2**) and (**inv3**), where (**inv3**) states that a gear cannot be extended and retracted at the same time:

> **inv2:** $gear\_retracted\_p \in PositionsDG \rightarrow BOOL$
> **inv3:** $\forall po.(po \in PositionsDG \Rightarrow$
> $\qquad \neg(gear\_extended\_p(po) =TRUE \wedge gear\_retracted\_p(po) =TRUE))$

Consequently, the event **Make_GearExtended** is refined by adding the guard ($gear\_retracted\_p(po)$ =FALSE), and we define the two following new events to make a gear start extending (it becomes no longer retracted) or complete its closing.

Start_GearExtending	Make_GearRetracted
ANY *po* **WHERE**	**ANY** *po* **WHERE**
$po \in PositionsDG$	$po \in PositionsDG$
$gear\_retracted\_p(po)$ =TRUE	$gear\_extended\_p(po)$ =FALSE
THEN	$gear\_retracted\_p(po)$=FALSE
$gear\_retracted\_p(po)$:=FALSE	**THEN**
END	$gear\_retracted\_p(po)$:=TRUE
	END

3.2 Doors Modeling: The Second and Third Refinements

In this part, we present the modeling of the doors. To this aim, we have proceeded like for the gears by defining two levels. In the first level, we define a new variable *door_open_p* to know if a door is open or not. Then, we refine, in the second level, the state where a door is not open by adding a new variable *door_closed_p* to state if the door is closed or partly-open.

– the third refinement: we define the variable $door\_open\_p$ and express an invariant to state that when a gear is partly-extended then all the doors are open. In other words, it is not possible to start the extending/retracting of a gear until all the doors are open.

> **inv4:** $door\_open\_p \in$ PositionsDG $\rightarrow$ BOOL
> **inv5:** $\exists po.(po \in$ PositionsDG $\land gear\_extended\_p(po) =$ FALSE$\land$
> $gear\_retracted\_p(po) =$ FALSE$) \Rightarrow door\_open\_p =$PositionsDG$\times\{$TRUE$\}$

In order to preserve invariant (**inv5**), we refine the events Start_GearExtending and Start_GearRetracting by adding the guard ($door\_open\_p$ =PositionsDG$\times$ {TRUE}). We also define two events to make a door open and start closing.

Make_DoorOpen	Start_DoorClosing
ANY po **WHERE**	**ANY** po **WHERE**
$door\_open\_p(po)$ =FALSE	$door\_open\_p(po)$ =TRUE
THEN	($gear\_extended\_p$ =PositionsDG $\times$ {TRUE} $\lor$
$door\_open\_p(po)$:=TRUE	$gear\_retracted\_p$ =PositionsDG$\times$ {TRUE})
END	**THEN**
	$door\_open\_p(po)$:= FALSE
	END

– the fourth refinement: in this level, we define the variable $door\_closed\_p$ and express that a door cannot be open and closed at the same time:

> **inv6:** $door\_closed\_p \in$ PositionsDG $\rightarrow$ BOOL
> **inv7:** $\forall po.(po \in$ PositionsDG $\Rightarrow$
> $\neg(door\_open\_p(po) =$TRUE $\land door\_closed\_p(po) =$TRUE$)$

In order to preserve invariant (**inv7**), we refine the event Make_DoorOpen by adding the guard ($door\_closed\_p(po) =$ FALSE). We also define two new events to make a door start opening (it becomes no longer closed) or accomplish its closing.

Start_DoorOpening	Make_DoorClosed
ANY po **WHERE**	**ANY** po **WHERE**
$door\_closed\_p(po)$ =TRUE	$door\_closed\_p(po)$ =FALSE
THEN	$door\_open\_p(po)$ =FALSE
$door\_closed\_p(po)$:=FALSE	**THEN**
END	$door\_closed\_p(po)$:=TRUE
	END

3.3   Cylinders Modeling: The Fourth Refinement

The motion of the gears and the doors is performed by a set of cylinders. A door (resp. gear) cylinder is locked when the door is closed (resp. extended or retracted). Of course, before starting moving, the cylinder, associated with the door/gear, should not be locked. So in the next refinement, we define two new variables $door\_cylinder\_locked\_p$ and $gear\_cylinder\_locked\_p$ with the following invariant:

> **inv8:** $door\_cylinder\_locked\_p \in$ PositionsDG $\rightarrow$ BOOL
> **inv9:** $gear\_cylinder\_locked\_p \in$ PositionsDG $\rightarrow$ BOOL
> **inv10:** $\forall po.(door\_cylinder\_locked\_p(po) =$TRUE $\Rightarrow door\_closed\_p(po) =$TRUE$)$
> **inv11:** $\forall po.(gear\_cylinder\_locked\_p(po) =$TRUE $\Rightarrow$
> $(gear\_extended\_p(po) =$TRUE $\lor gear\_retracted\_p(po) =$TRUE$))$
> **inv12:** $\forall po.(gear\_cylinder\_locked\_p(po) =$FALSE $\Rightarrow door\_open\_p=$PositionsDG$\times\{$TRUE$\})$

In order to satisfy (**inv11**), we have refined the events *Start_GearExtending* and *Start_GearRetracting* by adding the guard (*gear_cylinder_locked_p(po)* = FALSE). Similarly, we have refined the event *Start_DoorClosing* by adding the guard (*gear_cylinder_locked_p* =PositionsDG × {TRUE}) to make (**inv12**) satisfied. Finally, we have defined four new events to lock/unlock door/gear cylinders. For the sake of space, we provide only those associated with gears.

UnlockGearCylinder
ANY *po* **WHERE**
  po ∈ PositionsDG
  gear_cylinder_locked_p(po) =TRUE
  gear_extended_p(po) =TRUE ∨
  gear_retracted_p(po)=TRUE
  door_open_p =PositionsDG × {TRUE}
THEN
  gear_cylinder_locked_p(po) :=FALSE
END
	LockGearCylinder
	ANY *po* **WHERE**
	  po ∈ PositionsDG
	  gear_cylinder_locked_p(po)=FALSE
	  gear_extended_p(po) =TRUE ∨
	  gear_retracted_p(po) =TRUE
	THEN
	  gear_cylinder_locked_p(po) :=TRUE
	END

3.4 Handler/Switch/Shock Absorbers/Hydraulic Circuit Modeling: The Fifth Refinement

In this step, we continue the modeling of the monitored variables by introducing the handler, the analogical switch, the shock absorbers and the hydraulic circuit. First, we extend the context by defining two new sets `PositionsHandler` and `PositionsSwitch` to denote respectively the possible positions for the handler, *up* and *down*, and for the switch, *open*, *closed*. So, we define two Boolean variables *handler_p* and *analogical_switch_p* to model the position of the handler and the switch respectively. Since the analogical switch closes each time the handler changes its position, we add a Boolean variable *handle* which memorizes the handler shift. The events we define for the handler are: `PutHandlerUp` and `PutHandlerDown`. For instance, under the guard *handler_p* = *down*, the event `PutHandlerUp` sets the variable *handler_p* to *up* and assigns TRUE to the variable *handle*.

To model the physical behavior of the analogical switch depicted in Figure 2, we define two additional Boolean variables *Intermediate$_1$* and *Intermediate$_2$* that cannot be true at the same time as follows:

inv13: ¬(*Intermediate$_1$* =TRUE ∧ *Intermediate$_2$* =TRUE)
inv14: (*Intermediate$_1$*=TRUE ∨ *Intermediate$_2$* =TRUE) ⇒ *analogical_switch_p* = *open*

Each transition is translated into an event whose guard corresponds to its source state and includes (*handle*=TRUE) if it is triggered by the handler shift. The action of this event consists in assigning FALSE to the source state and TRUE to the target one. For the sake of space, we only provide the Event-B translation of two transitions.

close_Switch
WHEN
  Intermediate$_1$ =TRUE
THEN
  analogical_switch_p := *closed*
  Intermediate$_1$:=FALSE
END
	HandleFromIntermediate2ToIntermediate1
	WHEN
	  Intermediate$_2$ =TRUE
	  handle =TRUE
	THEN
	  handle :=FALSE
	  Intermediate$_2$:=FALSE
	  Intermediate$_1$:=TRUE
	END

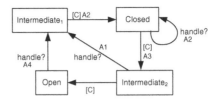

C: currentTime =deadlineSwitch
A1: deadlineSwitch:=currentTime+(8-2/3*(deadlineSwitch-currentTime)
A2: deadlineSwitch:=currentTime+200
A3: deadlineSwitch:=currentTime+12
A4: deadlineSwitch:=currentTime+8

Fig. 2. Physical behavior of the analogical switch

The hydraulic circuit is modeled with a Boolean variable $circuit\_pressurized\_p$, and two events *Unpressurise* and *Pressurise*. For instance, under the guard $(circuit\_pressurized\_p{=}\text{TRUE})$, the event *Unpressurise* sets the variable $circuit\_pressurized\_p$ to FALSE. In addition, we have refined each event related to the doors/gears/ motion and lock/unlock cylinders by adding a guard $(circuit\_pressu\,rized\_p = \text{TRUE})$. Finally, we model gears shock absorbers by a Boolean variable that gives for each position the state of its associated shock absorber according to the following invariant stating that a gear shock absorber is on ground only if its gear is extended:

$\boxed{\textbf{inv15:}\ \forall po.(po \in \texttt{PositionsDG} \wedge gear\_shock\_absorber\_p(po) {=}\text{TRUE} \Rightarrow gear\_extended\_p(po){=}\text{TRUE})}$

So, to preserve invariant (**inv15**), the event **Start_GearRetracting** is refined by adding an action that set the variable $gear\_shock\_absorber\_p(po)$ to FALSE. In addition, to make the state of a shock absorber evolve, we have defined two new events: a first to set it to FALSE and a second to TRUE under the guard that its gear is extended.

4   Modeling the Controlled Variables: The Sixth Refinement

This section deals with the modeling of valves and lights that are controlled by the system (Component *ValvesLights*). We describe how a valve becomes active/not active and how a light becomes on/off. Each valve is modeled with a Boolean variable ($general\_EV\_p$, $open\_EV\_p$, $close\_EV\_p$, $extend\_EV\_p$, $retract\_EV\_p$) and two events to make it active or not. For the sake of space, we describe the events that activate the open door valve and deactivate the extend valve; the others are very similar.

MakeOpenDoorValveActive	MakeExtendValveActive
WHEN	**WHEN**
$open\_EV\_p{=}$ FALSE	$extend\_EV\_p{=}$ FALSE
$circuit\_pressurized\_p{=}$ TRUE	$circuit\_pressurized\_p{=}$ TRUE
THEN	**THEN**
$open\_EV\_p{:=}$ TRUE	$extend\_EV\_p{:=}$ TRUE
END	**END**

In addition, we refine each event related to the motion of doors/gears by adding a guard to specify that the corresponding valve is active and its opposite is deactivated. For instance, we refine the event Start_GearExtending by adding the guard ($extend\_EV\_p$ = TRUE $\land$ $retract\_EV\_p$ = FALSE). We also refine the events related to lock/unlock door/gear cylinders by adding the adequate guard. For instance, we refine the event LockGearCylinder by adding the guard:

$$(gear\_extended\_p(po) = \text{TRUE} \land extend\_EV\_p = \text{TRUE}) \lor$$
$$(gear\_retracted\_p(po) = \text{TRUE} \land retract\_EV\_p = \text{TRUE})$$

Finally, we refine the event Pressurise_HydrolicCircuit (resp. Unpressurise_HydrolicCircuit) by adding the guard ($general\_EV\_p$ = TRUE) (resp. $general\_EV\_p$ = FALSE).

The lights are dealt with similarly to the valves. We model each of them by a Boolean variable ($greenLight\_p$, $orangeLight\_p$, $redLight\_p$) and define two events for green and orange lights; one to set the light on and the other to set it off. For the red light, only the event that makes it on is defined since this state is kept forever.

5 Modeling the Controller/Output Variables: The Seventh Refinement

In this section, we describe how the controller takes its decisions about the setting of the light and the activation/deactivation of the valves according to the information it gets from the sensors that it periodically reads (Component *Sensor*). To do that, the controller reads the status of the handler, the switch, the hydraulic circuit, the doors and the gears[2]. So, we introduce for each of these elements a new variable that represents its state as seen by the controller. Such variables are suffixed by "$\_ind$" and are of the same type and have the same constraints as their associated variables suffixed by "$\_p$". For instance, a door cannot be seen open and closed at the same time. The controller acquires information from the sensors as follows:

```
ReadInput
  ANY
     handler_sensor_value , analogical_switch_sensor_value, circuit_pressurized_sensor_value,
     gear_extended_sensor_valueF, gear_extended_sensor_valueL, gear_extended_sensor_valueR,
        ...
  WHERE
     handler_sensor_value ∈ PositionsHandler
        ...
     gear_extended_sensor_valueF ∈ BOOL ∧
        gear_extended_sensor_valueF=TRUE ⇒
        gear_extended(front)=TRUE ∧ gear_cylinder_locked_p(front)=TRUE
        ...
  THEN
     handler_sensor_ind:=handler_sensor_value
        ...
     gear_extended_sensor_p:= {front ↦ gear_extended_sensor_valueF,
        left ↦ gear_extended_sensor_valueL,right ↦ gear_extended_sensor_valueR}
        ...
  END
```

---

[2] In this paper, we make the assumption that there is a unique sensor on each of these elements.

The key point of the event ReadInput is that each sensor does not give information that goes against the security of the system (the sensors are intrinsically safe), that means that if it says that a door/gear is {open, close}/{extended/retracted} then it is really the case. If the sensor is faulty, it should say: I do not know!, that is, it will return FALSE for the doors and the gears. From these inputs, the controller takes decisions about sending orders to the valves. Each order to a valve is modeled by a Boolean variable ($general\_EV$, $close\_EV$, etc.) such that:

```
inv16: ¬(open_EV=TRUE ∧ close_EV=TRUE)//Req R41
inv17: ¬(extend_EV=TRUE ∧ retract_EV=TRUE)//Req R42
inv18: (open_EV =TRUE ∨ close_EV =TRUE ) ⇒ general_EV =TRUE
inv19: (extend_EV =TRUE ∨ retract_EV =TRUE) ⇒ open_EV =TRUE//inv18 + inv19 = R51
```

For instance, the controller sends orders to the general and extend valves as follows:

– when the analogical switch is closed, it sends a start stimulation to the general valve if it reads that the handler is up (resp. down) but the gears are not locked up (resp. down). It should also maintain the stimulation of the general valve if the open/close valve is still stimulated. The event that model starting/stopping the stimulation of the general valve is as follows:

```
OutputGeneralValve
  ANY general_EV_value WHERE
    general_EV_value =bool((analogical_switch_ind =closed
       ∧ ((handler_ind=down ∧ gear_extended ≠PositionsDG × {TRUE}) ∨
      (handler_ind=up ∧ gear_retracted_ind ≠ PositionsDG × {TRUE}))) ∨
      (open_EV =TRUE ∨ close_EV =TRUE))
    general_EV ≠ general_EV_value THEN
    general_EV := general_EV_value
  END
```

– if the open door valve is stimulated and the doors are seen open, it sends a stimulation order to the extend valve if it sees that the handler is down but one of the gear is not extended and locked in the down position, otherwise it stops it:

```
OutputExtendGearValve
  ANY extend_EV_value WHERE
    extend_EV_value =bool(handler_ind =down ∧
    gear_extended_ind ≠ PositionsDG×{TRUE} ∧
    open_EV =TRUE ∧ retract_EV =FALSE ∧
    door_open_ind=PositionsDG×{TRUE})
    extend_EV ≠ extend_EV_value THEN
    extend_EV := extend_EV_value
  END
```

Similarly to the valves, the controller sends orders to the lights. At this level, we only introduce the order to the green and orange lights; the red one is achieved later when we model failures. For instance, when the controller sees the gears extended and locked, it sends order $gears\_locked\_down$ as follows:

```
gears_locked_down :=bool(gear_extended_sensor_valueF =TRUE ∧
                         gear_extended_sensor_valueL =TRUE ∧
                         gear_extended_sensor_valueR =TRUE)
```

In this step, we refine each event related to making a valve active/not active by adding a guard to specify that its related order has been sent from the controller. We also refine the event acting on the lights by adding a guard that expresses that the setting order has been received from the controller.

6   Introducing Timing Aspects: The Eighth Refinement

In this system, timing aspects are four folds: (1) the analogical switch takes time to move from open to close and vice versa (2) the start/stop stimulation of valves should be separated by some time, (3) the valves take time to be active, the cylinders take time to move and be locked/unlocked, (4) the controller has to read some inputs at given moments to be sure that the system behaves correctly as expected or not. In this section, we deal with the first three aspects (Component *TimedAspects*) and postpone the last one to the next section. Let us notice that real-time cannot be explicitly modeled in Event-B, thus we approximate it by using discrete time: a natural variable *currentTime* represents the current time.

6.1   Timing Constraints on the Analogical Switch

To introduce timing constraints on the switch, we add a natural variable *deadline Switch* that represents the deadline at which the switch changes its state according to Figure 2. To move from a state to another, *currentTime* should be equal to *deadlineSwitch*, then the deadline is updated adequately. For instance, the event `HandleFromIntermediate2ToIntermediate1` is refined by adding the action $deadlineSwitch := currentTime + (8 - (2/3) \times (deadlineSwitch - currentTime))^3$. Similarly, the event `close_Switch` is refined by adding the guard $currentTime = deadlineSwitch$ and action $deadlineSwitchcurrentTime + 200$.

6.2   Timing Constraints on the Start/Stop Stimulation of Valves

In this system, the time between starting the stimulation of the general valve and the others should be separated by at least 2 *u.t* (units of time). Since the open valve is the first to stimulate just after the general valve, it is sufficient to respect this time between them. Similarly, the time between stopping the stimulation of the general valve and the others should be separated by at least 10 *u.t*. Since the open/close valve is the last valve that stops stimulation just before stopping the general valve, it is sufficient to respect this time only between them. In addition, the stimulation of contrary orders should be separated by at least 1 *u.t*. So, we have defined five natural variables *allowedStopGeneralEv*, *allowedStartOpenEV*, *allowedStartCloseOpenEV*, *allowedStartExtedEV* and *allowedStartRetractEV* that are updated as follows: when the general (resp. open, close, extend, retract) valve is stimulated, then the variables *allowedStartOpenEV* and *allowedCloseOpenEV* (resp. *allowedCloseOpenEV*, *allowedStartOpenEV*, *allowedStartRetractEV*, *allowedStartExtedEV*) are updated with the adequate value. In addition, when open (resp. close) valve is stopped then the variable *allowedStopGeneralEv* is also updated with the adequate value. So, the event

---

[3] Since, the type *Real* is not provided in Event-B, all computations are done in fixed-point arithmetic with a scale of 10.

$\mathtt{OutputGeneralValve}$ has been refined by adding the guard $(currentTime \geq allowedStopGeneralEv)$ and actions:

$$allowedStartOpenEv := \{\text{FALSE} \mapsto \text{TRUE} \mapsto currentTime + 2, \text{TRUE} \mapsto \text{FALSE} \mapsto 0\}$$
$$(general\_EV \mapsto general\_EV\_value)$$

6.3   Timing Constraints on the Activation of the Valves

A valve takes some time to be active/not active after starting/stopping its stimulation. So, we have associated with each kind of valves (general, door, gear) a natural variable that states the time at which the valve can be active/not active. For instance, we have defined for the extend/retract valves the variable $deadlineStimulationRetractExtendEv$ that is updated to the adequate time when the controller sends an order for these valves, and it is reset to 0 when the valve becomes active/not active. Basically, we have refined the event $\mathtt{OutputExtendGearValve}$ by adding the action:

$$deadlineStimulationRetractExtendEv := \{\text{FALSE} \mapsto \text{TRUE} \mapsto currentTime + 10$$
$$\text{TRUE} \mapsto \text{FALSE} \mapsto currentTime + 36\}(extend\_EV \mapsto extend\_EV\_value)$$

Finally, we have refined the events that make the extend/retract valve active/not active by adding the guard $(currentTime = deadlineStimulation RetractExtendEv)$ and action $(deadlineStimulationRetractExtendEv := 0)$ to reset the deadline after executing the event.

6.4   Timing Constraints on Cylinders

The gears/door cylinders take some time to lock/unlock but also to move from high to down and vice versa. To consider the time taken by a gear cylinder to lock/unlock, we have defined a variable $deadlineUnlockLockGearsCylinders$. This variable is set by events that make extend and retract valves active in order to launch the deadline for unlocking the cylinders, and the events $\mathtt{Make\_GearExended}$ and $\mathtt{Make\_GearRetracted}$ to launch the deadline for locking the cylinders. Similarly, we have defined a variable $deadlineGearsRetractingExtending$ to consider the time tacken by the gear to move from down to up and vice versa. So, the event $\mathtt{MakeExtendValveActive}$ is refined by adding the guard $(currentTime = deadlineStimulationRetractExtendEv)$ and the two following actions that permit to reset the deadline and to set the moment at which the gear cylinders become unlocked.

$$deadlineStimulationRetractExtendEv := 0$$
$$deadlineUnlockLockGearsCylinders := PositionsDG \times \{currentTime + 4\}$$

In addition, we refine the event $\mathtt{Start\_GearExtending}$ by adding the action:

$$deadlineGearsRetractingExtending(po) :=$$
$$\{front \mapsto currentTime + 12, left \mapsto currentTime + 16, right \mapsto 16\}(po)$$

and the guard $(deadlineUnlockLockGearsCylinders(po) = 0)$. Finally to make the time progress, we have defined the event $\mathtt{passingTime}$ that increases the variable $currentTime$ when there is at least one non-null deadline. The time progresses by an amount $step$ without exceeding any non-null deadline in order to avoid the starvation problem. More details can be found at:

http://www-public.it-sudparis.eu/~mammar_a/LandingGearsSystem.html

7 Introducing Failures: The Ninth Refinement

7.1 Modeling Failures

So far, we have considered all the physical elements as working correctly as expected. However in practice, each of them can fail: the switch, the cylinders and the valves can fail at any time. To take such failures into account, we have added for each of these elements an event that makes it fail (Component *Failures*). For example, for the switch and the door cylinders, we have defined the two following events where the variables *analogical_switch_fail* and *door_cylinder_fail* denote Boolean variables that say respectively whether the switch or a door cylinder has failed:

MakeSwitchFail
  WHEN *analogical_switch_fail* =FALSE
  analogical_switch_fail :=TRUE
END
	MakeDoorCylinderFail
	  ANY *po* **WHERE** *po* ∈ PositionsDG **THEN**
	  door_cylinder_fail(po) :=TRUE
	END

Consequently, we refine each event related to the behavior of the switch, the valves and the cylinders by adding a guard stating that the element change its status only if it has not failed. For instance, we have added the guard (*door_cylinder_fail(po)* :=FALSE) for the events Make_DoorOpen, Start_Door-Opening, Start_DoorClosing, etc.

7.2 Detecting Anomalies

As stated in the previous section, physical elements can fail. The controller does not have any information about that but it can deduce it by monitoring the status of the switch, the doors, and the gears. In fact, if the controller sends an order to stimulate the open valve but the doors are not seen open after a given time, then it can assert that a problem has happened (in at least one physical element) by displaying the *anomaly* information to the pilot. To this aim, the controller has to read, through the sensors, the status of these elements at well-defined times. For instance, the controller has to verify that the switch is closed 10 *u.t* after the handler has changed its position otherwise an anomaly is detected. To model that, we add a natural variable *nextInputReadForOpenSwitch* that memorizes the time at which the controller must not see the switch open. This variable is updated by the event ReadInput which we refine by adding the following action:

nextInputReadForOpenSwitch :=
    {FALSE ↦ *nextInputReadForOpenSwitch*, TRUE ↦ *currentTime+10*}
                (**bool**(*handler_ind* ≠ *handler_sensor_value*))

As for other deadlines, to avoid the starvation problem, we refine the event passingTime by adding a guard stating that if *nextInputReadForOpenSwitch* is not null then the time can progress but without exceeding it. In addition, the event ReadInput resets the variable *nextInputReadForOpenSwitch* when this deadline is reached and the verification performed. So, we add the following actions to the event ReadInput:

$$\begin{array}{l} nextInputReadForOpenSwitch := \\ \quad \{FALSE \mapsto nextInputReadForOpenSwitch, \text{ TRUE} \mapsto 0\} \\ \qquad\qquad\qquad\qquad (\mathbf{bool}(currentTime = nextInputReadForOpenSwitch)) \\ anomaly := \mathbf{bool}(currentTime = nextInputReadForOpenSwitch \land analogical\_switch\_ind = open) \end{array}$$

The other anomalies on the doors, the gears, the hydraulic circuit are dealt with similarly. In addition, we have refined the event ReadInput and the events sending orders to the valves by adding the guard ($anomaly = FALSE$) in order to stop the system. Indeed according to the description of the system, the anomaly message has to be maintained forever. From a modeling point of view, we introduce a deadlock such that no operation becomes possible.

8   Properties Verification: The Tenth Refinement

Most properties to verify are temporal properties that refer to several moments of the system. A model checker like ProB [7] would be very useful for such purpose. Nevertheless, we have chosen to stay in a same framework of proof by modeling them as invariants (Component *PropertyVerification*). Moreover to distinguish the specification of the system from the verification of properties, we have created a new refinement level that defines such properties as invariants. For the sake of space, this paper illustrates the verification of the properties through one example, the verification of the other properties can be found at:

http://www-public.it-sudparis.eu/~mammar_a/LandingGearsSystem.html

R_{74}. *If one of the three gears is not seen locked in the down position more than 10 seconds after stimulating the outgoing electro-valve, then the Boolean output normal mode is set to false.*

To specify this property, we have defined a new variable *TimeStimulationExtendRetractEv* to memorize the time at which the extend/retract valve is stimulated. This variable is set by the event OutputExtendGearValve by adding the action ($TimeStimulationExtendRetractEv := currentTime$). Then, the property is specified as follows:

$$\begin{array}{c} (currentTime > TimeStimulationExtendRetractEv + 100 \land extend\_EV = TRUE) \Rightarrow \\ (anomaly = TRUE \lor gear\_extended\_ind = PositionsDG \times \{\text{TRUE}\}) \end{array}$$

To discharge this invariant, the following intermediate lemmas have been added:

$$\begin{array}{c} (currentTime > TimeStimulationExtendRetractEv + 100 \land extend\_EV = \text{TRUE}) \Rightarrow \\ nextInputReadForGearEndExtendingRetracting = 0 \\[4pt] (nextInputReadForGearEndExtendingRetracting = 0 \land extend\_EV = TRUE) \Rightarrow \\ (anomaly = \text{TRUE} \lor gear\_extended\_ind = PositionsDG \times \{\text{TRUE}\}) \end{array}$$

The first invariant ensures that the time does not progress beyond the deadline ($TimeStimulationExtendRetractEv + 100$) without reading the state of the gears since the variable *nextInputReadForGearEndExtendingRetracting* is reset when the gears are read. The second one states that the controller sets the variables *anomaly* and *gear_extended_ind* correctly when the deadline is reached. Table 1 gives the results of the verification activities.

Table 1. Verification results

Requirement	Verified?	Method	Comment
R_{11}	✓	Animation	Proof seems to be too hard since it needs several intermediate lemmas.
R_{12}	✓	Animation	Proof seems to be too hard since it needs several intermediate lemmas.
R_{21}	✓	Proof	It is verified from the instant where the controller sees the position of the handler down
R_{22}	✓	Proof	It is verified from the instant where the controller sees the position of the handler up
R_{31}	✓	Proof	It is not valid on the physical elements since the controller can start extending/retracting the gears when the doors are actually open but the close valve does not stop completely. Thus, we express it according to the internal variables.
R_{32}	✓	Proof	It is not valid on the physical elements since the controller can start opening/closing the doors when the gears are actually extended/ retracted but the extend/retract valve does not stop completely. Thus, we express it according to the internal variables.
R_{41}, R_{42}, R_{51}	✓	Proof	
$R_{61}, R_{62}, R_{63}, R_{64}$	✓	Proof	
$R_{71}, R_{72}, R_{73}, R_{74}$	✓	Proof	

9 Conclusion: Limits and Future Work

In this paper, we have presented a modeling of a landing gear system in the formal language Event-B. To this aim, we have proceeded into 3 main phases: (1) modeling the system without timed concerns and possible failures; (2) taking timed concerns into account; (3) considering the possible faults on the different elements of the system. From a design point of view, the main difficulty was to define a method to tackle the complexity of the case study. The combination of the four-variable model of Parnas and of the Event-B refinement process has proved very relevant for this type of problem. The former allows to classify the variables that represent the system and its environment and the latter allows to gradually introduced these variables. This approach has been used by Butler [4] but with a very simple case study. Contrary to Butler's work, we have chosen to consider time constraints later in the design, since it seemed to us simpler for the proof activity. Finally, failures have been introduced at the end of the process following the idea of considering first the nominal system behavior as advised by [6,9]. From a technical point of view, we have defined 66 variables and 48 events split into 10 refinement levels that give rise to 285 proof obligations, 72% of which have been discharged automatically; we have accomplished the remaining proofs interactively thanks to the Atelier B, SMT and ML provers which are Rodin plugins. We think the modeling can be improved if Event-B and the Rodin framework, under which this development has been achieved, offer real-time aspects. In addition, it would be interesting to deeper study the use of one of the structuring mechanisms proposed for Event-B: decomposition [10] or modularization [5], in order to structure the specification into logical units.

As stated before, regarding the description of the case study, we make the assumption that each sensor is unique and not triplicated. This is not a strong assumption and does not affect the modeling; it can be easily relaxed by only adapting the event ReadInput. For the handler for instance, we will define two functions $handler\_sensors$ and $handler\_sensors\_valid$ to memorize the values of the sensors and its validity:

$$\boxed{handler\_sensors \in 1..3 \longrightarrow \text{BOOL} \wedge handler\_sensors\_valid \in 1..3 \longrightarrow \text{BOOL}}$$

Then, the event ReadInput is updated as follows (value TRUE (resp. FALSE) represents position up (resp. down)):

$$
\begin{array}{l}
\textbf{ANY}\ handler\_ind\_value, handler\_sensor\_valid\_value\ \textbf{WHERE} \\
\quad handler\_ind\_value = \\
\quad\quad ((card(handler\_sensor\_valid^{-1}[\{\text{TRUE}\}])=3\ \wedge \\
\quad\quad\quad ((handler\_sensor(1)=\text{TRUE}\ \wedge\ (handler\_sensor(2)=\text{TRUE}\ \vee\ handler\_sensor(3)=\text{TRUE}))\ \vee \\
\quad\quad\quad\quad \vee\ (handler\_sensor(2)=\text{TRUE}\ \wedge\ handler\_sensor(3)=\text{TRUE}))) \\
\quad\quad \vee\quad (card(handler\_sensor\_valid^{-1}[\{\text{TRUE}\}])=2\ \wedge \\
\quad\quad\quad\quad\quad\quad card(handler\_sensor[handler\_sensor\_valid^{-1}[\{\text{TRUE}\}]])=1))) \\
\quad handler\_sensor\_valid\_value=\dots\ \textbf{THEN} \\
\quad\quad handler\_ind:=\{\text{TRUE} \mapsto \text{up}, \text{FALSE} \mapsto \text{down}\}(handler\_ind\_value) \\
\quad\quad handler\_sensor\_valid := handler\_sensor\_valid\_value \\
\quad\quad \dots
\end{array}
$$

References

1. Abrial, J.-R.: The B-book, Assigning Programs to Meanings, pp. I–XXXIV, 1–779. Cambridge University Press (2005)
2. Abrial, J.-R.: Modeling in Event-B - System and Software Engineering, pp. I–XXVI, 1–586. Cambridge University Press (2010)
3. Boniol, F., Wiels, V.: The Landing Gear System Case Study. In: Boniol, F. (ed.) ABZ 2014 Case Study Track. CCIS, vol. 433, pp. 1–18. Springer, Heidelberg (2014)
4. Butler, M.: Using Event-B Refinement to Verify a Control Strategy, Working Paper. ECS, University of Southampton (2009)
5. Iliasov, A., Troubitsyna, E., Laibinis, L., Romanovsky, A., Varpaaniemi, K., Ilic, D., Latvala, T.: Supporting reuse in event B development: Modularisation approach. In: Frappier, M., Glässer, U., Khurshid, S., Laleau, R., Reeves, S. (eds.) ABZ 2010. LNCS, vol. 5977, pp. 174–188. Springer, Heidelberg (2010)
6. Jeffords, R.-D., Heitmeyer, C.-L., Archer, M., Leonard, E.-I.: Model-Based Construction and Verification of Critical Systems using Composition and Partial Refinement. Formal Methods in System Design 37(2-3), 265–294 (2010)
7. Leuschel, M., Butler, M.-J.: ProB: An Automated Analysis Toolset for the B Method. STTT 10(2), 185–203 (2008)
8. Lorge Parnas, D., Madey, J.: Functional Documents for Computer Systems. Sci. Comput. Program. 25(1), 41–61 (1995)
9. Miller, S.-P., Tribble, A.-C.: Extending the Four-Variable Model to Bridge the System-Software Gap. In: Proceedings of the 20th Digital Avionics Systems Conferene (DASC 2001), Daytona Beach, Florida (2001)
10. Silva, R., Pascal, C., Hoang, T.-S., Butler, M.: Decomposition tool for Event-B. Softw., Pract. Exper. 41(2), 199–208 (2011)

Offline Model-Based Testing and Runtime Monitoring of the Sensor Voting Module

Paolo Arcaini[1], Angelo Gargantini[1], and Elvinia Riccobene[2]

[1] Dipartimento di Ingegneria, Università degli Studi di Bergamo, Italy
{paolo.arcaini,angelo.gargantini}@unibg.it
[2] Dipartimento di Informatica, Università degli Studi di Milano, Italy
elvinia.riccobene@unimi.it

Abstract. Formal specifications are widely used in the development of safety critical systems, as the Sensor Voting Module of the Landing Gear System. However, the conformance relationship between the formal specification and the concrete implementation must be checked. In this paper, we show a technique to formally link a Java class with its Abstract State Machine formal specification, and two approaches for checking their conformance: an offline model-based testing approach and an online runtime monitoring approach.

1 Introduction

For safety critical components, formal verification and validation of models must be combined with the validation of the implementation. The user wants to gain confidence that the system has been implemented as specified, i.e., it *conforms* to its requirements. Indeed, regardless the correctness of the model (guaranteed by formal verification, simulation and so on), the implemented system must be validated itself. As aptly stated by Ed Brinksma in his 2009 keynote at the Dutch Testing Day and Testcom/FATES, "Who would want to fly in an airplane with software proved correct, but not tested?".

We here focus on the model-driven design and validation of the sensor voting module (SVM) in a landing gear system [7]. A sensor voting system, similar to that presented in our case study, is verified in [16] using the UML Verification Environment. In this paper, we describe the validation activity of a Java implementation of the SVM, using the Abstract State Machines (ASMs) as formal language. For a complete description of the modeling of the whole landing gear system case study using ASMs through the ASMETA framework, we refer to [5].

In this paper, we first introduce the SVM case study, and give a brief introduction to two conformance validation techniques, model-based testing and runtime monitoring, reporting some related literature (Section 2). Then, we show the ASM model for the SVM and which activities the designer should perform, even before the conformance checking is started, to be sure that the model is correct (Section 3.1). We then implement the SVM in Java (Section 3.2) and we validate it against the ASM model. We describe how the formal specification

F. Boniol et al. (Eds.): ABZ 2014 Case Study Track, CCIS 433, pp. 95–109, 2014.

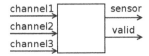

Fig. 1. Sensor Voting Module Interface

can be linked with the implementation (Section 3.3), and then we present the application of model-based testing (Section 4) and of runtime monitoring (Section 5) to the case study. Finally, we compare the strengths and the weaknesses of the two approaches through some experiments (Section 6), and conclude the paper in Section 7.

2 Background

2.1 The Sensor Voting Module

The Landing Gear System (LGS) has proposed in the ABZ conference as a real-life case study [7] with the aim of showing how different formal methods can be used for the specification, design and development of a complex system.

In the LGS the state of the equipments (i.e., doors and gears) is computed by a set of discrete sensors; the digital part of the landing gear system takes decisions and sends commands (e.g., stimulating the electro-valves) relying on the sensor values. In order to prevent sensor failures, each sensor value is based on the values of three *micro-sensors* [7]; a sensor receives the values of the three micro-sensors from three channels. The duty of the Sensor Voting Module (SVM) is to select one of these three values according to the following policy.

Let X be a sensor and $X_i(t)$ ($i = 1, 2, 3$) the values for X received at time t:
- If at t the three channels are considered as valid and are equal, then the value considered by the control software is this common value.
- If at t one channel is different from the two others for the first time (i.e., the three channels were considered as valid up to t), then this channel is considered as invalid and is definitely eliminated. Only the two remaining channels are considered in the future. At time t, the value considered by the control software is the common value of the two remaining channels.
- If a channel has been previously eliminated, and if at t the two remaining channels are not equal, then the sensor is definitely considered as invalid.

We can represent an SVM by the black box reported in Fig. 1. It has three inputs corresponding to the three channels for the sensor and two outputs: one that represents the value of the sensor and one that informs whether the sensor is valid or invalid.

2.2 Model-Based Off-line Testing

Model-based conformance testing [13,17] of reactive systems consists in taking benefit from the model for mechanizing both test data generation and verdicts computation (i.e., to solve the oracle problem). In off-line approaches, test suites are pre-computed from the model and stored under a format that can be later executed on the System Under Test (SUT). The model can be used both to guide the test generation, in order to discover which aspects of the model must be covered, and to decide when to stop testing, when coverage of the model has reached a certain level.

A classical technique to generate tests from models exploits the use of model checkers. In this case, the model of the system is translated to the language of the model checker, and a suitable property (also called *trap property*) is proved false by the model checker by means of a counterexample. This counterexample represents a possible system behavior and it can be translated to a test through a concretization process.

MBT for ASM. For ASMs, we have developed a tool, called ATGT [11], which is capable of generating tests from ASMs following several testing criteria [10], like rule coverage, update rule coverage, parallel rule coverage, etc.

For example, a test suite satisfies the *rule coverage* criterion if, for every rule r_i, there exists at least one state in a test sequence in which r_i fires and there exists at least one state in a test sequence (possibly different from the previous one) in which r_i does not fire.

2.3   Runtime Monitoring

According to [14], *runtime monitoring* (also *runtime verification*) is "the discipline of computer science that deals with the study, development, and application of those monitoring techniques that allow checking whether a run of a system under scrutiny satisfies or violates a given correctness property".

The aim of runtime monitoring is to check that the observed executions of a system ensure some correctness properties. Runtime monitoring is a *lightweight* verification technique that, considering the ability to detects faults, can be classified halfway between those techniques that try to ensure universal correctness of systems – as model checking and theorem proving – and those techniques like testing that ensure the correctness only for a fixed set of executions.

The main difference with techniques like model checking is that, whereas these techniques check all possible executions of a program, runtime monitoring only checks those executions that are actually performed by the program under scrutiny. So, it is possible that, although the program contains a fault, its executions never produce a failure that evidences that fault.

The main difference with testing, instead, is that the number of executions over which the program is checked is not fixed. Sometimes, runtime monitoring is seen as the process of testing the system *forever* [14], since, as in testing, the actual output is checked with respect to an expected output (usually described by an *oracle*), but, unlike testing, every execution of the system is checked.

Finally, whereas traditional validation and verification activities are only executed *offline*, i.e., before the deployment, runtime monitoring can also be executed *online*, i.e, after the deployment of the program.

In order to describe the expected correctness properties, several formalisms have been used in literature as, for example, temporal logics [12,6], extended regular expressions [8], and Z specifications [15].

Coma: Conformance Monitoring between ASMs and Java. In [3] we propose *CoMA*, runtime *Conformance Monitoring* of Java code *by ASM specifications*. The CoMA monitor allows *online* monitoring, namely it considers executions in an incremental fashion. It takes as input an executing Java software system and an ASM formal model. The monitor observes the behavior of the Java system and determines its correctness w.r.t. the ASM specification working as an oracle of the expected behavior. While the software system is executing, the monitor checks conformance between the observed state and the expected state.

2.4   Comparing Offline Testing and Runtime Monitoring

Offline testing is much simpler than runtime monitoring: once the tests are generated, they can be easily reused as long as the model does not change. The test generation time may be an issue, especially if the model is large and the model checker takes a lot of resources for test generation; however, efficient test generator tools can generate tests also for big models. Once the tests are obtained, they can be launched and, if the SUT passes all the tests, the tester can be confident that the implementation is correct and therefore the system can be deployed.

However, the system could strongly depend on the environment in which it is executed [9]. If such environment is not available at testing time or, although available, it is not practically possible to interact with it (because maybe too much time consuming), testing the system could become difficult. In unit testing this problem is sometimes mitigated by using *mock objects* that mimic the behavior of the environment: nonetheless, if the actions of the environment are not fully predictable, also using mock objects could be not useful. Moreover, safety-critical systems as medical devices, aircraft flight controls, nuclear systems, etc., although tested and verified deeply, could require an additional degree of confidence that they behave as expected. Runtime monitoring here acts as a double check that everything goes well [14].

Furthermore, in the presence of nondeterministic systems, an MBT approach, as that described in Section 4, is not suitable because it is not able to correctly judge the implementation output: the implementation could deviate from a test case, taking a different but valid execution path, and the test case would *falsely* fail. For such kind of systems, a runtime monitoring approach able to deal with nondeterminism, as that described in Section 5, can also benefit the testing [4].

3   Specification and Implementation of the SVM

The following sections describe the ASM model (Section 3.1) and the Java implementation (Section 3.2) for the SVM. The ASM and the Java implementation have been developed independently: once we have agreed upon the interface, one author has developed the ASM and another one the Java code. In this way, the two artifacts may be quite different. Finally, Section 3.3 describes how to link the Java code with the ASM; such linking will be exploited in Section 4 and Section 5 for the testing and the runtime monitoring of the implementation.

3.1   ASM Model of the SVM

Code 1 reports the ASM model. The signature of the ASM contains the enumerative domain Channel representing the three input channels of the sensor; one unary monitored function channel represents the signals coming from the three channels. The controlled unary function validCh keeps track if each channel is still valid; in the initial state all the channels are valid. The output value of the sensor is computed by the machine and recorded with the function sensor, while its validity is simply defined as a derived function valid, which is true if there exist two different channels still valid.

In the main rule, if the sensor is not valid, the machine state is no longer updated. Otherwise, if the sensor is valid, the following rules are called:

- r_allValidChannels checks if all the channels are still valid and, in this case, it controls if the values of the three channels are equal. Since the comparison is performed by considering each pair of channels, r_allValidChannels calls r_threeValidChannels three times, in order to actually compare each pair ($vc1 and $vc2); if they are equal, it also checks the third channel ($vc3) and, if necessary, it updates its validity. The sensor value is updated to the majority value of the three channels.
- r_twoValidChannels checks if two channels are still valid, in case the third channel ($nvc) is no longer valid; the rule is called three times, one for each pair of channels. The sensor value is updated only if the two valid channels are equal.

Note that the specification can be easily extended in case there are more than three channels.

Model Validation. We have performed the following preliminary activities over the ASM model using the framework ASMETA[1], in order to be sure that the model exactly captures the intended behavior of the system. In fact, in model-based testing and in runtime monitoring, it is of extreme importance that the models are correct, otherwise faults in the model jeopardize the entire activity of the implementation validation.

Simulation. Through simulation with the ASM simulator AsmetaS, we have simulated the scenarios of a channel becoming invalid and then the entire sensor becoming invalid. Simulation is useful to gain confidence that the specification actually captures the intended behavior. The simulator, at each step, checks

---

[1] http://asmeta.sourceforge.net/

```
asm SensorVotingModule

signature:
    enum domain Channel = {ONE | TWO | THREE}
    dynamic monitored channel: Channel −> Boolean
    dynamic controlled validCh: Channel −> Boolean
    dynamic controlled sensor: Boolean
    derived valid: Boolean

definitions:
    function valid =
        (exist $c1 in Channel, $c2 in Channel with $c1!=$c2 and validCh($c1) and validCh($c2))

        rule r_threeValidChannels($vc1 in Channel, $vc2 in Channel, $vc3 in Channel) =
            if channel($vc1) = channel($vc2) then
                par
                    sensor := channel($vc1)
                    if channel($vc1) != channel($vc3) then
                        validCh($vc3) := false
                    endif
                endpar
            endif

        rule r_allValidChannels =
            if (forall $c in Channel with validCh($c)) then
                par
                    r_threeValidChannels[ONE,TWO,THREE]
                    r_threeValidChannels[TWO,THREE,ONE]
                    r_threeValidChannels[THREE,ONE,TWO]
                endpar
            endif

        rule r_twoValidChannels($nvc in Channel, $vc1 in Channel, $vc2 in Channel) =
            if not(validCh($nvc)) then
                if channel($vc1) = channel($vc2) then
                    sensor := channel($vc1)
                else
                    par
                        validCh($vc1) := false
                        validCh($vc2) := false
                    endpar
                endif
            endif

        invariant over validCh: size({$c in Channel | validCh($c) : $c}) != 1

        main rule r_Main =
            if valid then
                par
                    r_allValidChannels[]
                    r_twoValidChannels[ONE,TWO,THREE]
                    r_twoValidChannels[TWO,THREE,ONE]
                    r_twoValidChannels[THREE,ONE,TWO]
                endpar
            endif

default init s0:
    function validCh($c in Channel) = true
```

Code 1. ASM specification of the SVM

that all the specified invariants are satisfied. In the model (before the main rule), we have introduced an invariant specifying that it is not possible that only one single channel is valid. The requirements indeed specify that at least two

```
rule r_twoValidChannels($vc1 in Channel, $vc2 in Channel, $vc3 in Channel) =
    if not(validCh($vc1)) then
        if channel($vc2) = channel($vc3) then
            sensor := channel($vc2)
        else
            par
                validCh($vc1) := false //error
                validCh($vc2) := false
            endpar
        endif
    endif
```

Code 2. Faulty model – Error in the rule r_twoValidChannels

channels must be valid, otherwise the entire sensor must be considered invalid (i.e., all the channels must be considered invalid).

Model Advisor. During the development of the model, we have applied the model advisor [2], a tool we developed for looking for common errors that are usually introduced in the model development using ASMs. The model advisor has discovered an error in the model. Code 2 shows the faulty implementation of rule r_twoValidChannels. The model advisor signals that, when the update validCh($vc1) := false is executed, the location validCh($vc1) is always yet *false*. Indeed, the model is faulty and the location that should be updated to *false* is validCh($vc3). We have fixed the error, and we have given more meaningful names to the rule parameters, as shown in Code 1.

Formal Property Verification. We have been able to formally prove some properties by using the model checker AsmetaSMV [1]. The first property simply checks that the specified invariant is satisfied in all the states. Indeed, by default AsmetaSMV translates each invariant φ in the Computation Tree Logic (CTL) formula $\mathbf{ag}(\varphi)$.
The following temporal properties have also been proved:
- Once the sensor becomes invalid, then it will always remain invalid in the future:
  CTLSPEC ag(not(valid) implies ag(not(valid)))
- There exists a path in which the sensor eventually becomes invalid:
  CTLSPEC ef(not(valid))
- There exists a path in which the sensor always remains valid:
  CTLSPEC eg(valid)

3.2 Java Implementation

Code 3 shows the Java implementation of the SVM. The method computeSensorValue, given the values of the three parameters s1, s2, and s3 (representing the input channels), updates the value of the sensor and marks if the sensor is no more valid (field sensorValid). The boolean array chValid records which channels are still valid. Two methods return the values of fields value and sensorValid.

```
@Asm(asmFile = "models/SensorVotingModule.asm")
public class Sensor {
    private boolean value;
    private boolean sensorValid;
    private boolean[] chValid;

    @StartMonitoring
    public Sensor() {
        sensorValid = true;
        chValid = new boolean[]{true, true, true};
    }

    @RunStep
    public void computeSensorValue(@Param(func = "channel", args={"ONE"}) boolean s1,
                                   @Param(func = "channel", args={"TWO"}) boolean s2,
                                   @Param(func = "channel", args={"THREE"}) boolean s3) {
        if (sensorValid) {
            if (chValid[0] && chValid[1] && chValid[2]) {
                if (s1 == s2 && s2 == s3) {
                    value = s1;
                } else if (s1 != s2 && s2 == s3) {
                    chValid[0] = false; // first channel invalid
                    value = s2;
                } else if (s2 != s1 && s1 == s3) {
                    chValid[1] = false; // second channel invalid
                    value = s3;
                } else {
                    chValid[2] = false; // third channel invalid
                    value = s1;
                }
            } else if (!chValid[0]) {
                if (s2 == s3)
                    value = s2;
                else
                    sensorValid = false;
            } else if (!chValid[1]) {
                if (s1 == s3)
                    value = s1;
                else
                    sensorValid = false;
            } else if (!chValid[2]) {
                if (s1 == s2)
                    value = s2;
                else
                    sensorValid = false;
            }
        }
    }

    @MethodToFunction(func = "sensor")
    public boolean getValue() {
        return value;
    }

    @MethodToFunction(func = "valid")
    public boolean isValid() {
        return sensorValid;
    }
}
```

Code 3. Java implementation of the SVM

3.3   Linking Java Code and ASM Specifications

Linking a Java code with its ASM formal specification permits to establish a conformance relation between the ASM and the implementation. In the following, we provide an informal description; a complete description of the technique with all the formal definitions can be found in [3].

We use *Java annotations* to establish this link; Java annotations are metadata tags that can be used to add some information to code elements as class declarations, field declarations, etc. In addition to the standard ones, annotations can be defined by the user similarly as classes. For our purposes, we have defined a set of annotations [3]. The retention policy (i.e., the way to signal how and when the annotation can be accessed) of all our annotations is *runtime*: annotations can be read by the compiler and by any program through reflection. In the tools developed for supporting our model-based testing and runtime monitoring approaches, we read the annotations in order to discover the relation between the ASM and the Java code.

In order to link a Java class with its corresponding ASM specification, first the class must be annotated with the annotation @Asm, having the path of the ASM model as string attribute (asmFile). The Java class Sensor (Code 3) is linked to the ASM specification SensorVotingModule (Code 1).

Then the class data must be connected with the signature of the ASM. A field of the Java class can be connected with a function/location of the ASM, through the field annotation @FieldToFunction; the annotation has a mandatory attribute func for specifying the function name, and an optional attribute args, for specifying the arguments' values (if one wants to connect the field to a specific location). Moreover, it is also possible to link a pure method[2] with a function/location, using the method annotation @MethodToFunction, having the same attributes of @FieldToFunction. In the presented case study, pure methods getValue and isValid are respectively linked to functions sensor and valid.

Linked fields (those annotated with @FieldToFunction) and linked methods (those annotated with @MethodToFunction) constitute the *observed Java state*. In the case study, the observed Java state is given by the methods getValue and isValid.

Finally, the execution of the Java code must be linked with an execution (i.e., a run) of the ASM. The annotation @StartMonitoring is used to select one constructor[3] which builds the desired observed initial state of the object. The annotation @RunStep, instead, permits to identify the method (called *changing* method) that changes the observed state, i.e., the values of the linked fields and the return values of the linked pure methods[4]. Both linked constructors and linked methods can have some parameters, that can be linked to the ASM as well. The annotation @Param can be used to link parameters to monitored functions/locations of the ASM; it has a mandatory attribute func to specify the name of a monitored function of the ASM model, and an optional attribute args to specify the function arguments. In the case study, the parameters of method computeSensorValue are linked to the locations of function channel.

---

[2] Pure methods are side effect free methods with respect to the object/program state. They return a value but do not assign values to fields.

[3] We do not consider the default constructor. If the class does not have any constructor, the user has to specify an empty constructor and annotate it with @StartMonitoring.

[4] The user can identify several changing methods, but, in this case, each changing method must be linked with a different monitored value by the two annotation attributes setFunction, specifying the name of a 0-ary monitored function of the ASM model, and toValue, specifying a value of the function codomain. setFunction should have the same value in all the annotations, while toValue must assume different values.

State and Step Conformance. The linking previously described allows the following notion of conformance between an instance O_C of a class C and the ASM specification ASM_C linked to C.

Definition 1. *State conformance.* *We say that* a state s_J *of* O_C *conforms to a state* s_A *of* ASM_C*, i.e.,* $conf(s_J, s_A)$*, if all the observed elements of* C *(fields annotated with* @FieldToFunction *and methods annotated with* @Method-ToFunction*) have values in* O_C *conforming to the values of the functions in* ASM_C *linked to them.*

Intuitively, the Java state and the ASM state are conformant, if the values of the linked fields and the values returned by linked methods are equal to the values of the corresponding functions/locations.

Definition 2. *Step conformance.* *Given the execution of a* changing *method* m *(i.e., a method annotated with* @RunStep*) and a step of simulation of the ASM, we say that the Java step* (s_J, s'_J) *and the ASM step* (s_A, s'_A) *are conformant if* $conf(s_J, s_A)$ *and* $conf(s'_J, s'_A)$*.*

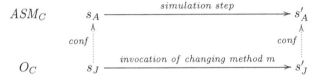

Intuitively, a Java object is step conformant with the corresponding ASM specification, if their states are conformant before and after the changing method execution and the ASM simulation step.

4 Offline Testing

4.1 Test Generation

We have used ATGT to generate tests from the SVM model, using the basic rule coverage (BRC) and the update rule coverage (URC). BRC requires that every rule is executed at least once, while URC requires that every update is executed at least once without being trivial, i.e., by actually changing the value of the location that it updates. For every coverage goal (e.g., a rule to execute in BRC), ATGT computes a *test predicate* which is a predicate over the state of the machine, representing the condition that must be reached to cover that particular goal. For instance, the basic rule coverage of the update rule in the inner conditional rule of rule r_threeValidChannels is specified by the following test predicate.

BR_r_threeValidChannels_TTT21:
valid and (validCh(ONE) and validCh(TWO) and validCh(THREE)) and
(channel(ONE) = channel(TWO)) and (channel(ONE) != channel(THREE))

ATGT has derived, for the entire specification, 38 test predicates (20 for the BRC and 18 for the URC). For every test predicate tp, ATGT has built, if possible, an abstract test sequence, which is a valid sequence of states, leading to a state where tp becomes true. ATGT exploits the SPIN model checker and its capability to produce counterexamples upon property violations. If a test predicate cannot be covered, we say that it is *unfeasible* and it means that there is no valid system behavior that can cover that case. Unfeasible test predicates must be discarded and no longer considered. For the SVM, we found no unfeasible test predicates.

In order to reduce the test suite size, ATGT can perform a coverage evaluation of the tests, by checking if a test sequence, generated for a test predicate, unintentionally covers also other test predicates. Without coverage evaluation, ATGT produces 38 test sequences, while, with coverage evaluation, ATGT produces only 11 test sequences.

4.2   Test Concretization

We devise a novel technique that derives a concrete Java test, consisting of a sequence of method calls with suitable checks (i.e., asserts), from each abstract test sequence ATS; in this work, we automatically build JUnit tests. The test concretization leverages the linking between the Java class and the ASM (see Section 3.3) and the definitions of state conformance (Def. 1) and step conformance (Def. 2).

First, it identifies the constructor annotated with @StartMonitoring, builds an instance of the class, and associates it to the reference variable sut. For example, given a class C whose constructor without parameters is annotated with @StartMonitoring, the produced statement is C sut = **new** C();

If the constructor has some parameters, these must be annotated with @Param. The technique identifies the actual parameters to use in the object instantiation by reading, in the first state of the abstract test sequence, the values of the monitored functions that are linked with the parameters.

The procedure that identifies the inputs in the ATS and maps them in method invocations with values for their parameters exploits the Java annotations @RunStep and @Param. For each state of the ATS, the method annotated with @RunStep is called[5]. The (possible) actual parameters in the method invocation are fixed by the values of the monitored functions/locations linked in the @Param annotations of the method formal parameters. For instance, the formal parameters s1, s2 and s3 of changing method computeSensorValue are connected to the monitored locations channel(ONE), channel(TWO), and channel(THREE).

After each method invocation and after the object instantiation, the oracle is built, exploiting the annotations @FieldToFunction and @MethodToFunction. For each state of the ATS:

---

[5] If there are several changing methods, the value v of the monitored function/location linked in the @RunStep annotations identifies what method must be called (the method having value v in the annotation argument toValue). In our case study, since only method computeSensorValue is annotated with @RunStep, it is always called.

```
---- state 0 -----
-- controlled --
valid = true
-- monitored --
channel(ONE) = false
channel(TWO) = false
channel(THREE) = true
---- state 1 -----
-- controlled --
sensor = false
valid = true
```

```
@Test
public void test() {
  // state 0
  Sensor sut = new Sensor();
  assertEquals(true, sut.isValid());
  sut.computeSensorValue(false, false, true);
  // state 1
  assertEquals(false, sut.getValue());
  assertEquals(true, sut.isValid());
}
```

(a) Abstract test sequence   (b) JUnit test case

Fig. 2. Example of test concretization for BR_r_threeValidChannels_TTT21

- given a function/location linked with an annotation, we obtain its value v from the ATS;
- if the annotation annotates a field f, we build an assertion as follows: assertEquals(v, sut.f);
- if the annotation annotates a pure method m, we build an assertion as follows:
  assertEquals(v, sut.m());

Fig. 2 shows the translation of the ATS built for covering the test predicate BR_r_threeValidChannels_TTT21 (Fig. 2a) in a JUnit test case (Fig. 2b).

5   Runtime Monitoring

Although a model-based testing approach as that described in Section 4 can give enough confidence that the implementation is correct, for safety-critical systems as the sensor voting module, we may want to continue checking the conformance of the implementation with respect to its specification also after the deployment.

We propose CoMA [3], a runtime monitoring approach for Java code using ASMs. The schema of the proposed runtime framework is shown in Fig. 3. The monitor is composed of: an *observer* that evaluates when the Java (observed) state is changed (1), and leads the abstract ASM to perform a machine step (2), and an *analyzer* that evaluates the step conformance between the Java execution and the ASM simulation (3). When the monitor detects a violation of conformance, it reports the error. It can also produce a trace in form of counterexample, which may be useful for debugging. Note that the use of CoMA can be twofold, since also faults in the specification can be discovered by monitoring the software. For instance, by analysing and re-executing counterexamples, faults in the model can be exposed.

The technique exploits the linking described in Section 3.3 and the definitions of state conformance (Def. 1) and step conformance (Def. 2). In the following, we give the definition of runtime conformance.

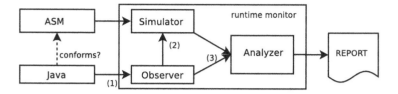

Fig. 3. The CoMA runtime monitor for Java

Definition 3. *Runtime conformance.* *We say that C is runtime conforming to its specification ASM_C if the following conditions hold:*
1) *the initial state s_J^0 of the computation of O_C conforms to one and only one initial state s_A^0 of the computation of ASM_C, i.e., $\exists! s_A^0$ initial state of ASM_C such that $conf(s_J^0, s_A^0)$;*
2) *for every Java step (s_J, s'_J) induced by the execution of a changing method m, $\exists! (s_A, s'_A)$ step of ASM_C with s_A the current state of ASM_C, such that the two steps are conformant.*

The runtime framework has been implemented using AspectJ. By means of an *aspect*, AspectJ allows to specify different *pointcuts*, i.e., points of the program execution one wants to capture. For each pointcut, it is possible to specify an *advice*, i.e., the actions that must be executed when a pointcut is reached (*before* or *after* the execution of the code specified by the pointcut). In our runtime framework, we have defined some pointcuts for identifying the instantiation of a class under monitoring (when a constructor annotated with @StartMonitoring is called) and the execution of a changing method (i.e., a method annotated with @RunStep). Moreover, for each pointcut we have defined an advice actually implementing the monitoring:
- when a monitored object is instantiated, the corresponding advice creates an instance of the ASM simulator AsmetaS;
- when a changing method is executed, the corresponding advice forces a step of simulation of the ASM, and it checks the conformance between the obtained Java state and the ASM states that can be reached in one step.

6 Experimental Comparison

We have executed the 38 Junit tests, obtained as explained in Section 4, and applied CoMA, as explained in Section 5. In CoMA, we have simulated the environment by instantiating 10 times a new sensor and computing 10 times the sensor value by the method `computeSensorValue`, passing three random values as inputs for the three channels. We have measured the code coverage by EclEmma and the mutation score by PIT[6]. In both cases, we found line and branch code coverage of 100%, and mutation score of 57 killed mutants over 74.

---

[6] `http://www.eclemma.org/` and `http://pitest.org/`

The not killed mutants involve code inserted by AspectJ and are not relevant for the case study. We can state that both techniques are equivalent regarding detecting faults inserted by the standard PIT mutation operators. However, we have simulated a delayed short circuit fault that causes isValid to return true after 5 times it is called. We have modified the code as follows:

```
int nvCount = 0;
boolean isValid() {
    return valid | nvCount++ > 5;
}
```

The tests produced from the specification do not detect this fault, since the rule coverage of the specification does not imply the coverage of this faulty behavior in the implementation. However, monitoring the code with CoMA exposes the failure by any run in which valid becomes false and isValid is called at least 5 times. In general, we can assume that unforeseen and unspecified anomalous behaviors of the implementation are better detected by runtime monitoring than by MBT.

7   Conclusions

We have presented the model-driven development and validation activity of a critical module in the Landing Gear System. We have applied the formal method of ASMs from the design to the conformance checking of the implementation. We have presented two methodologies for actual system validation (model-based testing and runtime monitoring) and briefly compared them.

References

1. Arcaini, P., Gargantini, A., Riccobene, E.: AsmetaSMV: A way to link high-level ASM models to low-level nuSMV specifications. In: Frappier, M., Glässer, U., Khurshid, S., Laleau, R., Reeves, S. (eds.) ABZ 2010. LNCS, vol. 5977, pp. 61–74. Springer, Heidelberg (2010)
2. Arcaini, P., Gargantini, A., Riccobene, E.: Automatic Review of Abstract State Machines by Meta Property Verification. In: Muñoz, C. (ed.) Proceedings of the Second NASA Formal Methods Symposium (NFM 2010), pp. 4–13. NASA (2010)
3. Arcaini, P., Gargantini, A., Riccobene, E.: CoMA: Conformance monitoring of Java programs by Abstract State Machines. In: Khurshid, S., Sen, K. (eds.) RV 2011. LNCS, vol. 7186, pp. 223–238. Springer, Heidelberg (2012)
4. Arcaini, P., Gargantini, A., Riccobene, E.: Combining model-based testing and runtime monitoring for program testing in the presence of nondeterminism. In: IEEE Sixth International Conference on Software Testing, Verification and Validation Workshops (ICSTW), pp. 178–187 (2013)
5. Arcaini, P., Gargantini, A., Riccobene, E.: Modeling and analyzing using ASMs: The Landing Gear System case study. In: Boniol, F. (ed.) ABZ 2014 Case Study Track. CCIS, vol. 433, pp. 36–51. Springer, Heidelberg (2014)
6. Bauer, A., Leucker, M., Schallhart, C.: Runtime verification for LTL and TLTL. ACM Transactions on Software and Methodology (TOSEM) 20 (2011)

7. Boniol, F., Wiels, V.: The Landing Gear System Case Study. In: Boniol, F. (ed.) ABZ 2014 Case Study Track. CCIS, vol. 433, pp. 1–18. Springer, Heidelberg (2014)
8. Chen, F., D'Amorim, M., Roşu, G.: A formal monitoring-based framework for software development and analysis. In: Davies, J., Schulte, W., Barnett, M. (eds.) ICFEM 2004. LNCS, vol. 3308, pp. 357–372. Springer, Heidelberg (2004)
9. Colin, S., Mariani, L.: Run-time verification. In: Broy, M., Jonsson, B., Katoen, J.-P., Leucker, M., Pretschner, A. (eds.) Model-Based Testing of Reactive Systems. LNCS, vol. 3472, pp. 525–555. Springer, Heidelberg (2005)
10. Gargantini, A., Riccobene, E.: ASM-Based Testing: Coverage Criteria and Automatic Test Sequence Generation. J. Universal Computer Science 7, 262–265 (2001)
11. Gargantini, A., Riccobene, E., Rinzivillo, S.: Using Spin to Generate Testsfrom ASM Specifications. In: Börger, E., Gargantini, A., Riccobene, E. (eds.) ASM 2003. LNCS, vol. 2589, pp. 263–277. Springer, Heidelberg (2003)
12. Havelund, K., Roşu, G.: Efficient monitoring of safety properties. International Journal on Software Tools for Technology Transfer 6, 158–173 (2004)
13. Hierons, R., Derrick, J.: Editorial: special issue on specification-based testing. Software Testing, Verification and Reliability 10(4), 201–202 (2000)
14. Leucker, M., Schallhart, C.: A brief account of runtime verification. Journal of Logic and Algebraic Programming 78(5), 293–303 (2009)
15. Liang, H., Dong, J., Sun, J., Wong, W.E.: Software monitoring through formal specification animation. Innovations in Systems and Software Engineering 5, 231–241 (2009)
16. Mrugalla, C., Robbe, O., Schinz, I., Toben, T., Westphal, B.: Formal verification of a sensor voting and monitoring UML model. In: Houmb, S.H., Jürjens, J., France, R. (eds.) Proceedings of the 4th International Workshop on Critical Systems Development Using Modeling Languages (CSDUML 2005), Technische Universität München (September 2005)
17. Utting, M., Legeard, B.: Practical Model-Based Testing: A Tools Approach. Morgan Kaufmann (2006)

Model-Checking Real-Time Properties
of an Aircraft Landing Gear System Using Fiacre*

Bernard Berthomieu[1,2], Silvano Dal Zilio[1,2], and Łukasz Fronc[1,2]

[1] CNRS, LAAS, 7 avenue du colonel Roche, F-31400 Toulouse, France
[2] Univ de Toulouse, LAAS, F-31400 Toulouse, France

Abstract. We describe our experience with modeling the landing gear system of an aircraft using the formal specification language Fiacre. Our model takes into account the behavior and timing properties of both the physical parts and the control software of this system. We use this formal model to check safety and real-time properties on the system but also to find a safe bound on the maximal time needed for all gears to be down and locked (assuming the absence of failures). Our approach ultimately relies on the model-checking tool Tina, that provides state-space generation and model-checking algorithms for an extension of Time Petri Nets with data and priorities.

1 Introduction

We describe our experience with modeling the landing gear system of an aircraft using the formal specification language Fiacre [1]. This case study has been submitted as a problem to be solved by the participants of the Case Study Track at the 4th International ABZ Conference. Our answer to this challenge is based on the use of a model-checking tool for an extension of Time Petri Nets with data and priorities. All the requirements were checked using a dense (continuous) time model, without resorting to discrete time verification methods. The Fiacre models used in this study are available online at `http://projects.laas.fr/fiacre/examples/landinggear.html`.

The purpose of the control system is to manage and monitor the hydraulic and mechanical parts operating the movement of the gears—and their associated doors—on a modern aircraft: activation of the electrical and hydraulic power; opening of the locks and doors; extension or retraction of the gears; ... A full description of the system is given in [2].

The control (digital) part of the system is fairly complex, since there are several subsystems involved—each associated with their own set of timing constraints—and many safety requirement to be satisfied. Some of these requirements are quite straightforward, like for instance that "gears should not be extended if the doors are closed", but other requirements depend on the architecture of the system. For instance that "the controller should not attempt to power the doors without first stimulating the general electro-valves" or that

---

* This work was partly supported by the ITEA2 Project OpenETCS.

F. Boniol et al. (Eds.): ABZ 2014 Case Study Track, CCIS 433, pp. 110–125, 2014.
© Springer International Publishing Switzerland 2014

"stimulation of the electro-valves should be separated by at least 200ms". Another source of complexity stems from the multiple redundancies put in place as a contingency in case of mechanical failure. Actually, one of the main tasks of the control system is to identify the occurence of failures in order to warn the pilot of any anomalous behavior. This is a major safety requirement, since the pilot should be warned as soon as possible that he needs to engage his emergency extension system.

Our formal model takes into account the behavior and timing properties of the mechanical and control parts of the system, both in its normal and failure mode of operation. We study several versions of the model, each of growing complexity, by strengthening our assumptions on the system. The different versions are used to check safety and real-time properties on the system but also to find a safe bound on the maximal time needed for all gears to be down and locked (assuming the absence of failures). Therefore we experiment here with another interesting application of model-checking, that is as a tool for architecture exploration (dimensioning).

This case study is interesting for several reasons. First, it is well-suited for component-based modeling languages (since the description is highly modular) and it is a good example for real-time verification methods (since the specification has plenty of timing constraints). Also, a similar case study was used by Boniol et al. in 2006 [3], where they compared the use of several model-checking tools: a majority of tools based on the synchronous language Lustre, and one tool, Uppaal, based on timed automata. It is interesting to revisit these results that are nearly ten years old.

2   Fiacre and Tina

We describe the language and tools used to check the behavior of the system. Our approach is based on Fiacre (http://www.laas.fr/fiacre/), a specification language designed to represent compositionally both the behavioral and timing aspects of embedded and distributed systems for the purposes of formal verification or simulation. The language comes equipped with a set of dedicated tools, such as a compiler to the input format of the model-checking tool Tina [4].

2.1   The Fiacre Language

Fiacre is a modeling language for behavioral verification, with a textual notation, in the vein of Promela or BIP. It can be used for model-checking but is not tied to any particular toolset. The language supports two of the most common coordination paradigms: communication through shared variable (shared-memory) and synchronization through synchronous communication ports (message-passing). A formal definition of the language is given in [5].

Fiacre programs are stratified in two main notions: *processes*, which are well-suited for modeling structured activities, and *components*, which describe a system as a composition of processes, possibly in a hierarchical manner.

We give a simple example of a Fiacre specification in Fig. 1. It is the model of a computer mouse driver with double-click. A more complex example of Fiacre process, extracted from the case study, is given in Fig. 4. The behavior of the computer mouse is to emit the event double if it receives more than two click events in strictly less than one unit of time (u.t.). Note that the semantics of the language is based on a dense, "dimensionless", notion of time. This approach is consistent with several of the state space abstraction techniques used in our tools [6]. Indeed, the "geometric methods" based on the use of Difference Bound Matrices (DBM) are insensitive to the scaling of time (this is not true for methods based on a discrete time approach that may also be used in Tina).

```
process Push [click  : none,          component Mouse [click : none,
              single : none,                           once  : none,
              double : none,                           twice : none] is
              delay  : none] is
                                      port delay : none in [1,1]
states s0, s1, s2
                                      priority delay > click
var dbl : bool := false
                                      par
from s0 click; to s1                      Push [click, once, twice, delay]
                                      end
from s1
  select                             //- - - - - - - - - - - - - - - - - - - - - - - - - - - -
    click; dbl := true; loop
  [] delay; to s2                    component Main is
  end
                                      port click, once, twice, thrice : none
from s2
  if dbl then double                 par
  else single end;                       once → Mouse [click, once, twice]
  dbl := false; to s0                  || once → Mouse [once, twice, thrice]
                                      end
```

Fig. 1. A double-click example in Fiacre

Processes: a process is defined by a set of parameters and control states, each associated with a set of *complex transitions* (introduced by the keyword from). The initial state of a process is the state corresponding to the first from declaration. Complex transitions are expressions that declare how variables are updated and which transitions may fire.

Expressions are built from deterministic constructs available in classical programming languages (assignments, conditionals, sequential composition, ...); non-deterministic constructs (such as external choice, with the select operator); communication on ports; and jump to a state (with the to or loop operators). For example, in Fig. 1, we declare a process named Push with four communication ports (click to delay) and one local boolean variable, dbl. Ports may send and receive typed data. The port type none means that no data is exchanged; ports of type none simply act as synchronization events. Regarding complex transitions, the expression for s1, for instance, declares two possible behaviors when in state s1: first, on a `click` event, set `dbl` to true and stay in state s1; second, on a `delay` event, change to state s2.

Data variables are not restricted to simple boolean values. The language provides rich datatypes, such as natural numbers, arrays, queues, records, ... For instance, in the model of the landing gear system (see Sect. 3), we use records and arrays of booleans to represent the signals from the replicated sensor probes. The language is strongly typed, meaning that type annotations are exploited in order to guarantee the absence of unchecked run-time errors.

Components: a component is built from the parallel composition of processes and/or other components, expressed with the operator `par P`$_0$ `|| ... || P`$_n$ `end`. Components are the unit for process instantiation and for declaring ports and shared variables. The syntax of components allows to associate timing constraints with communications and to define priority between communication events. The ability to express directly timing constraints in programs is a distinguishing feature of Fiacre. For example, in the declaration of component `Mouse` (see Fig. 1), the `port` statement declares a local event `delay` with a punctual timing constraint [1, 1]. As a consequence, a transition from state s1 to s2 in the mouse cannot be delayed more than one unit of time. A behavior similar to the synchronization on a local, time-constrained port like `delay` (basically a timeout) can be obtained using the expression `wait` [1, 1]. Additionally, the `priority` statement asserts that a transition on event `click` cannot occur if a transition on `delay` is also possible.

2.2   Behavioral Verification with Tina

Tina [4], the TIme Petri Net Analyzer, provides a software environment to edit and analyze Time Petri Nets and their extensions. It is particularly well suited to the verification of systems subject to real time constraints, such as the landing gear system studied in this paper. The core of the Tina toolset is an exploration engine used to generate state space abstractions that are fed to dedicated model checking and transition system analyzer tools. The front-ends to the exploration engine convert models into an internal representation — the abstract Time Transition Systems (TTS) — that is an extension of Time Petri Nets (TPN) handling data and priorities [7]. We can use the *frac* compiler to convert Fiacre description into TTS and therefore to model-check Fiacre specifications.

We give the graphical representation of a TTS in Fig. 2. This example corresponds to the interpretation of the Fiacre process `Push` from the computer mouse example of Sect. 2.1. A TTS can be viewed as a Time Petri Net where transitions are decorated with guards and actions on data variables; the `pre` and `act` expressions inside dotted rectangles. Data is managed within the `act` and `pre` expressions and refer to a fixed set of variables that form the *store* of the TTS. In comparison with a TPN, a transition in a TTS is enabled if there is both: (1) enough tokens in the places of its pre-condition; and (2) the predicate `pre` is true. When a transition fires, the store is updated atomically by executing the corresponding action `act`. For example, when the token reaches the place s_2 in the TTS of Fig. 2, we use the value of dbl to test whether we should signal a double click or not. We can also see in this example the use of read arcs and priorities between transitions (dashed arrow between transitions).

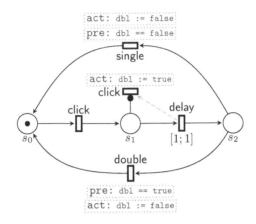

Fig. 2. Interpretation of the process Push in TTS

Time Transition Systems is the low level formalism used for model-checking. State space abstractions are vital when dealing with timed systems, such as TTS, that have in general infinite state spaces (because we work with a dense time model). Tina offers several abstract state space constructions that preserve specific classes of properties like absence of deadlocks, reachability of markings, linear time temporal properties, or bisimilarity.

In the case of the landing gear, most of the requirements can be reduced to safety properties, that is, checking that some bad state cannot occur. In this case, we do not need to generate the whole state class graph of the system and we can use "more aggressive" abstractions. Tina implements two main state-space abstraction methods, a default method that preserves the set of states and traces of the system, and a method that preserves the states but not the traces. While this abstraction gives an over-approximation of the set of execution traces of the system, it is often much more efficient than the default exploration mode. This second method can be used in Tina with the command line options -M or -E. The state-space abstraction corresponding to -M usually has a better space complexity than -E, but the latter is necessary when using models that have priorities between transitions.

For more complex properties, Tina provides several back-ends to convert its output into physical representations readable by external model checkers. In the context of this study, we need to check LTL properties in the case of failure mode requirements. Broadly speaking, we need to check that, after the failure of a mechanical part (the system is in a fail state), every event that triggers the part (say evt) will eventually lead to the anomaly being detected (the probe normal_mode is set to false). Since the system stays in a fail state when it reaches it, this property could be defined as follows in LTL:

[]((fail /\ evt) => <>(not normal_mode)) .

We can use *selt*, the model-checker distributed with the Tina toolbox, to check this kind of properties on a Fiacre model. It is a model-checker for an enriched version of State/Event-LTL, a linear time temporal logic supporting both state and transition properties. For the properties found false, we can compute a timed counter example and replay it in a TTS simulator.

3   Model of the Landing Gear System

We take benefit from the compositional and hierarchical nature of Fiacre to model the landing gear system. Each component described in the informal spec-ification [2] is encoded using a Fiacre component and we use the instantiation mechanism to efficiently model the redundancies and symmetries of the system.

The digital and mechanical parts are all modeled using separate components. Only the pilot interface remains implicit as a set of shared boolean variables that can be triggered by the component modeling the system's environment. We also assume that two separate stimuli from the environment cannot occur in less than 100ms. This value of 100ms is taken from the timing constraints information provided by the landing gear specification document (Sect. 4.2 of [2]), namely that "two contrary orders (closure / opening doors, extension / retraction gears) must be separated by at least 100ms". The document does not specify any timing constraints on the movement of the handle or, equivalently, on the reactivity of the pilot/environment. We chose to apply the same constraints of 100ms here to avoid unrealistic scenarios in which the handle could be moved infinitely often in a finite amount of time.

The whole model—when taking into account the maximal level of details— amounts to about 1200 lines of Fiacre. Most of it was programmed in the course of one week by a model-checking specialist that was novice with Fiacre. When compiled into a Time Transition System (see Sect. 2.2) we obtain a net with about 100 places and 150 transitions. These numbers give a rough idea of the complexity of the "coordination" aspect of the system. Concerning the functional complexity of the model, we have about 60 variables in the resulting TTS, but many of these variables are correlated (at least in normal mode, because of the redundancies). This is close to the 54 discrete sensor values declared in the specification and the 5 electrical outputs (called *electrical orders* in the specifi-cation [2]) emitted by each computing module.

We describe the structure of the Fiacre specification starting from the data types used in the model. The main data types are almost word for word those given in the informal specification of the system. Different parts of the system interact using electrical orders, hydraulic pressure or sensors. Our model repre-sents this information as boolean values. For example we observe the presence or absence of hydraulic pressure but not its transition phase (growing up / going down). However the time needed by this transition phase is always taken into account and adequately modeled in different parts.

To simplify the model, we also use arrays of sensors for closed/open door sensors, extended/retracted gear sensors and gear shock absorbers sensors. This allows to reduce the number of variables handled by different processes and to reduce the code size of our model without modifying the generated state space.

3.1   Digital Part

No timing constraints are given on the speed of the digital part of the system. (Actually, the description of the system is quite heavily oriented toward a synchronous architecture rather than, say, a time-triggered one.) Since the speed of digital signals is incommensurate with the speed of mechanical parts, we have chosen a null response time for every interaction with the digital part. Thus the digital component computes new outputs instantaneously each time a sensor value changes. However, electro-valve order delays are considered (we adopt the same timing constraints than in the use case specification, see Sect. 4.2 of [2]):

- the simulation of the general electro-valve and the maneuvering electro-valves must be separated by 200ms;
- orders to stop the general electro-valve and the maneuvering electro-valves must be separated by 1s;
- two opposite electro-valve orders must be separated by 100ms.

The digital part is modeled using two instances of the same computing module component and an electrical "OR" process making the composition of computing modules orders. To keep the model simple, each computing module is divided in four processes: the computing process responsible for detecting failures and ordering electro-valves; a process handling general electro-valve timing constraints; and two processes handling contrary orders and their timing constraints. This architecture has been faithfully mimicked in our model even if it is redundant in the normal operation mode given the 100ms delay between stimuli and because both computing processes should behave in the same manner. We illustrate the structure of a computing module component in Fiacre in Fig. 3. (The whole model uses two copies of this component).

3.2   Hydraulic Part

The hydraulic part is modeled using a component handling doors and gears circuits. The component is composed of two electro-valves and three cylinders; each part in the hydraulic architecture (valve, cylinder, ...) is modeled using a Fiacre process. The timing constraints used in the Fiacre processes are the one given by the specification (see e.g. Sect. 3.2 of [3]). For instance, an electro-valve changes its state from open to close in 1 second and from close to open in 3,6 seconds. The process for the cylinders is parametric and configured based on specification times. As for electro-valves, each cylinder motion can be reversed

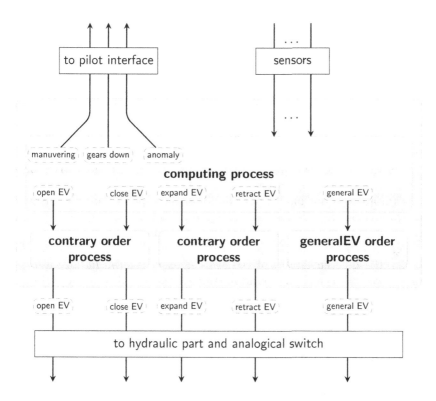

Fig. 3. Computing module implementation

at any time. We consider the whole extension or retraction time in each case and take into account the 20% time variation mentioned in the specification (Sect. 3.3 of [2]). The main simplification with regards to the specification is that we do not discretize the behavior of the valve and always consider the worst possible execution time. In the *experimental results* section of this paper (see Sect. 4), we also give some results on a "discrete" version of the model where we record the progress of the cylinders between a closing and opening requests and follow the physical behavior defined by the specification (see e.g. Fig. 8 of [2]). The discrete model use a sampling time of 100ms between every event. The size of the state space for this discrete model is quite big when compared to our abstracted model.

We used model-checking to compute the worst-case gear retraction time in our system. This time obtained with the discrete version of the model is the same than with our abstract version; actually we obtain a value that is marginally higher with the discrete model due to an accumulation of errors originating from the "time quantum".

3.3   Analogical Switch

The analogical switch is responsible for interfacing digital orders with the general electro-valve and protecting it from erratic orders. It is enabled each time the handle is moved. We model the closing and the opening of the switch by waiting a certain fixed amount of time (taken from the specification), that is, we do not discretize the state of the switch and always use the worst-case time when changing state.

We list the Fiacre process corresponding to the analogical switch process in Fig. 4. The process AnalogicalSwitch is parametrized with variables shared between processes which are used to update sensor states or pass electrical orders. We consider that these operations are immediate and thus are seen as shared boolean variables in our model. The values of these probes are used as guards on the transitions of the process (using the operator on).

The Fiacre process directly implements the state diagram for the analog switch that is given in Fig. 8 of the specification [2]. For instance we use the same names for the different states of the switch: *open*, *intermediate1*, *closed* and *intermediate2*. The last transition from state closed (line 33 of the code) models the fact that, when the switch is closed, the input of the electro-valve (the value of out_EV) should be equal to the output of the digital module (in_EV). This transition is implicit in the state diagram of [2]. Actually, the transition was missing in initial versions of our model and this modeling error raised no obvious inconsistencies during model-checking. The missing behavior was spotted by a reviewer familiar with the landing gear system. This is proof that subtle errors in modeling can be introduced when we use an informal language to describe the behavior of a system, like with the choice of graphical notation in [2].

3.4   Handling Failures

The physical parts in the system have multiple ways to fail. In our model, we only consider cylinder failures by allowing gear and door cylinders to get stuck in their current position indefinitely. We also assume that a part cannot leave a failure state once it has entered it (no transient failure). We consider only one possible type of failure at a time since adding all the possible cases—and all their combinations—could lead to an intractable model.

To address failure mode requirements, we have added failure handling mechanisms in each computing module, allowing to detect failures and to notify the pilot. In the current model, the only notification mechanism is to set the shared variable normal_mode to false. This is done by watching sensor states with adequate timeouts. We focused on failures induced by the requirements $R_{7\star}$ which are stronger than $R_{6\star}$, however requirements $R_{6\star}$ could be easily implemented (we use the notation $R_{6\star}$ to stand for requirements R_{61} to R_{64}). So, requirements $R_{6\star}$ and $R_{8\star}$ were not addressed but could be added with no effort. We made this choice to limit state space sizes.

```
1  process AnalogicalSwitch(&handle : sensor,
2                           &in_EV : electrical_order,
3                           &out_EV : electrical_order,
4                           &analogical_switch : sensor) is
5     states open, intermediate1, closed, intermediate2
6     var last_handle : bool := HANDLE_DOWN
7
8     from open
9        wait [0,0];
10       on (handle.value <> last_handle); // handle state has changed
11       last_handle := handle.value;
12       to intermediate1 // move to state intermediate1
13
14    from intermediate1
15       wait [0,800]; // wait 800ms... then deliver power
16       out_EV := in_EV;
17       analogical_switch.value := SWITCH_CLOSED;
18       to closed // move to state closed
19
20    from closed
21       select
22          wait [20000,20000]; // wait 20s but only if...
23          on (handle.value = last_handle); // handle did not move
24          // then cut power and start intermediate2
25          analogical_switch.value := SWITCH_OPEN;
26          out_EV := false;
27          to intermediate2
28       [] wait [0,0];
29          on (handle.value = last_handle); // if handle did not move...
30          on (out_EV <> in_EV); // but the input value had changed
31          out_EV := in_EV; // update the output
32          loop // stay in this state without but do not reset
33       [] wait [0,0];
34          on (handle.value <> last_handle);
35          // otherwise if handle state has changed...
36          // reset immediately this state
37          last_handle := handle.value;
38          out_EV := in_EV;
39          to closed
40       end
41
42    from intermediate2
43       select
44          wait [0,1200]; // wait 1.2s if handle did not move
45          on (handle.value = last_handle);
46          analogical_switch.value := SWITCH_OPEN;
47          to open // move to state open
48
49       [] wait [0,0]; // otherwise if handle did move
50          on (handle.value <> last_handle);
51          last_handle := handle.value;
52          to intermediate1 // move to state intermediate1
53       end
```

Fig. 4. The AnalogicalSwitch Process in Fiacre (see Fig. 8 of [2]). Full model available at http://projects.laas.fr/fiacre/examples/landinggear.html.

3.5 Optimizations

Because model checking is highly sensitive to state space explosion, our model embeds a certain number of optimizations. The electrical orders, hydraulic pressure, and sensors are abstracted to boolean values, so we can control the number of operations involved when a value changes. For example, we will trigger a component from the digital part of the system (a computing module) only when the change in its input probes leads to a change in the values that it writes. This is useful because it helps reduce the number of transitions in our system. Also, one can remark that computing modules are fully symmetric. Therefore, in normal mode, we will always observe the same values twice; once for each copy of the module. To avoid this unnecessary source of interleaving, we have added priorities between copies of the same component.

Priorities have also been added between the components of the hydraulic system so as to fix an arbitrary order between operations of the electro-valves and cylinders. This optimization is correct because all these devices are independent; hence we limit the interleaving between independent actions but do not rule out any possible scenario.

4 Experimental Results

We follow a methodology similar to the one adopted by Boniol et al. in a previous experiment with model-checking of a landing gear control system [3]. We define several versions of our model that corresponds to different abstractions or optimizations on the system. We define three sets of assumptions and, by combining these parameters, consider different cases of growing complexity.

Parameter V. We consider two configurations for the gear-door sets, a version with only one gear-door set (denoted V_1) and a complete version, with all three gear-door sets (V_3).

Parameter H. We consider several versions for the environment that stimulates the pilot handle. The most general case where the only constraint on handle movements is a $100ms$ delay between two stimuli is denoted H_2. We also consider simpler scenarios where the pilot can move the handle at most k times. This assumption is denoted $H_1(k)$.

Parameter N/F. We use the notation N for models that are restricted to the normal mode, where no failures can happen, and the notation F for models that include failures.

With these parameters defined, it is possible to refer to a version of the model with a triplet, for instance $(V_1, H_1(2), N)$. This is the simplest possible, meaningful case: only one gear-door set; two actions on the handle; and no failures. The most complex case is (V_3, H_2, F).

Because of the complexity of the system, we considered only cylinder failures. Since we only consider cylinder failures, we do not duplicate the computing component in the digital part, however we provide a version of our model allowing this duplication. For checking behavioral properties, we assume that, in the initial state of the system, gears are extended and doors are opened. We also assume that gear absorbers are always relaxed, i.e. we assume that the plane is flying.

4.1 Normal Mode Requirements

The properties corresponding to normal mode requirements (see [2]) can be expressed as reachability properties. Indeed checking requirements $R_{2\star}$, $R_{3\star}$, $R_{4\star}$, $R_{5\star}$ corresponds to looking for a state were some condition is not satisfied, and requirement $R_{1\star}$ can be expressed with an observer of the system (waiting $15s$) and a reachability condition. This allows for efficient verification using the faster state-space abstraction of Tina (option -E) that preserves reachable states without building the whole class graph.

All these properties are expected to be true on our model. This is the worst possible case when checking reachability since it means that we need to generate the whole set of reachable states of the system. We give below the computation times and the memory usage for generating the whole state graph. We also give the complexity using the number of "markings" and "classes" that have been generated in each case. A marking corresponds to a particular value for every variable and state for each process in the system. A class adds timing constraints on the possible transitions enabled from a marking (hence there are always more classes than markings.) Markings are enough to decide the requirements $R_{1\star}$ to $R_{5\star}$, but we need to compute a set of classes in order to compute an exact set of reachable markings.

Normal mode state space computation times and memory usage							
		H_2	$H_1(10)$	$H_1(11)$	$H_1(12)$	$H_1(13)$	$H_1(14)$
V_1	time	$41s$	$56s$	$71s$	$88s$	$105s$	$123s$
	memory	$24MB$	$47MB$	$54MB$	$62MB$	$69MB$	$76MB$
V_3	time	$262s$	$248s$	$331s$	$415s$	$507s$	$602s$
	memory	$127MB$	$202MB$	$241MB$	$282MB$	$323MB$	$364MB$

Normal mode markings and classes sizes							
		H_2	$H_1(10)$	$H_1(11)$	$H_1(12)$	$H_1(13)$	$H_1(14)$
V_1	markings	$16 \cdot 10^3$	$56 \cdot 10^3$	$63 \cdot 10^3$	$71 \cdot 10^3$	$79 \cdot 10^3$	$86 \cdot 10^3$
	classes	$153 \cdot 10^3$	$252 \cdot 10^3$	$303 \cdot 10^3$	$356 \cdot 10^3$	$411 \cdot 10^3$	$468 \cdot 10^3$
V_3	markings	$90 \cdot 10^3$	$242 \cdot 10^3$	$283 \cdot 10^3$	$325 \cdot 10^3$	$367 \cdot 10^3$	$409 \cdot 10^3$
	classes	$979 \cdot 10^3$	$1\,125 \cdot 10^3$	$1\,409 \cdot 10^3$	$1\,701 \cdot 10^3$	$2\,015 \cdot 10^3$	$2\,333 \cdot 10^3$

We can observe that the infinite behavior scenario (H_2) is easier to handle than bounded ones when the bound is at least 10 handle moves for V_1 and 11 handle moves for V_3. This is mainly due to the fact that bounding the number of interactions is performed by implementing a counter that may increase the number of reachable states.

For our next experiment, we study the requirement R_{11} and try to find the smallest time, say t_{min}, for the gears to be fully extended and locked in open position. This property can be reduced to a simple reachability property since there is a specific state, s_i, in the process modeling the pilot behavior that is reached when the pilot stay idle for a time t_{min}. Indeed, it is enough to check that there are no states where the pilot is in s_i and the gears are not fully open. The following table gives the computation time and memory usage for different value of t_{min}, for the configuration (N, H_2, V_3) (no failures, no assumptions on pilot behavior, and the complete gear-door sets). The best time for which the property is true is 8.5s. We can observe that the computation time is much smaller for values below this threshold since the property is false in this case (and the state space exploration can be stopped). So, the computation is quasi-immediate when the time bound is below the 8.5s threshold but the whole state space needs to be computed above it.

Checking requirement R_{11} on (N, H_2, V_3) for different time limits t_{min}				
t_{min}	$15s$	$9s$	$8.5s$	$8.4s$
result	valid	valid	valid	falsified
time	$268s$	$268s$	$268s$	$2s$
memory	$127MB$	$127MB$	$127MB$	$5MB$

We also considered a discretized version of our model where all intermediate movement states were computed, for example the cylinder extension ratio, and where we used the exact (hybrid) physical behavior given in the specification. This discretization was made using a sampling time of 100ms. Because of the number or possible combinations of cylinders, analogical switch and electrovalves, the number of states grow much faster than with our abstract (non discrete) version. Actually the discretized version was our first attempt, because we initially believed that it was giving more precise bounds. However, the 100ms sampling time was not enough to provide better results than the non discrete version. With the discrete version, the configurations $(N, H_1(5), V_1)$ and above were not computable in reasonable times (less than 8 hours).

Normal mode state space computation times and memory usage (discrete)			
	$H_1(2)$	$H_1(3)$	$H_1(4)$
V_1 time	$17s$	$804s$	$19\,887s$
memory	$33MB$	$1\,132MB$	$8\,982MB$

Normal mode markings and classes sizes (discrete)			
	$H_1(2)$	$H_1(3)$	$H_1(4)$
V_1 markings	$158 \cdot 10^3$	$5\,097 \cdot 10^3$	$112\,094 \cdot 10^3$
classes	$217 \cdot 10^3$	$8\,648 \cdot 10^3$	$202\,266 \cdot 10^3$

These experiments show the interest of having different kind of abstractions implemented in the same tool (like having different symbolic methods available). The most complex configuration we tried to analyze with the default options of Tina (that preserves linear time properties) is (N, H_2, V_3). We stopped the analysis after 36 hours of computation and more than 2 billion state classes.

The same model can be analyzed with the time-abstracted semantics (option -M) in two hours (7355s), then with the same option and after removing duplication of the digital component in 422s. Our results also show the interest of priorities to reduce the state space size. For instance, after adding priorities between independent devices and removing duplication of the digital component, we can analyze the same system in 262s (option -E). To see the impact of different optimizations we considered a smaller case $(N, H_1(8), V_3)$ with different configurations and all without computing module duplication, the results are shown in the table below.

Impact of optimizations on markings and classes.			
$(N, H_1(8), V_3)$	-E	priorities only	no priorities
time	$119s$	$5\,237s$	$12\,383s$
memory	$126MB$	$2\,204MB$	$5\,467MB$
markings	$160 \cdot 10^3$	$160 \cdot 10^3$	$292 \cdot 10^3$
classes	$619 \cdot 10^3$	$54\,342 \cdot 10^3$	$108\,302 \cdot 10^3$

4.2 Failure Mode Requirements

As mentioned in section 3.4, we focused on requirements $R_{7\star}$: "If one of the three doors is not seen locked in the open position more than 7 seconds after stimulating the opening electro-valve, then the boolean output normal mode is set to false". To check that we satisfy these requirements we need to consider LTL formula.

We can express the requirement R_{71} quite naturally using LTL: after a failure (`fail_c1`), if at least one door is closed (`not open_d1`) and we later try to stimulate the opening electro-valve (`<>open_EV`) then the boolean *normal_ mode* is eventually set to false.

```
[]((fail_c1 /\ (not open_d1) /\ (<>open_EV)) => <>(not normal_mode)).
```

We can observe that the 7 seconds delay does not appear explicitly in the formula. Indeed, this delay is part of the behavior of the digital module. This formula is false when checked on the model. After looking at the counter-example provided by the model-checker, we find that the problematic scenario corresponds to a situation where the pilot continuously moves the handle, waiting less than 7 seconds between each movement. We can modify the property in order to rule out this scenario; i.e. ask that the pilot does not move the handle up. We solve this issue by adding an *idle* state to our pilot that can be reached after moving the handle. If this idle state is reached then the pilot will not move the handle again. With this new state added, the correct formula is

```
[]((pilot_idle /\ handle_down /\ fail_c1 /\ (not open_d1)
               /\ (<>open_EV)) => <>(not normal_mode)).
```

We were not able to model-check the system with the configuration H_2. Even if the number of reachable states remains quite small in this case, the number of classes is too large to address it in reasonable time. We give below the results obtained with a "bounded" pilot $(H_1(k))$ and an incomplete or full gear-door set (configurations with V_1 or V_3).

Failure mode, time and memory usage results for bounded scenarios				
		$H_1(3)$	$H_1(4)$	$H_1(5)$	$H_1(6)$
V_1	time	$2s$	$7s$	$15s$	$32s$
	memory	$7MB$	$17MB$	$34MB$	$54MB$
V_3	time	$70s$	$304s$	$968s$	$2418s$
	memory	$169MB$	$611MB$	$1544MB$	$2925MB$

Failure mode, markings and classes counts for bounded scenarios				
		$H_1(3)$	$H_1(4)$	$H_1(5)$	$H_1(6)$
V_1	markings	$12 \cdot 10^3$	$30 \cdot 10^3$	$54 \cdot 10^3$	$83 \cdot 10^3$
	classes	$17 \cdot 10^3$	$49 \cdot 10^3$	$108 \cdot 10^3$	$200 \cdot 10^3$
V_3	markings	$317 \cdot 10^3$	$1153 \cdot 10^3$	$2822 \cdot 10^3$	$5073 \cdot 10^3$
	classes	$458 \cdot 10^3$	$1725 \cdot 10^3$	$4967 \cdot 10^3$	$10847 \cdot 10^3$

4.3   Comparaison with a Previous, Similar Study

A similar case study was used by Boniol et al. in 2006 [3], where they compared the use of several model-checking tools: a majority of tools based on the synchronous language Lustre, and one tool, Uppaal, based on timed automata. It is interesting to revisit these results that are nearly ten years old. This comparison is not very significant though. Indeed, even if the specification used in our work derives from the use case of [3], it is not clear if they are totally equivalent. Also, we do not know what optimizations were used in the other models. In particular, our use of an abstract (non discrete) behavior for the analog switches and the cylinders may account for most of our good results.

In the study of [3], no tools were able to deal with the failure mode requirements. For the nominal case, the most complex problem configuration studied is equivalent to (N, H_2, V_3) with our notation. With this configuration, Lustre-SMV requires $414MB$ of memory and 16mn 40s to compute its result. We give the running time for information only, since it is not meaningful to compare computers that are ten years apart. On the opposite, the memory consumption offers a more reliable point of comparison. Using Tina on our model for (N, H_2, V_3) we need only $127MB$ and 5mn.

Uppaal, that is based on timed automata, provides the formalism that is the closest to Time Petri Nets from all the tools considered in this study. At the time, Uppaal gave no results on the configuration with three gears. On a configuration with only one gear, equivalent to (N, H_2, V_1) with our notation, it takes $761MB$ and nearly 6 hours to return a result. Unfortunately we do not have access to the model and do not know the number of states that were generated, so we cannot use this information as a basis for our comparison. This can be compared to the $24MB$ of memory that are needed in our experiment (and 41s, with the same caveat than previously).

5   Conclusion

We have illustrated the use of Fiacre for checking the real-time properties of a fairly large and complex real-life case study. We have provided a formal model that is as faithful as possible to the informal, reference specification, at the risk of obtaining intractable model-checking problems. This model could be further optimized in order to obtain better computation times when checking a specific set of properties, for example by reducing the inherent level of redundancies when it does not modify the behavior of the system. Nonetheless, even without further optimizations, it is possible to check most of the requirements that are part of the specification.

Other solutions for checking larger, more complex configurations of our model are worth pursuing. A first possibility will be to take benefit from the symmetries of the system (for instance, the two rear gears are interchangeable). Another solution will be to simplify the transient transitions of the model, that is the internal, instantaneous transitions that are only used for modeling purpose and have no "physical meaning" in the system. This simplification can be compared to what we already obtain by adding priorities between independent devices, but would be more efficient and simpler to define at the model level. Unfortunately, our toolset does not provide this optimization. A first investigation (by reducing the state class graph afterward) show that, this way, we could reduce the memory usage by a factor of about 20.

References

1. Berthomieu, B., Bodeveix, J.P., Farail, P., Filali, M., Garavel, H., Gauffilet, P., Lang, F., Vernadat, F.: Fiacre: an intermediate language for model verification in the topcased environment. In: Embedded Real Time Software (ERTS) (2008)
2. Boniol, F., Wiels, V.: The Landing Gear System Case Study. In: Boniol, F. (ed.) ABZ 2014 Case Study Track. CCIS, vol. 433, pp. 1–18. Springer, Heidelberg (2014)
3. Wiels, V., Boniol, F., Ledinot, E.: Experiences in using model checking to verify real time properties of a landing gear control system. SIA/Articles Techniques (2006)
4. Berthomieu, B., Ribet, P.O., Vernadat, F.: The tool Tina – construction of abstract state spaces for Petri Nets and time petri nets. International Journal of Production Research 42 (2004)
5. Berthomieu, B., Bodeveix, J.P., Filali, M., Garavel, H., Lang, F., Peres, F., Saad, R., Stoecker, J., Vernadat, F.: The syntax and semantics of fiacre. Repport LAAS N 07264 (2007)
6. Berthomieu, B., Vernadat, F.: State Space Abstractions for Time Petri Nets. In: Lee, I., Leung, J.Y.-T., Son, S. (eds.) Handbook of Real-Time and Embedded Systems. CRC Press, Boca Raton (2007)
7. Abid, N., Dal Zilio, S., Le Botlan, D.: A formal framework to specify and verify real–time properties on critical systems. International Journal of Critical Computer-Based Systems 5, 4–30 (2014)

The Landing Gear Case Study in Hybrid Event-B

Richard Banach

School of Computer Science, University of Manchester,
Oxford Road, Manchester, M13 9PL, U.K.
banach@cs.man.ac.uk

Abstract. A case study problem based on a set of aircraft landing gear is examined in Hybrid Event-B (an extension of Event-B that includes provision for continuously varying behaviour as well as the usual discrete changes of state). Although tool support for Hybrid Event-B is currently lacking, the complexity of the case study provides a valuable challenge for the expressivity and modelling capabilities of the formalism. The size of the case study, and in particular, the number of overtly independent subcomponents that the problem domain contains, both significantly exercise the multi-machine and coordination capabilities of Hybrid Event-B, requiring the use of novel coordination mechanisms.

1 Introduction

This paper reports on a treatment of the landing gear case study using Hybrid Event-B. Hybrid Event-B [4] is an extension of the well known Event-B framework, in which continuously varying state evolution, along with the usual discrete changes of state, is admitted. There is a *prima facie* case for attempting such an exercise using Hybrid Event-B, since aircraft systems are replete with interactions between physical law and the engineering artifacts that are intended to ensure appropriate aircraft behaviour. In the case of landing gear systems specifically, a good idea of the real complexity of such systems can be gained from Chapter 13 of [16].

Given that landing gear is predominantly controlled by hydraulic systems (see Chapter 12 of [16]), it might be imagined that the requirements for the present case study [6], would feature relevant physical properties quite extensively. Hybrid Event-B would be ideally suited to describe the interactions between these and the control system — for example on the basis of the theory and models detailed in [10,1,11]. However, it is clear that the requirements in [6] have been heavily slanted to remove such aspects almost completely, presumably because the overwhelming majority of tools in the verification field would not be capable of addressing the requisite continuous aspects. Instead, the relevant properties are reduced to constants (perhaps accompanied by margins of variability) that delimit the *duration* of various physical processes, these being relevant to a treatment centred on discrete control events. Such an approach reduces the modelling workload, but the penalty paid for it is the loss of the ability to *justify* the values of these constants during the verification process, whether this be on the basis of deeper theory or of values obtained from lower level phenomenological models.

Despite this reservation, a small number of simple continuous behaviours are left within the requirements in [6], these being confined to simple linear behaviours of some

F. Boniol et al. (Eds.): ABZ 2014 Case Study Track, CCIS 433, pp. 126–141, 2014.

parts of the physical apparatus. Yet, these are enough to demonstrate many essential capabilities of the Hybrid Event-B formalism in dealing with continuous phenomena and their interaction with discrete events.

The reduced workload of the restricted requirements was in fact welcome, since the limited resources available for the present work meant that a treatment including all failure modes could not be included. However, the nominal regime study that is presented here is sufficient to bring out the main benefits of the approach, and some comments on the failure cases are included in the latter parts of this paper.

Since there is presently no specific tool support for Hybrid Event-B, our case study is primarily an exploration of modelling capabilities. As explained below, a major element of this is the challenge of modelling physically separate components in separate machines, and of interconnecting all these machines in ways appropriate to the domain, all supported by relevant invariants. This requires novel machine interconnection mechanisms, introduced for pure Event-B in [2]. The suitability of proposals for such mechanisms can only be tested convincingly in the context of independently conceived substantial case studies like this one, so it is gratifying that the mechanisms exercised here fare well in the face of the complexities of the given requirements.

The rest of this paper is as follows. Section 2 briefly overviews the landing gear requirements. Section 3 gives an overview of Hybrid Event-B, while Section 4 covers the case of multiple machines and our modelling strategy for complex systems. A description of our development appears in Section 5. Section 6 summarises the lessons learned from this exercise and concludes.

2   Landing Gear Overview

The landing gear case study is presented in [6]. Here we give the gist of it, focusing on features of most interest to the Hybrid Event-B treatment. Fig. 1, reproduced from [6], shows the architecture of the system.

The sole human input to the system is the pilot handle: when pulled up it instructs the gear to retract, and when pulled down it instructs the gear to extend. The signal from the handle is fed both to the (replicated) computer system and to the analogical switch, the latter being an analogue device that gatekeeps powerup to the hydraulic system, to prevent inappropriate gear movement even in the case of computer malfunction. In a full treatment, including faulty behaviour, there are further inputs from the sensors, which can behave in an autonomous manner to introduce faults. But in our purely nominal treatment, sensor behaviour is a deterministic consequence of other actions, so does not constitute independent influence from the environment. A further point concerns the shock absorber sensors, which are modelled using a guard rather than as inputs. The relevant issue is discussed at the beginning of Section 5.

The analogical switch passes a powerup command from the computers to the general electro-valve. [1] This pressurises the rest of the landing gear hydraulic system, ready for specific further commands to manipulate its various parts, these being the doors of the cabinets that contain the gear when retracted, and the gear extension and retraction mechanisms themselves. Beyond this, both the analogical switch and the output

---

[1] As a rule, commands from the two computers are ORed by the components that obey them.

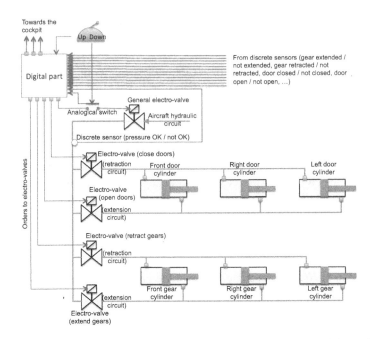

Fig. 1. Architectural overview of the landing gear system, reproduced from [6]

of the general electro-valve are monitored by (triplicated) sensors that feed back to the computer systems, as is discernible from Fig. 1[2].

What is particularly interesting about the system so far, is that the arrangement of these various interconnections between system components is evidently quite far from the kind of tree shape that facilitates clean system decomposition. Thus, the handle is connected to the computers, and the handle is connected to the analogical switch. But the analogical switch is also connected to the computers, so 'dividing' the computers from the analogical switch in the hope of 'conquering' structural complexity will not work, and obstructs the clean separation of proofs into independent subproofs concerning analogical switch and computers separately. This poses a major challenge for our modelling methodology, and gave rise to the need for new interconnection mechanisms, discussed in Section 4.

Beneath the level of the general electro-valve, it is a lot easier to see the system as comprised of the computers on the one hand, and the remaining hydraulic components on the other, connected together in ways that are tractable when the new interconnection mechanisms are available.

3   Hybrid Event-B, Single Machines

In this section we look at Hybrid Event-B for a single machine. In Fig. 2 we see a bare bones Hybrid Event-B machine, *HyEvBMch*. It starts with declarations of time

---

[2] A large number of other sensors also feed back to the computers, but this not relevant to the point we are making just now.

```
MACHINE HyEvBMch              ...  ...                      ...  ...
TIME t                        MoEv                          PliEv
CLOCK clk                     STATUS ordinary               STATUS pliant
PLIANT x, y                   ANY i?, l, o!                 INIT iv(x, y, t, clk)
VARIABLES u                   WHERE                         WHERE grd(u)
INVARIANTS                      grd(x, y, u, i?, l, t, clk) ANY i?, l, o!
  x, y, u ∈ ℝ, ℝ, ℕ           THEN                          COMPLY
EVENTS                          x, y, u, clk, o! :|           BDApred(x, y, u,
  INITIALISATION                BApred(x, y, u, i?, l, o!,       i?, l, o!, t, clk)
  STATUS ordinary               t, clk, x′, y′, u′, clk′)   SOLVE
  WHEN                        END                             𝒟 x =
    t = 0                     ...  ...                         φ(x, y, u, i?, l, o!, t, clk)
  THEN                                                         y, o! :=
    clk, x, y, u := 1, x₀, y₀, u₀                             E(x, u, i?, l, t, clk)
  END                                                       END
...  ...                                                    END
```

Fig. 2. A schematic Hybrid Event-B machine

and of a clock. In Hybrid Event-B, time is a first class citizen in that all variables are functions of time, whether explicitly or implicitly. However time is special, being read-only. Clocks allow more flexibility, since they are assumed to increase like time, but may be set during mode events (see below). Variables are of two kinds. There are mode variables (like u) which take their values in discrete sets and change their values via discontinuous assignment in mode events. There are also pliant variables (such as x, y), declared in the PLIANT clause, which typically take their values in topologically dense sets (normally $\mathbb{R}$) and which are allowed to change continuously, such change being specified via pliant events (see below).

Next are the invariants. These resemble invariants in discrete Event-B, in that the types of the variables are asserted to be the sets from which the variables' values *at any given moment of time* are drawn. More complex invariants are similarly predicates that are required to hold *at all moments of time* during a run.

Then, the events. The *INITIALISATION* has a guard that synchronises time with the start of any run, while all other variables are assigned their initial values as usual.

Mode events are direct analogues of events in discrete Event-B. They can assign all machine variables (except time itself). In the schematic *MoEv* of Fig. 2, we see three parameters $i?, l, o!$, (an input, a local parameter, and an output respectively), and a guard grd which can depend on all the machine variables. We also see the generic after-value assignment specified by the before-after predicate *BApred*, which can specify how the after-values of all variables (except time, inputs and locals) are to be determined.

Pliant events are new. They specify the continuous evolution of the pliant variables over an interval of time. The schematic pliant event *PliEv* of Fig. 2 shows the structure. There are two guards: there is iv, for specifying enabling conditions on the pliant variables, clocks, and time; and there is grd, for specifying enabling conditions on the mode variables. The separation between the two is motivated by considerations connected with refinement.

The body of a pliant event contains three parameters $i?, l, o!$, (again an input, a local parameter, and an output) which are functions of time, defined over the duration of the pliant event. The behaviour of the event is defined by the COMPLY and SOLVE clauses. The SOLVE clause specifies behaviour fairly directly. For example the behaviour of pliant variable y and output $o!$ is given by a direct assignment to the (time dependent) value of the expression $E(...)$. Alternatively, the behaviour of pliant variable x is given by the solution of the first order ordinary differential equation (ODE) $\mathcal{D}x = \phi(...)$, where $\mathcal{D}$ indicates differentiation with respect to time. (In fact the semantics of the $y, o! = E$ case is given in terms of the ODE $\mathcal{D}y, \mathcal{D}o! = \mathcal{D}E$, so that x, y and $o!$ satisfy the same regularity properties.) The COMPLY clause can be used to express any additional constraints that are required to hold during the pliant event via its before-during-and-after predicate $BDApred$. Typically, constraints on the permitted range of values for the pliant variables, and similar restrictions, can be placed here.

The COMPLY clause has another purpose. When specifying at an abstract level, we do not necessarily want to be concerned with all the details of the dynamics — it is often sufficient to require some global constraints to hold which express the needed safety properties of the system. The COMPLY clauses of the machine's pliant events can house such constraints directly, leaving it to lower level refinements to add the necessary details of the dynamics.

Briefly, the semantics of a Hybrid Event-B machine is as follows. It consists of a set of *system traces*, each of which is a collection of functions of time, expressing the value of each machine variable over the duration of a system run. (In the case of *HyEvBMch*, in a given system trace, there would be functions for clk, x, y, u, each defined over the duration of the run.)

Time is modeled as an interval $\mathcal{T}$ of the reals. A run starts at some initial moment of time, t_0 say, and lasts either for a finite time, or indefinitely. The duration of the run $\mathcal{T}$, breaks up into a succession of left-closed right-open subintervals: $\mathcal{T} = [t_0 \ldots t_1), [t_1 \ldots t_2), [t_2 \ldots t_3), \ldots$. The idea is that mode events (with their discontinuous updates) take place at the isolated times corresponding to the common endpoints of these subintervals t_i, and in between, the mode variables are constant and the pliant events stipulate continuous change in the pliant variables.

Although pliant variables change continuously (except perhaps at the t_i), continuity alone still admits a wide range of mathematically pathological behaviours. To eliminate these, we insist that on every subinterval $[t_i \ldots t_{i+1})$ the behaviour is governed by a well posed initial value problem $\mathcal{D}xs = \phi(xs \ldots)$ (where xs is a relevant tuple of pliant variables and $\mathcal{D}$ is the time derivative). 'Well posed' means that $\phi(xs \ldots)$ has Lipschitz constants which are uniformly bounded over $[t_i \ldots t_{i+1})$ bounding its variation with respect to xs, and that $\phi(xs \ldots)$ is measurable in t. Moreover, the permitted discontinuities at the boundary points t_i enable an easy interpretation of mode events that happen at t_i.

The differentiability condition guarantees that from a specific starting point, t_i say, there is a maximal right open interval, specified by t_{MAX} say, such that a solution to the ODE system exists in $[t_i \ldots t_{MAX})$. Within this interval, we seek the earliest time t_{i+1} at which a mode event becomes enabled, and this time becomes the preemption point beyond which the solution to the ODE system is abandoned, and the next solution is sought after the completion of the mode event.

In this manner, assuming that the *INITIALISATION* event has achieved a suitable initial assignment to variables, a system run is *well formed*, and thus belongs to the semantics of the machine, provided that at runtime:

- Every enabled mode event is feasible, i.e. has an after-state, and on its comple- (1)
tion enables a pliant event (but does not enable any mode event).[3]
- Every enabled pliant event is feasible, i.e. has a time-indexed family of after- (2)
states, and EITHER:

(i) During the run of the pliant event a mode event becomes enabled. It pre-
empts the pliant event, defining its end. ORELSE
(ii) During the run of the pliant event it becomes infeasible: finite termination.
ORELSE
(iii) The pliant event continues indefinitely: nontermination.

Thus in a well formed run mode events alternate with pliant events. The last event
(if there is one) is a pliant event (whose duration may be finite or infinite). In reality,
there are a number of semantic issues that we have glossed over in the framework just
sketched. We refer to [4] for a more detailed presentation.

We point out that the presented framework is quite close to the modern formulation
of hybrid systems. See eg. [15,12] for representative modern formulations, or [8] for a
perspective stretching further back.

4 Top-Down Modelling of Complex Systems, and Multiple Cooperating Hybrid Event-B Machines

The principal objective in modelling complex systems in the B-Method is to start with
small simple descriptions and to refine to richer, more detailed ones. This means that, at
the highest levels of abstraction, the modelling must **abstract away from concurrency**.
By contrast, at lower levels of abstraction, the events describing detailed individual
behaviours of components become visible. In a purely discrete event framework, like
conventional Event-B, there can be some leeway in deciding whether to hold all these
low level events in a single machine or in multiple machines — because all events
execute instantaneously, isolated from one another in time (in the usual interpretation).

In Hybrid Event-B the issue is more pressing. Because of the continuous behaviour
that is represented, *all* components are always executing *some* event. Thus an integrated representation risks hitting the combinatorial explosion of needing to represent
each possible combination of concurrent activities within a separate event, and there is
a much stronger incentive to put each (relatively) independent component into its own
machine, synchronised appropriately. Put another way, there is a very strong incentive
to **not abstract away from concurrency**, an impulse that reflects the actual system architecture. In Hybrid Event-B, there is thus an even greater motivation than usual for the
refinement methodology to make the step from monolithic to concurrent convincingly.

This is accomplished by using normal Hybrid Event-B refinement up to the point
where a machine is large enough and detailed enough to merit being split up. Then, the
key concept in the decomposition is the INTERFACE. This is adapted from the idea in
[9] to include not only declarations of variables, but of the invariants that involve them,

---

[3] If a mode event has an input, the semantics assumes that its value only arrives at a time strictly
later than the previous mode event, ensuring part of (1) automatically.

INTERFACE $Level7\_AnSw\_IF$
READS $Level7\_Comp\_IF$
REFERS $Level7\_Comp\_IF$
CLOCK clk_AnSw
VARIABLES
  $AnSwClosed, sens\_AnSw_i$
PLIANT
  $answ2genev$
INVARIANTS
  $AnSwClosed \in$ BOOL
  $answ2genev \in$ BOOL
  $(AnSw\_CLOSED\_INIT < clk\_AnSw <$
    $AnSw\_CLOSED\_FIN) \Rightarrow AnSwClosed$
  $\neg(AnSw\_CLOSED\_INIT \leq clk\_AnSw \leq$
    $AnSw\_CLOSED\_FIN) \Rightarrow \neg AnSwClosed$
$\cdots \quad \cdots \quad \cdots \quad \cdots$

$\cdots \quad \cdots \quad \cdots \quad \cdots$
$\bigwedge_i sens\_AnSw_i \in \{OPEN, CLOSED\}$
$\bigwedge_i AnSwClosed \Rightarrow sens\_AnSw_i = CLOSED$
$\bigwedge_i \neg AnSwClosed \Rightarrow sens\_AnSw_i = OPEN$
$answ2genev \Rightarrow cmp2answ_1 \lor cmp2answ_2$
$answ2genev \Rightarrow AnSwClosed$
INITIALISATION
BEGIN
  $clk\_AnSw := BIGT$
  $AnSwClosed := FALSE$
  $||_i \, sens\_AnSw_i := OPEN$
  $answ2genev := FALSE$
END
END

Fig. 3. Level 7 interface for the analogical switch, from the case study

and their initialisations. A community of machines may have access to the variables declared in an interface if each machine CONNECTS to the interface. All events in the machines must preserve all of the invariants in the interface, of course. An important point is that *all* invariants involving the interface's variables must be in the interface.

Well, not quite all; an exception is needed. Invariants of the form $U(u) \Rightarrow V(v)$, where variables u and v belong to different interfaces, are also allowed. Such *cross-cutting* invariants (which we call type 2 invariants, t2is) are needed to express fundamental dependencies between subsystems which are coupled in a nontrivial manner (such couplings invariably arise in multicomponent systems). In a t2i, the u and v variables are called the local and remote variables respectively. By convention a t2i resides in the interface containing its local variables.

Fig. 3 shows an example of the preceding taken from the landing gear case study. It is an interface, $Level7\_AnSw\_IF$, primarily intended for some variables of the *A*nalogical *Sw*itch. It contains some, by now, familiar ingredients, such as a clock clk_AnSw, and some mode and pliant variables, $AnSwClosed, sens\_AnSw_i, answ2genev$. These model the state of the analogical switch, the state of its sensors, and the signal from the switch to the general electro-valve. It also contains statements READS $Level7\_Comp\_IF$ and REFERS $Level7\_Comp\_IF$.

The first of these says that the interface contains a t2i (specifically $answ2genev \Rightarrow cmp2answ_1 \lor cmp2answ_2$) for which the local variables (i.e. $answ2genev$) are found in $Level7\_AnSw\_IF$, and the remote variables (i.e. $cmp2answ_1, cmp2answ_2$) are found in $Level7\_Comp\_IF$, which is another interface, predominantly concerned with variables (and their invariants) belonging to the computer systems.

The second expresses the converse idea, namely that there is a t2i in $Level7\_Comp\_IF$ for which the local variables are in $Level7\_Comp\_IF$, and the remote variables are in $Level7\_AnSw\_IF$.

By restricting to t2is as the only means of writing invariants that cross-cut across two interfaces (and, implicitly, across the machines that access them), we can systematise, and then mechanise, the verification of such invariants. Thus, for a t2i $U(u) \Rightarrow V(v)$ it is sufficient for events that update the u variables to preserve $\neg U$ (if it is true in the before-state) and for events that update the v variables to preserve V (if it is true in the before-state). A more comprehensive treatment of the notion of interface used here appears in [2].

As well as sharing variables via interfaces, multi-machine Hybrid Event-B systems need a synchronisation mechanism — one that is more convenient than creating such a thing *ab initio* from the semantics. For this the shared event paradigm [7,14] turns out to be the most convenient. In this scheme, identically named (mode) events in two (or more) machines of the system are deemed to be required to execute simultaneously. In practice, it means that for each such event, its guard is re-interpreted as the conjunction of the guards of all the identically named events. Below, in Section 6, we say rather more more about mode event synchronisation. In particular, we point out the need for a more flexible method of identifying events which are to be synchronised than pure name identity. (In fact, a more flexible mechanism has been implemented in the Rodin Tool [13] than is described in the literature. However, we stick, for simplicity and comparability with the published literature, to the simple and static identical name scheme.)

5 Model Development

Having discussed the technical preliminaries, in this section, we overview the development of the landing gear case study. To clarify some minor inconsistencies in the spec [6], we assume that the pilot controls the gear via a *handle* for which handle *UP* means gear up, and handle *DOWN* means gear down. We also assume that in the initial state the gear is down and locked, since the aircraft does not levitate when stationary on the ground, presumably. Connected with this requirements aspect is the absence of provision in [6] of what is to happen if the pilot tries to pull the handle up when the aircraft is not in flight. Presumably the aircraft should not belly-flop to the ground, so we just incorporate a suitable guard on the handle movement events, based on the value of the shock absorber sensors. This leaves open the question of what *actually* happens if the pilot pulls the handle up when the plane is on the ground. Does the handle resist the movement, or does gear movement remain pending until released by the state of the shock absorber sensors, or ...?

This issue, in turn, raises a further interesting question. Although the fact just pointed out causes no special problem for an event-by-event verification strategy like the B-Method, the absence of any explicit requirement that allows the shock absorber to change value, would be equivalent to the aircraft never leaving the ground, leading to the absence of nontrivial traces for a trace based verification strategy to work on (unless suitable additional events were introduced into the model, just for this purpose).

Pursuing the technical strategy discussed earlier, implies that in the final development, each component that is identifiable as a separate component in the architectural model, should correspond to a machine in its own right. Thus, at least, the pilot subsystem (handle and lights), the two computers, the analogical switch, the general electro-valve, and the individual movement electro-valves (and their associated hydraulic cylinders), should all correspond to separate machines at the lowest level of development. The nontrivial interdependencies between these subsystems give rise to enough cross-cutting type 2 invariants between the corresponding machines to thoroughly exercise the modelling capabilities of our formal framework.

A further technical goal in this development is, as far as possible, to use variables that correspond directly to quantities discussed in the requirements document. The aim is to strive for the closest possible correspondence between requirements and formal model, in the belief that this improves the engineering process. Allied to this is the fact that the present work is the most complex case study attempted in Hybrid Event-B to date, so, a certain amount of experimentation was carried out during the case study in order to evaluate different modelling approaches to various features found in [6]. Consequently, the same kind of situation is not always approached in the same way.

5.1   The Nominal Regime

With these remarks made, we turn to the development itself. This is too big to include in full here of course; the details can be found at [3]. In this section we summarise the essentials, pausing to discuss interesting issues as they arise.

We focus on the nominal regime. For the faulty regime, see below. Adhering to the vision of the B-Method, the development starts very simply, and proceeds to add detail via layers of refinement. As different parts of the system require different numbers of refinement steps in order to reach their final degree of detail, in [3], the various syntactic constructs are labeled with a level number, and the caption accompanying each construct states which constructs constitute the system at the current level of development.

Level 0 gives the simplest, pilot-level view of the system, and consists of just one machine: *Level0_PilotAndLightsNominal*. There are mode events for raising and lowering the handle, and for switching the green and orange lights on and off (the red light is ignored in the nominal regime). For example:

PilotGearUP
  ANY *in*?
  WHERE *in*? = *pilotGearUP_X* ∧ *handle* = *DOWN*
  THEN *handle* := *UP*
  END

This is identical to normal Event-B, aside from the input parameter *in*?, which is required to be *pilotGearUP_X*, and which is furthermore unused in the event. The explanation for this is that while in normal Event-B, events are assumed to execute *lazily*, i.e. *not* at the very instant they become enabled (according to the normal interpretation of how event occurrences map to real time), in Hybrid Event-B, mode events execute *eagerly*, i.e. as soon as they are enabled (in real time).

This is because physical law is similarly eager: if a classical physical system reaches a state in which some transition is enabled, it is overwhelmingly the case that energetics and thermodynamics force the transition to take place straight away. Hybrid Event-B, in being designed to model physical systems, must therefore conform to this. As a consequence, typical Event-B models, in which a new after-state immediately enables the next transition, would cause an avalanche of mode event occurrences if interpreted according to Hybrid Event-B semantics.

To avoid this, and yet to allow modelling convenience in Hybrid Event-B, the undesirable avalanche of mode event occurrences is avoided at runtime by building a delay into the semantics. The delay lasts as long as a required input parameter remains absent, and the semantics *assumes* that the input does not arrive until after some positive (but otherwise unspecified — unless more precisely constrained in the guard) period of time has elapsed.

There is also a default pliant event *PliTrue* to define behaviour between occurrences of the mode events. It merely stipulates COMPLY *INVARIANTS*.

Level 1 is a simple refinement of level 0, and just introduces some additional variables. Aside from minor details of syntax, it is just a discrete Event-B refinement of *Level0_PilotAndLightsNominal* to *Level1_PilotAndLightsNominal*.

Level 2 begins the process of splitting things into smaller components. The level 1 machine is split into *Level2_PilotNominal* and *Level2_CompNominal*. Each event of *Level1_PilotAndLightsNominal* is split into a pair of synchronised events in the two machines. The former reflects the pilot's view, in which the pilot is responsible for handle events (so the earlier *in*? = *pilotGearUP_X* goes into the *Pilot* machine), and the computer is responsible for the lights events (so the inputs for those events go into the *Comp* machine). The rationale for the latter is that the occurrences of the lights events depend on as yet absent *Comp* details, so at this level of abstraction, they just appear as spontaneously generated events from *Comp*'s environment, to be eventually refined to the deterministic behaviour of a more complete computing machine. The relationship between *Level2_PilotNominal* and *Level2_CompNominal* is mediated by an interface, *Level2_Comp_IF*, which contains all the variables shared by the two machines. The decomposition of the level 1 machine into the two level 2 machines plus their interface constitutes a 'textbook' example of doing decomposition according to the scheme described earlier.

The next few levels are concerned with reconciling the pilot's view of a singular computing system behaviour with the reality of the duplicated computing modules of the architecture of Fig. 1. Again, while the system description is still small, a 'textbook' approach to the issue is taken. What we mean by this is that there will be a machine depicting a singular computing system behaviour for the pilot, connected with two actual computing modules which will be successively refined to include further implementation detail. The textbook approach to this is to refine the *Level2_CompNominal* machine to a machine, *Level3_CompNominal* that: firstly, duplicates the computer initiated events (to model potential asynchrony of the two computing modules[4]); secondly, replicates the relevant variables so that each representative machine will have its own copy of each relevant variable. This situation is supported by an enriched interface *Level3_Comp_IF*. That done, at level 4, we can decompose *Level3_CompNominal* into *Level4_CompNominal* (expressing the pilot's view), and *Level4_Comp₁Nominal* and *Level4_Comp₂Nominal* (the two 'real' computing modules-to-be).

The main outcome of this approach is to convince us of its extreme verbosity as a way of modelling the 'OR' of the two computing modules' commands whenever they must send a command to any external component. In the remainder of the development, such verbosity is avoided by having the receiving component simply react to the OR of the received signals in the guards of its events, even though this is slightly inaccurate architecturally (since, in reality, the OR is calculated outside the relevant component).

The next step is to introduce the analogical switch, whose functioning takes time, for which the *Level5_AnalogicalSwitchNominal* machine introduces a clock, *clk_AnSw*. The analogical switch is open by default. When stimulated by a handle event, it takes

---

[4] We allow for potential asynchrony, even though in our idealised modelling sphere, both computing modules will follow exactly the same trajectory.

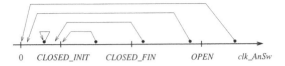

0   *CLOSED_INIT*   *CLOSED_FIN*   *OPEN*   *clk_AnSw*

Fig. 4. The analogical switch machine's transitions when interrupted by a fresh handle event

some time to close (from 0 till *CLOSED_INIT*), then stays closed for a while (from *CLOSED_INIT* till *CLOSED_FIN*), then takes some time to open once more (from *CLOSED_FIN* till *OPEN*). Fig. 4 indicates what happens to the clock value when a fresh handle event occurs before the previous sequence has completed. The handle events that intiate these activities are synchronised with the pilot's handle events (in machine *Level5_PilotNominal*, which is a copy of *Level2_PilotNominal* but including these additional synchronisations). This in order to model the fact that —according to the architecture of Fig. 1— the pilot's handle events reach the analogical switch directly, and not via the computing modules.

Thus far, the development is relatively tree-shaped. Practically speaking, this means that there is no need for nontrivial invariants involving variables that are not declared in the same place. For a development of modest size, it is always possible to arrange things so that this holds. However, as the size of the development increases, the prescience needed to arrange the development so that this remains true, and the need to appropriately separate concerns, both render this desire unrealistic. We see this in concrete terms in our development at level 6, which is concerned with introducing the analogical switch sensors. For clarity, these are introduced in a separate step to that which introduces the analogical switch itself. Since the analogical switch is by now in a separate machine from the computing modules, any invariant involving the sensors and computing variables becomes a cross-cutting t2i. This applies to $\bigwedge_i gearsMoving_k \Rightarrow sens\_AnSw_i = CLOSED$ which states that various landing gears do not start moving until the the analogical switch is sensed to be closed. This t2i appears in the *Level6_Comp_IF* interface, using the t2i machinery discussed above. This necessitates a partitioning of *Level5_AnalogicalSwitchNominal* in that a new interface, *Level6_AnSw_IF* is needed to house some of the *Level5_AnalogicalSwitchNominal* variables, so as to conform to the syntactic conventions for t2is, yielding also machines *Level6_AnalogicalSwitchNominal* and *Level6_Comp_kNominal*.

A similar process can be followed for introducing the general electro-valve. This is carried out at level 7, rather as for the analogical switch at level 5. What is interesting though, for the general electro-valve, is that the requirements [6] do specify some continuous behaviour for this component, albeit that this is simple linear behaviour. The opportunity is taken here to model this using nontrivial pliant events in machine *Level7_General_EV_Nominal*. For instance, the growth of pressure in the door and gear movement circuits is given by:

PressureIncreasingOrHIGH
   INIT *answ2genev*
   SOLVE
      $\mathcal{D}\ genEVoutput = PressureIncRate \times bool2real((genEVoutput < HIGH) \wedge answ2genev)$
   END

This says that the time derivative of *genEVoutput* is constant as long as *genEVoutput* does not exceed *HIGH* and the control signal *answ2genev* is true. Once *genEVoutput* = *HIGH* is reached, the derivative drops to zero and so *genEVoutput* remains constant. Level 8, which introduces the sensors for the general electro-valve, is as interesting as level 7. The general electro-valve sensors only signal *HIGH* when *genEVoutput* actually reaches *HIGH*. This leads to a multi-step refinement of the level 7 pliant event *PressureIncreasingOrHIGH*. A first pliant event models the increasing episode during which the derivative is nonzero, and a second pliant event models the constant episode during which *genEVoutput* remains at *HIGH*. The two pliant events are separated by a mode event *PressureHIGH_reached*, that turns the sensors to *HIGH*. A similar state of affairs holds for the pressure decreasing regime, when the *answ2genev* signal goes false.

Even more interesting is the fact that due to pilot initiated handle events, the analogical switch's behaviour may be restarted before a previous behaviour has completed, leading to two possible mode events in the general electro-valve that synchronise with the analogical switch closure event: one for the normal case when the general electro-valve is depressured *AnSw_CLOSED_INIT_reached_1_S*, and another for when it is already pressured-up *AnSw_CLOSED_INIT_reached_2_S*.

And even more interesting than that, is the fact that the timing of pilot initiated handle events may be such that mode event *AnSw_CLOSED_INIT_reached_2_S* is scheduled to occur at exactly the same moment as the mode event that naturally separates the increasing and *HIGH* episodes in the general electro-valve, *PressureHIGH_reached*. The guards and actions of the two mode events are identical, which would cause trouble with respect to the semantics, were it not for the fact that one of the mode events is a synchronised event and the other is not.

Normally, the unproductive complications of such coincidences in the semantics are avoided in Hybrid Event-B by assuming *in the semantics* that inputs do not arrive at times which clash with other mode events (see the earlier discussion in Section 4). But the case we are discussing is not like this since the coincidence occurs *as a consequence* of an earlier mode event that is quite innocent. Clearly such coincidences are not statically computable in general, so cannot be avoided by some kind of static definition in the semantics. Then, rather than complicate the modelling as we have done in the present case study, a possible way forward is as follows.

During design and development, we neglect the possible existence of these issues of undesired coincidence of mode events. In an environment with proper tool support for Hybrid Event-B, the potential coincidences will invariably generate some unprovable necessary conditions for semantic soundness. These conditions can then be added as further hypotheses in a domain theory, leading to closure of the previously open proofs. Provided such conditions only occupy a portion of the parameter space that is of zero measure, no harm would be done to any practical implementation, since no practical implementation that behaves in a stable way can hit a portion of the parameter space of zero measure.

We proceed to level 9. Now that the general electro-valve can be powered up and down, this level introduces the individual movement electro-valves, and implicitly, the hydraulic cylinders that they manipulate. Each of the four movement electro-valves and

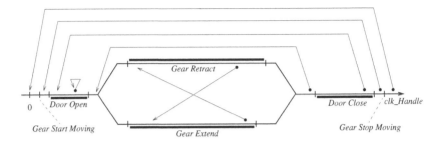

Fig. 5. The approximate timing diagram for the level 10 computing machine

cylinders gives rise to a new machine. Also there is *Level9_HydraulicCylinders_EV_IF*, a new interface that links them all to the computing modules. New synchronised events in the computing modules and electro-valve/cylinder machines command the initiation of the operation of the movement hydraulic cylinders, and timed events monitor the completion of the relevant operations via the relevant battery of sensors, given the variability in completion time described in [6]. All four operations are similar, so only one has been modelled in detail in [3]. The cross-cutting t2is that couple variables in *Level9_HydraulicCylinders_EV_IF* to those in the computing interface *Level9_Comp_IF* are handled in the by now familiar way.

Up to now, the impetus for executing any particular event that is potentially available in a machine has come from the environment, via the technique of using an external input that is created for that sole purpose. (Where there are synchronised families of events, one of them is allocated the external input and the rest are synchronised with it.) The final step in modelling the nominal regime is to remove this artifice, and replace it with explicit timing constraints. This is the job of level 10. Note that explicit timing information is already included in subsystems for which the description is relatively complete, such as the analogical switch, and the the general and movement electro-valves, so this development step only concerns the computing modules.

It was tempting to try to introduce the computing module timing constraints in a step by step fashion. However, it was soon realised that the complexity and interconnectedness of the constraints was such that a stepwise approach would need to allow guard *weakening* as well as guard strengthening. Since Event-B is not geared for guard weakening, the idea was abandoned in favour of a monolithic approach that introduced all of the timing machinery in one go.

Fig. 5 outlines the behaviour of the computing module's clock *clk_Handle*, when the handle is manipulated during the course of gear extending or retracting. Unlike Fig. 4 though, where the behaviour illustrated is close to what the model describes (since the analogical switch just responds to handle events in a self-contained way), Fig. 5 neglects important detail. For example, consider a *PilotGearUP_S* event while the gear is extending. Then, the retracting sequence has to be executed but only from the point that extending has reached. So first, *clk_Handle* is changed to stop the gear extending command. Then, *clk_Handle* is changed to a time sufficiently before the gear retracting command time that hydraulic hammer[5] has subsided. Once it is safe to activate the gear retracting command, the gear retracting command is activated, and then *clk_Handle* is changed again to advance the clock in proportion to the undone part of the gear extending activity. In effect, we use *clk_Handle* intervals as part of the state machine controlling the behaviour of the computing modules (along with additional internal variables). This proves especially convenient when the state transitions involved concern delays between commands that need to be enforced in order to assure mechanical safety (e.g. the hydraulic hammer case, just discussed). Such details are not visible in Fig. 5, but make the design of the level 10 events quite complicated. This completes our development of the nominal regime.

5.2 The Faulty Regime and the Imperative Closed Loop

Fig. 6.
The Tower
Pattern

Although we do not cover the faulty regime in detail in this study, we now indicate briefly how it would go in the context of a fuller Hybrid Event-B development. The structuring given by the nominal regime gives a good basis for considering the faulty regime. A great help here is the fact that the faults described in [6] are basically all *stuck_at* faults. To inject such faults into a nominal model is easy and systematic. For each potentially failing component we introduce a fault variable, and we additionally guard each preexisting event on the fault variable's falsehood. Furthermore, we introduce an event in the relevant machine to spontaneously make the fault variable true.

Having built up the nominal regime, the faulty regime would be constructed by retrenching the various nominal machines to include the needed faults in the manner just described. A great added benefit of this is that the suite of invariants built up for the nominal regime need not be changed in the face of *stuck_at* faults — retrenchment allows the invariants to be violated, after which further nominal behaviour ceases.

In a multistage development like the present one, the nominal and faulty versions would be related by *Tower Pattern* theorems such as can be seen in [5]. Fig. 6 shows the general scheme. The top-down nominal refinement-based development we have done appears as the bold left line, descending vertically through levels of abstraction as we have described. The faulty regime then takes a horizontal development step to the right, and builds up the analogous refinement chain bottom-up. This is indicated by the bold dashed line segments.

The ultimate product of an exercise like the present one, is to produce an iterative closed loop controller in a suitable imperative language, so that the control is reduced to the instructions of a suitable embedded processor. The modelling in this case study has not been carried that far, but we explain now why it would be easy to do.

We would just need a straightforward refinement. The reason for this is that the only continuous behaviour that is relevant to the case study is linear with respect to time

---

[5] Hydraulic hammer is the term for the collection of transient shock waves that propagate round the hydraulic system when relatively abrupt changes are inflicted on its control surfaces (i.e. the pistons in the various cylinders), and which are typically damped using a relatively elastic hydraulic accumulator somewhere in the hydraulic circuit in order to avoid damage to the hydraulic circuit components.

(whether this concerns a clock variable, or some other physical variable). Being linear, the behaviour becomes completely predictable over the duration of a sampling period. The needed refinement would thus need to simply replace the continuous behaviour of the pliant event that ran during the sampling period with a (continuous) skip, and augment the mode event that ran at the end of the sampling period with a discrete update that expressed the calculated changes in pliant variables over the sampling period just elapsed. The semantics of Hybrid Event-B would ensure that a straightforward retrieve relation was provable regarding this change of representation (see [4] for examples). This is indicated by the lowest vertical bold line segment in Fig. 6.

6   Review, Lessons Learned, and Conclusions

In the last few sections, we have overviewed the landing gear case study, and tackled the modeling challenges of capturing the resulting development using Hybrid Event-B. Although we restricted to the nominal regime, this provided a sufficient challenge to the modelling capabilities of Hybrid Event-B to reassure us of its suitability for this kind of system. In fact, with the nominal regime done, we were able to indicate that the faulty regime could be handled quite straightforwardly. A number of lessons emerged from this modelling exercise, which we summarise now.

[1] Doing an exercise like the present one by hand is *really* tricky. Almost every re-reading of some fragment of the development revealed another bug (although typically, such bugs would be easily picked up mechanically). Proper machine support is obviously vital when doing such a development in anger.

[2] Using a component's clock as an adjunct to its state machine proved very convenient in combination with conventional state variables. Modelling mechanical safety delays using pure state machine techniques would have made the state machines much more cumbersome. Simply adjusting the clock to allow a safety margin of time to elapse before the next required action was an elegant solution.

[3] The possibility of using t2is as a tool for breaking up complex architectures into more digestible components, while maintaining interdependencies, proved vital. This generic pattern showed itself to be both sufficiently expressive that needed dependencies could be captured, and sufficiently well structured that mechanisation across multiple machines and interfaces is feasible.

[4] Composition/decomposition mechanisms based on event name identity are inadequate to express the more dynamic synchronisations needed by complex system architectures. As noted already, the current Rodin Tool implementation of synchronised events goes beyond static event name identity, a need vividly illustrated in our case study.

[5] The tension between describing components as self-contained machines, utilising their own naming conventions as standalone entities, contrasts with the approach of regarding them *ab initio* as elements of the full system, adhering to system-wide naming conventions. In general, the synchronisation mechanisms referred to in [4] need to be combined with sufficiently flexible instantiation mechanisms to enable a proper component based approach to be pursued.

The need for the more flexible mechanisms mentioned in the last two points above is already apparent in some of the synchronisations used in the case study here, where it already proved impossible to do the needed job using purely static mechanisms. Such challenges, and others (for example, how to model edge-triggered behaviour in a formalism based primarily on states, or the more intensive use of input and output variables rather than shared variables), provide good inspiration for the further fine-tuning of the multi-machine version of the Hybrid Event-B formalism. Such insight will provide valuable guidance for subsequent tool building effort.

References

1. Akers, A., Gassman, M., Smith, R.: Hydraulic Power System Analysis. CRC Press (2010)
2. Banach, R.: Invariant Guided System Decomposition. These proceedings
3. Banach, R.: Landing Gear System Case Study in Hybrid Event-B Web Site (2013), `http://www.cs.man.ac.uk/~banach/some.pubs/ABZ2014LandingGearCaseStudy/LandingGearCaseStudy.html`
4. Banach, R., Butler, M., Qin, S., Verma, N., Zhu, H.: Core Hybrid Event-B: Adding Continuous Behaviour to Event-B (2012) (submitted)
5. Banach, R., Jeske, C.: Retrenchment and Refinement Interworking: the Tower Theorems. Math. Struct. Comp. Sci. (to appear)
6. Boniol, F., Wiels, V.: The Landing Gear System Case Study. In: ABZ 2014 Case Study Track. CCIS, vol. 433, pp. 1–18. Springer, Heidelberg (2014)
7. Butler, M.: Decomposition Structures for Event-B. In: Leuschel, M., Wehrheim, H. (eds.) IFM 2009. LNCS, vol. 5423, pp. 20–38. Springer, Heidelberg (2009)
8. Carloni, L., Passerone, R., Pinto, A., Sangiovanni-Vincentelli, A.: Languages and Tools for Hybrid Systems Design. Foundations and Trends in Electronic Design Automation 1, 1–193 (2006)
9. Hallerstede, S., Hoang, T.S.: Refinement by Interface Instantiation. In: Derrick, J., Fitzgerald, J., Gnesi, S., Khurshid, S., Leuschel, M., Reeves, S., Riccobene, E. (eds.) ABZ 2012. LNCS, vol. 7316, pp. 223–237. Springer, Heidelberg (2012)
10. Ionel, I.: Pumps and Pumping. Elsevier (1986)
11. Manring, N.: Hydraulic Control Systems. John Wiley (2005)
12. Platzer, A.: Logical Analysis of Hybrid Systems: Proving Theorems for Complex Dynamics. Springer (2010)
13. RODIN Tool, `http://www.event-b.org/`, `http://www.rodintools.org/`, `http://sourceforge.net/projects/rodin-b-sharp/`
14. Silva, R., Pascal, C., Hoang, T., Butler, M.: Decomposition Tool for Event-B. Software Practice and Experience 41, 199–208 (2011)
15. Tabuada, P.: Verification and Control of Hybrid Systems: A Symbolic Approach. Springer (2009)
16. U.S. Department of Transportation, Federal Aviation Administration, Flight Standards Service: Aviation Maintenance Technician Handbook — Airframe (2012), `http://www.faa.gov/regulations_policies/handbooks_manuals/aircraft/amt_airframe_handbook/`

Landing Gear System: An ASM-Based Solution for the ABZ Case Study

Felix Kossak

Software Competence Center Hagenberg GmbH,
Softwarepark 21, 4232 Hagenberg, Austria
felix.kossak@scch.at
http://www.scch.at

Abstract. We present an ASM model for the case study given as a challenge for the ABZ'14 conference, which specifies the digital part of a landing gear system for aircraft. We strove to make the formal model well understandable for humans. We note inconsistencies, ambiguities and gaps in the case study and summarise our experiences during modelling and the proof of safety properties.

Keywords: Formal specifications, Rigorous specifications, Abstract state machines, ASMs, Safety-critical software.

1 Introduction

We herewith present experiences while working on a solution to the case study by Boniol and Wiels given as a challenge for the ABZ'14 conference [1], which specifies the digital part of a landing gear system for aircraft. Our model is based on abstract state machines (ASMs) as presented in [2]. Throughout this paper, we will refer to the cited case study document by Boniol and Wiels as the "requirements document", and by default, page numbers refer to this requirements document.

We strove to make the formal specification well understandable for humans and traceable with respect to the requirements document. We use the same terms as given in the case study document whenever possible, and in general, we use long and telling identifiers. However, expecting all stakeholders to have a technical background, we assume them to be familiar with e.g. the usual set notation.

During our work on the model and the proofs, we have noted several inconsistencies or ambiguities in the requirements document, which we state in Section 2 on *Specification Issues*.

In Section 3, we present the basic design ideas behind an ASM ground model for the software, i.e. the digital part of the landing gear system. The full model is available in [3]. Several safetey requirements according to pp. 18-19 were manually proven and one requirement was refuted; the proofs and the refutation are also available in [3].

In the final section, we state our experiences collected while creating the ASM model and proving requirements.

F. Boniol et al. (Eds.): ABZ 2014 Case Study Track, CCIS 433, pp. 142–147, 2014.

2 Specification Issues

Formal specifications are made in order to avoid inconsistencies, ambiguities, and gaps. Thus a major part of specification work consists in the detection, documentation, and communication of such deficiencies in a given informal requirements document.

We found a few issues in the requirements document of the case study which would, in a real-life scenario, require discussions with representatives of the customer. These regard ambiguities or confusing wording as well as obvious errors. We summarise these issues in this section. A more detailed discussion can be found in [3].

2.1 Normal and Emergency Mode

We found the requirements document confusing regarding "normal" (or "nominal"?) mode and "emergency mode". And while the document states that "In this case study, we do not consider the emergency mode" (p. 1), there is an output variable "anomaly" to be set and the requirements require to set an output variable "normal_mode" to false in certain cases (see p. 19, "Failure mode requirements").

We interpret the remark on p. 3 (top), "... the green light ... must be on", such that the monitoring part of the specified system should still work even in case of "failure" (if possible). On the other hand, one can assume that the controlling part should *not* do anything anymore, i.e. should *not* send any commands to any valves anymore. In order to continue operating in principle while not sending any further commands, however, it is necessary to know whether the emergency mode is active or not, for which we use the variable "normal_mode", as mentioned. We interpret "failure" as synonymous with "anomaly".

2.2 Synchronous Parallelism

Two computing modules shall run "in parallel" (p. 5). However, it is not explicitly stated whether they shall be executed synchronously or asynchronously. We assume that they shall be executed *asynchronously*.

2.3 Obvious Errors in Monitoring Specification

We found two obvious errors in Section 4.3 of the requirements document on health monitoring, regarding *gears motion monitoring* (p. 17):

- In the first list item, it surely must read, "if the control software does not see the value $gear\_extended[x] = false$ [...] after stimulation of the retraction electro-valve [...]", instead of $gear\_retracted$.
- In the third list item, it must likewise read, "if the control software does not see the value $gear\_retracted[x] = false$ [...] after stimulation of the extension electro-valve [...]", instead of $gear\_extended$.

Furthermore, under *Gears motion monitoring* (p. 17), in the second, third, and fourth item, it is stated that "the doors are considered as blocked" when obviously it must read, "the *gears* are considered as blocked".

2.4 Inconsistencies in Timing

On p. 9 of the requirements document, it is stated that the analogical switch can take up to 0.8s (i.e. 800ms) to close. However, according to p. 16, an anomaly shall be detected already 160ms after the handle position has changed. We consider Section 4 of the requirements document to be authoritative (and Section 3 to be primarily informative), thus we assume 160ms.

2.5 Miscellaneous

In Section 5 (Requirements / Properties) of the requirements document (pp. 18–19), we encounter a "command button" which can be pushed "DOWN" or "UP". We assume that this is synonymous to the "handle" as mentioned e.g. on p. 2 or on p. 6.

In Section 3 of the requirements document, on p. 11, it is stated that "door cylinders are locked [...] only in closed position." This is corroborated on p. 5 (Section 2). However, on p. 6, we read that "$door\_open_i[x]$ is true if and only if the corresponding door is locked open". Likewise, in Section 5 (Requirements), e.g. in (R_{31}) (p. 18), there is talk of "when the three doors are locked open". In this paper, we consider "open" and "locked open" as synonymous in the context of doors.

3 A Ground Model for the Software

We developped an ASM ground model for the digital part of the landing gear system which is detailed in a technical report [3]. We laid an emphasis on traceability and general understandability, having experienced that lack of understandability for lay people, including domain experts, managers and potentially also lawyers, is a major deterrent for the use of formal methods in practice. Therefore we also use *long* names for rules, functions, and local variables rather than single letters or short abbreviations – except from abbreviations used consistently in the requirements document as well (such as "EV" for "electro-valve"). However, as a compromise with the need for brevity and a clear structure, we use common set and set operator notation, assuming that the major stakeholders in this case have a technical background.

The main part of the "normal mode" specification is given as enumerated lists of steps, for the "outgoing" and "retraction" sequences, respectively (pp. 14–15). To render our model fully traceable, we have decided to retain the structure given in the requirements document, including the step numbers. This led to admittedly long rules, in which the transitions between possible states of the landing gear are explicitly reflected, including transitions between the outgoing and retraction sequences. A snippet from one such rule may illustrate this:

rule OutgoingSequence(moduleNumber) =
  if EvaluateSensor(moduleNumber, handle) = down **and**
    EvaluateSensor(moduleNumber, analogical_switch) = closed **then**
    if state(moduleNumber) ∈ {lockedRetracted,
      retract_8_generalEValveOpening} **then**
    parallelblock
      CloseGeneralEV(moduleNumber)
      state(moduleNumber) := extend_1_1_generalEValveClosing
    endparallelblock
    else if state(moduleNumber) =
      extend_1_1_generalEValveClosing **then**
      ...

Apart from the given number of steps and some necessary intermediate steps – we have to distinguish between e.g. "opening" and "open" states – the number of possible transitions from an outgoing state to a retraction state contribute to the length of the rules (almost 3 pages in LNCS format per rule). Note that even the first step of the outgoing sequence can be made starting from an intermediate step of the retraction sequence. However, the original structure of the requirements is clearly visible this way.

An alternative for so long rules would have been a graphical notation for *control-state ASMs* as introduced in [2]. However, when you have a graph with 33 nodes and some 55 edges, one would need a large sheet of paper to keep this legible (including sensible state names), and even then it must be questioned whether this would yield more overview. Additionally and more generally, while a graph *may* indeed give a better overview in many cases, we think that it can be more easily misinterpreted when it comes to details, and it is much easier to accidentally overlook a part of it and forget to implement it. Therefore we decided against this option.

The monitoring part is much easier to modularise:

rule MonitorSystem(moduleNumber) =
parallelblock
    CheckSensors(moduleNumber)
    CheckAnalogicalSwitch(moduleNumber)
    CheckPressureSensor(moduleNumber)
    CheckDoorsMotion(moduleNumber)
    CheckGearsMotion(moduleNumber)
endparallelblock

A further note may be due on the modelling of temporal behaviour. According to the requirements document, only linear behaviour has to be modelled, which we do by simply subtracting points of time which are set using a monitored function "now". We think a naïve reliance on some system time to provide "now" is absolutely sufficient for the specification of the given requirements, and no further constraints are required. In such a closed system, we regard system time as a primitive available for the specification language. Constraints (axioms) concerning the "Time" universe may be required for the use of certain tools (in particular, theorem provers), but not for manual proving as we undertook.

4   Experiences and Conclusion

Modelling. Modelling the use case as an ASM was straight-forward, basically starting with the specification of the two different control sequences (pp. 14–15 of the requirements document) and then using stepwise refinement for larger steps and checks and later to include timing constraints as well as extra action required for health monitoring. Due to the flexibility of the ASM method and language, we met no method-specific obstacles.

Modelling temporal behaviour posed no problem in the given case due to assumed linear behaviour, as already mentioned in Section 3. (Non-linear behaviour would certainly pose a considerable challenge.)

We believe that we could also demonstrate that an ASM-based specification can be made well understandable also for people who are not familiar with this method or other rigorous software specification methods, or software development in general.

The lack of a *general* (i.e. not tool-specific) editor which can do at least simple syntax checks and identifier management was felt, but it was not seriously impeding work. In one case, however, a syntax checker would have prevented an error in the model which we only detected later when we were proving requirements.

Note that we advise against writing *specifications* in the language of a tool such as CoreASM due to (a) the restrictions of the specific language and (b) tool-specific overhead which is not necessary for human understanding and actually can be a bit irritating for non-expert stakeholders. Furthermore, a specification is typically part of a contract and should therefore be available in usual and printable document form. We have argued this case in detail in [4]. (This does not invalidate tools for other purposes, however, including validation!)

Errors in the Case Study. As can be seen in the section on *Specification Issues*, we have detected several obvious errors, inconsistencies and ambiguities in the original requirements document, even without interaction with other stakeholders. This is a common experience for us and once again documents one of the many advantages of formal specifications – in this case, of *the process of preparing* a formal specification. Even though it is not unlikely that a developer would have discovered these errors as well, it is much less likely that the necessary changes would have found their way into the specification, leading to a (possibly even undocumented) inconsistency between specification and implementation. Moreover, in a real-life setting, a developer might find it much more difficult to contact a relevant person of the customer than a specifier during the specification process.

Proving. We kept to manual proving. Proving (or refuting) a normal mode requirement was straight-forward, manually parsing (i.e., simulating) the relevant steps of the ASM. Manual proving went relatively fast, probably *much* faster than if we had used an automated theorem prover (even when we do not count the necessary translation into a respective language). The longest proof which we performed, of (R_{41}), took us about two working days (leading to more than 11 pages of output); the other proofs took considerably less time.

Proving a failure mode requirement was more complex, as several different parts of the ASM model are relevant: Amongst others, it is necessary to pick relevant lines somewhere within the very long rules *OutgoingSequence* and *RetractionSequence* as well as look at a rule in the *Monitoring* subsection and auxiliary rules in both the *Control* and *Auxiliary Subrules* subsections. Doing this manually is certainly prone to error, and will also make it hard for reviewers to check. And while it can be doubted that a tool could provide more oversight in a *printed* proof, it could certainly help to avoid errors such as missed, relevant lines in the model and make it easier to trace the proof for those who have the tool available.

It will be very interesting to compare such manual proofs with automated or tool-checked proofs of the same problems, especially with respect to time and legibility. For comparison, compiling the complete model for both control and monitoring as well as the proofs of requirements $(R_{11}\text{bis})$, (R_{21}), (R_{22}), (R_{31}), (R_{41}), (R_{61}), and (R_{71}) and the refutation of (R_{11}) (cf. pp.18–19 of the requirements document) took us estimatedly a bit more than one person month.

Conclusion. We have shown that the given case study can be modelled and verified with ASMs without tool support within reasonable time and effort, although tool support would have been helpful to some degree.

Acknowledgement. This publication has been written within the project "Vertical Model Integration". The project Vertical Model Integration is supported within the program "Regionale Wettbewerbsfähigkeit OÖ 2007-2013" by the European Fund for Regional Development as well as the State of Upper Austria.

References

1. Boniol, F., Wiels, V.: The Landing Gear System Case Study. In: Boniol, F. (ed.) ABZ 2014 Case Study Track. CCIS, vol. 433, pp. 1–18. Springer, Heidelberg (2014)
2. Börger, E., Stärk, R.: Abstract State Machines - A Method for High-Level System Design and Analysis. Springer, Heidelberg (2003)
3. Kossak, F.: Landing gear system: An ASM-based solution for the ABZ 2014 case study. Technical Report SCCH-TR-1401 with the complete model and proofs (2014), http://www.scch.at/en/rse-news/landing_gear
4. Kossak, F., Mashkoor, A., Geist, V., Illibauer, C.: Improving the understandability of formal specifications: An experience report. In: Salinesi, C., van de Weerd, I. (eds.) REFSQ 2014. LNCS, vol. 8396, pp. 184–199. Springer, Heidelberg (2014)

Co-simulation Environment for Rodin:
Landing Gear Case Study

Vitaly Savicks, Michael Butler, and John Colley

University of Southampton, United Kingdom

Abstract. This work in progress presents a prototype multi-simulation environment for the Rodin platform that enables import, co-modelling and co-simulation of dynamic models and formal Event-B specifications, which can help in the design of mixed discrete-event/continuous-time systems. The proposed solution is based on the Functional Mock-up Interface standard and ProB animator for Event-B. The involved technologies and co-simulation semantics are explained, followed by a demonstration of preliminary results, obtained from a landing gear case study.

1 Introduction

Hybrid system models are a mixture of discrete-event and continuous-time components that can be domain specific and therefore require different development tools [1]. At the same time the complexity of systems, in particular within a safety-critical domain, demands the application of formal methods [2]. Both challenges can be addressed by integrating the existing technologies [3]. We propose a simulation-based collaborative approach that combines the Event-B [4] development in the Rodin platform [5] and co-simulation with tool-independent physical components via the FMI interface [6]. The approach is demonstrated on a landing gear example, modelled in Event-B and Modelica [7], and co-simulated in the tool.

2 Modelica and FMI

The Modelica language and the Functional Mock-up Interface standard for Model Exchange and Co-simulation are designed to facilitate tool integration and interoperability. While the Modelica language provides an object-oriented equation-based notation that is natural for describing physical processes in a structural way, the FMI interface enables the exchange and co-simulation of models from any tool that supports the standard by exporting them as a shared library (FMU) with a common interface and model description format. The co-simulation of exported FMI units is performed by the master algorithm that must be designed by the simulation host.

F. Boniol et al. (Eds.): ABZ 2014 Case Study Track, CCIS 433, pp. 148–153, 2014.

3 Rodin Multi-simulation

Our co-simulation environment RMS (Rodin Multi-Simulation) provides a generic master algorithm and an extensible simulation component meta-model that currently implements Event-B and FMI components, which map to Event-B machines and FMI units, respectively. The environment allows diagrammatic composition of components via input/output ports and visualised simulation, coordinated by the master and executed in fixed-size simulation steps (communication points), which is a standard simulation approach. The simulation semantics of Event-B components is defined by the IO events, executed at the beginning of a simulation step to read the inputs, a sequence of proceeding events that master selects non-deterministically, and Wait events that mark the end of the step. The simulation of Event-B is performed via master by the ProB animator [8].

4 Landing Gear Experiment

RMS environment has been exercised on a landing gear system [9] that consists of a cockpit interface, a discrete controller and a continuous mechanical/hydraulic plant. The task of the system is to control the manoeuvring of landing gears based on the input from the cockpit and the sensors of the plant. The initial experiment uses a simplified version of the original specification, in a sense that it omits the triplication of each sensor and implements a single control module and a single manoeuvring sequence, i.e. gear extension. The plant (analogical switch, electro-valves and landing gear/door hydraulic cylinders) has been modelled in Modelica (Figure 1) and exported from the Dymola tool [10] as an FMU.

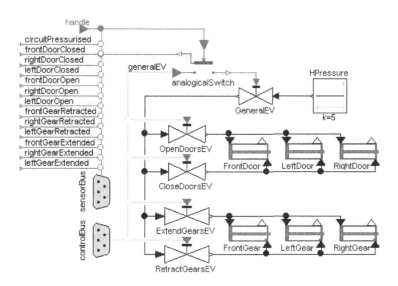

Fig. 1. Modelica model of the mechanical/hydraulic plant

In the model of Figure 1 there are Open, Close, Extend and Retract electro valves for the hydraulic supply to the doors and the gears, hydraulic cylinders for each of the doors and gears along with a source of hydraulic pressure, a general supply valve, and sensor and actuator ports. The behaviour of each component is defined by equations in Modelica. For example, an electro valve has the following specification:

```
model ElectroValve
  parameter Real closingtime = 1.0 "Closing duration";
  parameter Real openingtime = 3.6 "Opening duration";
protected
  parameter Real Rmax = 1.0 "Max opening";
  parameter Real dRcl = Rmax/closingTime "dR when closing";
  parameter Real dRop = -Rmax/openingTime "dR when opening";
  Real R(start = 0.0) "Current opening (0-open, 1-closed)";
  discrete Real dR(start = 0.0);
equation
  Hout = Hin*R;
  der(R) = dR;
algorithm
  // closing/opening event
  when E then
    dR := dRcl;
  elsewhen not E then
    dR := dRop;
  end when;
  // limiter of the R value
  when R <= 0 or R >= Rmax then
    dR := 0;
  end when;
end ElectroValve;
```

The controller was initially modelled in Modelica and StateGraph2 [11], and later in Event-B as a deterministic state machine (Figure 2) via the Statemachines plug-in for Rodin [12]. The *sExtending* state of the state machine comprises three parallel regions that model the state of the general electro-valve (top), doors (middle) and gears (bottom), and are synchronised by sensor-triggered transitions, such as *stopExtending*. The latter, for example, corresponds to the following Event-B event:

event *stopExtending*
where
$sDO = TRUE$
$sGE = TRUE$
$gearsExtended = TRUE$ // gears are extended (from sensor)
then
$sDO := FALSE$
$sGE := FALSE$
$sDelayDC := TRUE$

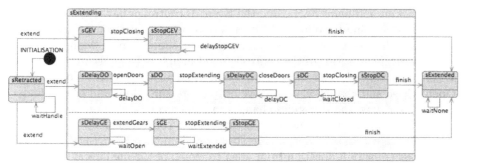

Fig. 2. State machine of the manoeuvring controller in Event-B

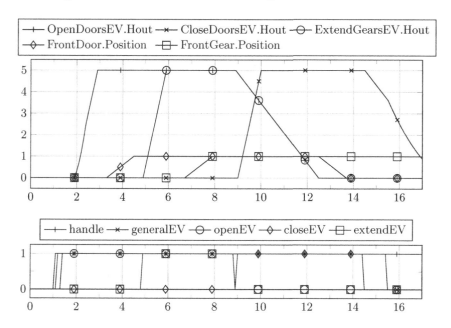

Fig. 3. RMS simulation results (time = 17s, step = 0.1s)

$sStopGE := TRUE$
$openEV := FALSE$ **// stop opening door**
$extendEV := FALSE$ **// stop gear extension**
$timerDC := 1$ **// start the 0.1s 'contrary order' delay (open/close door)**
end

Being the proof of concept the initial model does not yet incorporate safety and timing invariants and does not use the refinement. Refinement of state machines would allow us to refine the controller model towards an implementation and verify its correctness using the Rodin provers.

The cockpit and plant FMUs and the Event-B controller have been composed and successfully simulated in the RMS environment, demonstrating the expected behaviour when compared to a purely physical simulation in Modelica. The obtained results in terms of the controlled and monitored signals are illustrated in Figure 3, which shows the dynamic behaviour of the physical components (Open, Close and Extend electro valve output pressure, door and gear cylinder position) and how the dynamics changes in response to actuation signals from the Event-B controller. For instance, it is possible to observe a delay between the *generalEV* signal and the output pressure growth in the *OpenDoorsEV*, caused by the 0.8s transition duration from open to closed of the analogical switch.

5   Conclusion and Further Work

The presented work demonstrates the feasibility of a generic integration and co-simulation of Event-B formal models and multi-domain physical models that is aimed at combining formal verification and simulation-based analysis of hybrid systems. Our future R&D steps include a stronger formal analysis of the co-simulation semantics [13], development of an adaptive and deterministic master algorithm [14–16] and comparison of the proposed solution with traditional simulation approaches on a number of case studies, including the complete specification of the landing gear system.

Acknowledgement. This work is part of the ADVANCE Project (Advanced Design and Verification Environment for Cyber-physical System Engineering) funded by the European Commission (http://www.advance-ict.eu).

References

1. Lee, E.A.: Cyber physical systems: Design challenges. In: International Symposium on Object/Component/Service-Oriented Real-Time Distributed Computing (ISORC) (May 2008) (invited paper)
2. Gnesi, S., Margaria, T.: Formal Methods for Industrial Critical Systems. Wiley Online Library (2013)
3. Marwedel, P.: Embedded and cyber-physical systems in a nutshell. DAC. COM Knowledge Center Article 20(10) (2010)
4. Abrial, J.: Modeling in Event-B: System and software engineering. Cambridge University Press (2010)
5. Abrial, J., Butler, M., Hallerstede, S., Hoang, T., Mehta, F., Voisin, L.: Rodin: An open toolset for modelling and reasoning in Event-B. International Journal on Software Tools for Technology Transfer (STTT) 12(6), 447–466 (2010)
6. Blochwitz, T., Otter, M., Arnold, M., Bausch, C., Clauß, C., Elmqvist, H., Junghanns, A., Mauss, J., Monteiro, M., Neidhold, T., et al.: The Functional Mockup Interface for tool independent exchange of simulation models. In: Modelica 2011 Conference, pp. 20–22 (March 2011)
7. Fritzson, P., Engelson, V.: Modelica — a unified object-oriented language for system modeling and simulation. In: Jul, E. (ed.) ECOOP 1998. LNCS, vol. 1445, pp. 67–90. Springer, Heidelberg (1998)

8. Leuschel, M., Butler, M.: Prob: an automated analysis toolset for the B method. International Journal on Software Tools for Technology Transfer 10(2), 185–203 (2008)
9. Boniol, F., Wiels, V.: The Landing Gear System Case Study. In: Boniol, F. (ed.) ABZ 2014 Case Study Track. CCIS, vol. 433, pp. 1–18. Springer, Heidelberg (2014)
10. Brück, D., Elmqvist, H., Mattsson, S.E., Olsson, H.: Dymola for multi-engineering modeling and simulation. In: Proceedings of Modelica (2002)
11. Otter, M., Malmheden, M., Elmqvist, H., Mattson, S.E., Johnsson, C.: A new formalism for modeling of reactive and hybrid systems. In: Proceedings of the 7th International Modelica Conference, Linköping University, pp. 364–377. Electronic Press (2009)
12. Savicks, V., Snook, C., Butler, M.: Event-B wiki: Event-B Statemachines (2011), http://wiki.event-b.org/index.php/Event-B_Statemachines
13. Gheorghe, L., Bouchhima, F., Nicolescu, G., Boucheneb, H.: Formal definitions of simulation interfaces in a continuous/discrete co-simulation tool. In: Seventeenth IEEE International Workshop on Rapid System Prototyping, pp. 186–192 (June 2006)
14. Hines, K., Borriello, G.: Dynamic communication models in embedded system co-simulation. In: Proceedings of the 34th Annual Design Automation Conference, pp. 395–400. ACM (1997)
15. Schierz, T., Arnold, M., Clauß, C.: Co-simulation with communication step size control in an FMI compatible master algorithm. In: 9th International Modelica Conference, Munich (2012)
16. Broman, D., Brooks, C., Greenberg, L., Lee, E.A., Masin, M., Tripakis, S., Wetter, M.: Determinate composition of FMUs for co-simulation. In: 2013 Proceedings of the International Conference on Embedded Software (EMSOFT), pp. 1–12. IEEE (2013)

Modeling an Aircraft Landing System in Event-B

Dominique Méry[1,*] and Neeraj Kumar Singh[2]

[1] Université de Lorraine, LORIA, BP 239, Nancy, France
Dominique.Mery@loria.fr
[2] McMaster Centre for Software Certification, Hamilton, ON, Canada
singhn10@mcmaster.ca

Abstract. This paper presents a stepwise formal development of the landing system of an aircraft. The formal models include the complex behaviour, temporal behaviour and sequence of operations of the landing gear system. The models are formalized in Event-B modeling language, and then the ProB model checker is used to verify the deadlock freedom and to validate the behaviour requirements by animating the formalized models. This case study is considered as a benchmark for techniques and tools dedicated to the verification of behavioural properties of the complex critical systems.

Keywords: Landing System, Verification, Validation Refinement, Event-B.

1 Introduction

We present the stepwise formalization of the benchmark case study [1] landing system of an aircraft that is proposed in the ABZ'2014 Conference. The current work intends to explore problems related to modeling the sequence of operations of landing gears and doors associated with hydraulic cylinders under the real-time constraints and to evaluate the refinement process. A detailed version [2] of this paper includes formally proved Event-B models. Since the requirement for the length of this paper is limited at most 6 pages, we invite readers to use detailed version of this paper to understand the formal development and related refinements of the case study [2]. To understand the development of the case study, readers must require some basic knowledge of the Event-B, which is available in several publications [3–5].

2 Abstraction of the Landing System as an Automaton

The development is progressively designing the landing system by integrating observations and elements of the document [1]. We decompose the full development into sequences of refinement steps corresponding to our understanding of the system. The general process starts by a very abstract model and starts by an observation of the behaviour of the landing system. What is the goal of the system under modeling? The system is controlling mechanical parts of the landing system and the global resulting

---

* This work was supported by grant ANR-13-INSE-0001 (The IMPEX Project http://impex.loria.fr) from the Agence Nationale de la Recherche (ANR).

F. Boniol et al. (Eds.): ABZ 2014 Case Study Track, CCIS 433, pp. 154–159, 2014.

system should satisfy some requirements. Since we are using Event B for modeling the global system, so events will be used for formalizing the mechanical, hydraulic, and digital components including pilot interface. The construction of the final model starts by developing a first automaton (see Fig. 1) which expresses all the possible behaviours of the system in normal mode. In Fig. 1, the dashed and plain arrows present the distinction between two different types of actions. The dashed arrows indicate an action of the system, and the plain arrows show an action of the pilot. A sequence of refinement models (M1, M2, M3) lead to a general automaton that models the possible behaviours of the global system. A list of required properties (R11, R11bis,R12, R12bis, R22, R21) is checked in this abstract development when pilot does not take any action for modifying gear states. It should be noted that the ProB model checker is used for deadlock checking, and all the generated proof obligations are automatically discharged using Rodin prover. ProB allows us to validate the behavioural requirements of all the models through animation.

In the following section, we develop the subsequent refinement models by introducing numerous new features and associated components like electro-valves and cylinders including sensors, timing requirements and anomaly detection to formalize the global system requirements.

3   Chain of Refinements

3.1   Adding Sensors and Computing Module

In this refinement M4, we model the sensors reading, computing module and failure detection. We introduce the management of sensors by considering the collection of values of sensors and an abstract expression of the computing modules for analysing the sensed values. Moreover, the sensed values are also used for anomaly detection in the system. These sensors are introduced to sense current activities or states of various components of the landing system, such as *handle, analogical switch, gear extended, gear retracted, gear shock absorber, door open, door closed,* and *circuit pressurized.* These sensors are triplicated in order to prevent sensor failures. We define each sensor by a function from 1..3 into the sensors values. All these sensors are introduced in previously defined events corresponding to the components. A list of new events is introduced for modeling the system requirements. These new events are Analogical_switch_closed and Analogical_switch_open to update the general switch for protecting the system against abnormal behaviour of the digital part, Circuit_pressurized to manage the sensor of the pressure control, Computing_Module_1_2 to model in a very abstract way for computing and updating of electro-valve variables using sensors values, and Failure_Detection to detect any failure in the system. A list of safety properties is also introduced in this refinement in order to correct sensing and to guarantee for capturing the system requirements.

3.2   Managing Electro-Valves

In this refinement, we explore an idea for formalizing the behavior of physical mechanical systems like electro-valves. An electro-valve is an hydraulic equipment which

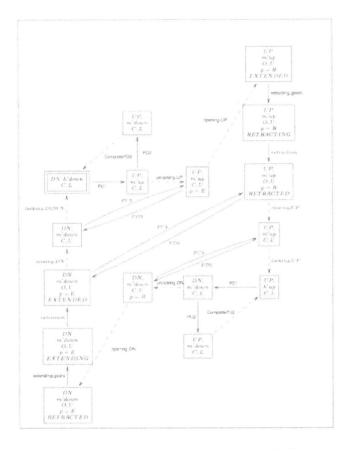

Fig. 1. State-based Automaton for the first sequence of refinements

contains two hydraulic ports (hydraulic input and output ports), and an electrical port with the current order (*True, False*). The behavior of the electro-valve depends on the value of the electrical order (E). These electro-valves produces some electrical outputs that are used to control other physical components like cylinders. Cylinders are pure hydraulic equipments, which can move when hydraulic pressure will be received, and it can stop to move when the pressure goes down. The moving behaviour of cylinders is controlled by the electro-valves. There are five electro-valves: *general EV, close EV, open EV, retract EV, and extend EV*. All these electro-valves are described formally in M5, where a new event Update_Hout presents an abstraction for calculating the current output states of electro-valves corresponding to the computing module outputs and hydraulic input pressure.

3.3   Integrating Cylinders Behaviours

Cylinders are hydraulic equipments. There are two types of cylinders (gear and door cylinders), which are used to control the movement of the gears and doors of the landing system. In this refinement M6, the next step is to integrate the cylinders behaviour according to the electro-valves circuit and to control the system process by computing the global state of the system using sensors values. Moreover, we strengthen the guards of events opening and closing doors and gears using cylinders sensors and hydraulic pressure (opening_doors_DOWN, opening_doors_UP, closing_doors_UP, closing_doors_DOWN, unlocking_UP, locking_UP, unlocking_ DOWN, locking_DOWN, retracting_gears, retraction, extending_gears, extension). However, after introducing the cylinders, we emphasis to maintain the sequential dynamic behaviours between components (i.e. electro-valves and sensors) using some control or flag variables. For instance, an event CylinderMovingOrStop models the change of the cylinders according to the pressure, when it is in *cylinder* state, and it leads to a next state which *activates* the computing modules.

3.4 Failure Detection

This is an important phase of refinements that allows to identify a list of anomalies by measuring the sensors values. The model M7 models the detection of different possible failures. Page 16 and page 17 of the case study have given a list of conditions for detecting anomalies: *Analogical switch monitoring, Pressure sensor monitoring, Doors motion monitoring, Gears motion monitoring, Expected behavior in case of anomaly.* The decision is to refine the event Failure_Detection into six events that model the different cases for failure detection: Failure_Detection_Generic_Monitoring, Failure_ Detection_Analogical_Switch, Failure_Detection_Pressure_Sensor, Failure_ Detection_Doors, Failure_Detection_Gears, Failure_Detection_Generic_Monitoring. However, we have also strengthened the guards of perviously defined events opening_doors_DOWN, opening_doors_UP, closing_doors_UP, closing_doors_ DO-WN, unlocking_UP, locking_UP, unlocking_DOWN, locking_DOWN by adding a condition $anomaly = FALSE$.

3.5 Timing Requirements

In this refinement, we introduce the timing requirements and health monitoring process of the landing system. Moreover this refinement step also enrich the previously defined events through introduction of the timing constraints and other requirements to realize the concrete behavior of the system. To introduce the temporal requirements, we use the existing timing pattern [6], where a detailed description is described. The time pattern [6] provides a way to add timing properties. The pattern adds an event tic_tock simulating the progression of time. Timing properties are derived from the document [1]. The timing requirements are defined for handle changing, electro-valve simulation, cylinders moving, and monitoring the health of gears motion, doors motion, analogical switch, generic switch, pressure circuit, etc. We agree with possible discussions on the modeling of time but it appears that further works are required to get a better integration of a *more real time* approach. However, we think that the current model M8 is an abstraction of another automaton with real time features [7].

3.6 Adding Lights

The last refinement of our development introduces the pilot interface. The pilot has a set of lights to indicate the current positions of gears and doors including the health of the system. The required inputs for these light are coming from the computing module that monitor the health of the system. The main outputs of computing module are *anomaly*, *gears maneuvering*, and *gears locked down* that directly connect to the light switches for indicating the various situations. These lights are green, red and orange. The green light indicates that gears are locked down, the red light shows that landing gear system failure, and the orange light indicates gears maneuvering. A list of events and safety properties are introduced to formalize the pilot interface: pilot_interface_Green_light_On (green light is on; when gears locked down is true); pilot_interface_Orange_light_On (orange light is on, when gears maneuvering is true); pilot_interface_Red_light_On (red light is on, when anomaly is detected (true)); pilot_interface_Green_light_Off (green light is off, when gears locked down is false); pilot_interface_Orange_light_Off (orange light is off, when gears maneuvering is false); pilot_interface_Red_light_Off (red light is off, when anomaly is detected (false)).

4 Conclusion

Validation and verification are processed by using the ProB tool [8] and Proof Statistics. *Validation* refers to gaining confidence that the developed formal models are consistent with the requirements, which are expressed in the requirements document [1]. The landing system specification is developed and formally proved by the Event-B tool support. The developed formal models are also validated by the ProB tool through animation and model checker tool support of the abstract and successive refined models under some constraints. These constraints are the selection of parameters for testing the given models, and avoiding the failure of the tool during animation or model checking. However, we use this tool on abstract and all the refined models to check that the developed specification is deadlock free from an initial model to the concrete model. Due to specific constraint of ProB (i.e. state explosion), we have used ProB to animate and to validate the behavioural requirements only for three models M1, M2 and M3. The model M4 and later models were not animatable due to introduction of several new variables, where specification states grow quickly.

The Table-1 expresses the proof statistics of the development in the Rodin tool. These statistics measure the size of the model, the proof obligations are generated and discharged by the Rodin platform, and those are interactively proved. The complete development of landing system results in 529(100%) proof obligations, in which 448(84,68%) are proved completely automatically by the Rodin tool. The remaining 81(15,31%) proof obligations are proved interactively using Rodin tool. In the models, many proof obligations are generated due to introduction of new functional and temporal behaviors. In order to guarantee the correctness of these functional and temporal behaviors, we have established various invariants in the stepwise refinements. Most of the proofs are automatically discharged and the interactively discharged proof obligations are discharged by simple sequence of using automatic procedures of Rodin.

Table 1. Table of requirements satisfied by models and proof statistics

Model	Requirements	Total PO	Auto	Man
M1	R11, R11bis,R12, R12bis	10	10	0
M2	R11, R11bis,R12, R12bis	33	33	0
M3	R11, R11bis,R12, R12bis, R22, R21	44	44	0
M4	R11, R11bis,R12, R12bis, R22, R21	264	252	12
M5	R11, R11bis,R12, R12bis, R22, R21	19	19	0
M6	R11, R11bis,R12, R12bis, R22, R21	49	20	29
M7	R11, R11bis,R12, R12bis, R22, R21	1	0	1
M8	R11, R11bis,R12, R12bis, R22, R21	56	23	33
M9	R11, R11bis,R12, R12bis, R22, R21	9	3	6
Total	R11, R11bis,R12, R12bis, R22, R21	529	448	81

The current version of the development is the nth version. The document describes a concrete system with sensors, mechanical parts and digital parts. The first attempt by one of the authors was to propose a sequence of refined models, which was closest to the description of requirement documents [1]. Then we try to have a global view of the system and to provide a very abstract initial model. In the second round of derivation of models, we got a wrong model, since we did not take into account the counter orders. Finally, the diagram of the Fig. 1 summarizes main steps of the system. From this model, we decide to make elements more concrete and we introduce sensors, computing modules and other required components. The timing requirements are added in the pre-last model M8 which is then equipped by lights in the model M9 as pilot interface. Our models are still refinable due to some abstract representation of system behaviours. In future, our plan is to consult with domain experts to revisit this case study and to identify possible modeling techniques considering refinement strategy for developing such type of a large complex critical system.

References

1. Boniol, F., Wiels, V.: The Landing Gear System Case Study. In: Boniol, F. (ed.) ABZ 2014 Case Study Track. CCIS, vol. 433, pp. 1–18. Springer, Heidelberg (2014)
2. Méry, D., Singh, N.K.: Modelling an Aircraft Landing System in Event-B (Full Report). Research report, MOSEL - LORIA, Department of Computing and Software - McMaster University (April 2014), http://hal.inria.fr/hal-00971787/PDF/full.pdf
3. Abrial, J.-R.: Modeling in Event-B: System and Software Engineering, 1st edn. Cambridge University Press, New York (2010)
4. Cansell, D., Méry, D.: The Event-B Modelling Method: Concepts and Case Studies. In: Logics of Specification Languages, pp. 33–140. Springer (2007)
5. Singh, N.K.: Using Event-B for Critical Device Software Systems. Springer-Verlag GmbH (2013)
6. Cansell, D., Méry, D., Rehm, J.: Time constraint patterns for event b development. In: Julliand, J., Kouchnarenko, O. (eds.) B 2007. LNCS, vol. 4355, pp. 140–154. Springer, Heidelberg (2006)
7. Alur, R., Dill, D.L.: A theory of timed automata. Theor. Comput. Sci. 126(2), 183–235 (1994)
8. Leuschel, M., Butler, M.: ProB: A model checker for B. In: Araki, K., Gnesi, S., Mandrioli, D. (eds.) FME 2003. LNCS, vol. 2805, pp. 855–874. Springer, Heidelberg (2003)

Author Index